ZENior CitiZEN

Mastering the Art of Aging

Sebastian de Assis

Blooming World Books

ZENior CitiZEN: Mastering the Art of Aging
Copyright © 2016 by Sebastian de Assis
All rights reserved

No part of this book may be used or reproduced, transmitted, or stored in whole or in part by any manner whatsoever without prior written permission from the publisher, except in the case of brief quotations embodied in critical articles and reviews.

Both names and chronological development of the events in this book have been altered to protect individual identities and to improve the flow of the narrative. The value of the content is the crux of this work and remains unaffected by these changes.

First Edition

ISBN 978-0-9700722-2-1 (pbk.)
ISBN 978-0-9700722-3-8 (Ebook)

Library of Congress Control Number: 2016909921

Published in the United States of America

Blooming World Books
P.O. Box 443
Corvallis, OR 97339-0443
www.bloomingworldbooks.com

Praise for *ZENior CitiZEN: Mastering the Art of Aging*

"Sebastian de Assis has performed an invaluable service to aging Boomers. As youth, Boomers sought inspiration from Eastern traditions. *ZENior CitiZEN* now provides us with an intelligent, intelligible, lucid resource. This aging Boomer delights in de Assis' guide to the art of aging."

🖉 W. Andrew Achenbaum, Ph.D., University of Houston
Author of *Older Americans, Vital Communities*

"I have found Sebastian de Assis' new book *ZENior CitiZEN: Mastering the Art of Aging*, to be a unique and valuable resource for those seeking to move consciously and fearlessly on the journey through the latter chapters of their lives...this is a book that inspires hope by showing how we can liberate ourselves from the shackles of fear of uncertainty and loss of control so we may live fully in each present moment...This book is meant to be read slowly and reflectively. It is full of deep wisdom and powerful practices that can make our journey through aging a time of liberation rather than fear."

🖉 Ron Pevny, Director of the Center for Conscious Eldering
Author of *Conscious Living, Conscious Aging*

"In *ZENior CitiZEN: Mastering the Art of Aging*, Sebastian de Assis has so artfully offered us an absolutely essential alternative path toward the process of aging...*ZENior CitiZEN* invites readers to the art of surrendering and living fully in the now...It is Zen at its best and here Sebastian de Assis invites us to what he calls Power Aging...This should be a required text for a course on gerontology."

🖉 Siroj Sorajjakool, Professor of Religion and Psychology,
Loma Linda University
Author of *Do Nothing: Reflections on Chang Tzu's Philosophy*

"In traditional Hindu cultures, the last phase of life is when we begin our spiritual journey. As an almost seventy-year-old Buddhist teacher, I welcome Sebastian de Assis' call to transform our senior years into the time of our lives."

🖋 Will Johnson, author of *Breathing Through the Whole Body*

"Sebastian de Assis wrestles powerfully with the angel of aging, bringing ideas from Zen and Taoism into the great struggle to understand what this angel wants from us. His story reminds us of our own struggles and invites us to see the journey of aging with new eyes...*ZENior CitiZEN: Mastering the Art of Aging* can be a great companion on a reflective afternoon to check in your own path."

🖋 John C. Robinson, Ph.D., author of *The Three Secrets of Aging*

"In this book Sebastian de Assis discusses his journey to find a Zen-like acceptance and strength for getting older. He masterfully shares his insights, which could be very useful for others to contemplate and practice. This book is for anyone who wants to be more mindful and gain insights that can help with the aging process. Scientists are finding that mindfulness can lead to measurable changes in mental and cognitive health among older adults, and de Assis adds a unique and valuable perspective to this approach."

🖋 Robert G. Winningham, Ph.D., Professor of Psychology and Gerontology, Western Oregon University
Author of *Train Your Brain: How to Maximize Memory Ability in Older Adulthood*

ALSO BY SEBASTIAN DE ASSIS

Teachers of the World, Unite!
rEvolution in Education
The Alchemy of Time

In memory of my mother, whom I never met but always have loved

Contents

Introduction
1

Chapter 1: The First Step of a Thousand-Mile Journey
7

Chapter 2: The Reawakening of Zen
21

Chapter 3: The Holy Trinity of Zen
39

Chapter 4: Dreaming of Being Awake
53

Chapter 5: The Awakened One
71

Chapter 6: The Dharma of Power Aging
87

Chapter 7: The Myths of Aging
121

Chapter 8: The Facts of Aging
143

Chapter 9: It's About TIME
163

Chapter 10: The Obstacles to Power Aging
189

Chapter 11: The Tao of Power Aging
219

Chapter 12: The Nirvana of Aging
263

Notes
285

About the Author

Introduction

Time goes by so quickly!

    I first heard this line when I was 18-years-old. I was sitting on a couch next to a lady who was 72 years my senior with my forearm resting juxtaposed to hers while we chatted. Noticing the stark contrast between her flaccid and wrinkled skin in comparison to my taut, tanned, and toned arm, I remember saying to myself in the privacy of my thoughts: "Yeh, right! It'll take an eternity till the day my skin gets to look like this."

    It didn't take an eternity, but a mere thirty-two years later for me to realize what she meant. It was not until I turned 50-years-old that I grasped the reality and wisdom of her words. What seemed to have happened rather hastily and without my being aware of it, suddenly I'd become a middle-aged man who recognized that time, like a fast-moving vehicle in the highway of life, had been rapidly zooming by as I watched my youthful years fade away in the rear mirror of my life journey. After driving by the milepost 50, I began reflecting on the nature and function of time; not only the time that has already passed, but even more importantly, the time that is yet to come. Then, I became aware that in another couple of decades, granted that I'd still be alive, I'd be the one telling a young person the truth that can only be understood in the latter stages of life: time goes by so quickly!

Although it seems like a long time since the days of my first job working at my father's nursing home, a place where I learned so much about aging at a very young age, my interest in the subject was reawakened in my middle-aged years when serendipity struck. After landing a job as the executive director of a nonprofit organization caring for the needs of older adults, I'd unexpectedly returned to the field of work of my very first job as though completing a full circle in my professional life. Having unwittingly reconnected with the challenging issues of the aging process, my interest in the critical latter decades of the individual human experience propelled me to commit my time to broadening my knowledge. The more I dedicated myself to expanding my know-how, the more confident I became in the comprehensive theoretical knowledge that I was accumulating. Thus, I began offering my expertise to several organizations that promoted the welfare of elders in my community and founded an aging services consulting agency. However, as soon as I established myself as a bona fide expert in social gerontology, I had an epiphany that rattled the foundation of my learning and compelled me to reevaluate what I thought I knew so well.

Based on my interactions with my generation cohorts (Baby Boomers), many of whom were caring for their elder parents, as well as my own personal experience in the fiftieth decade of my life, I had this revelation that old age is not the most frightful aspect of the latter years of life—the aging process itself is! It became evident to me that the fear of being old is not the main culprit of people's anxieties. Instead, it is the fretful fast-paced tour of terror of the ag-

～ Introduction ～

ing process that escalates the apprehension of arriving at the undesired destination. It is the dreadful journey of a continuously disempowered self marching toward the end of life that paves the way to unbearable fear of a future that may steal our health, vitality, and heavens forbid, our minds. Hence, the unrelenting angst of a future we cannot control becomes the actual thief that robs us from the present experience of living.

Taking for granted the truism of the words of the nonagenarian woman who warned me when I was a teenager that "time goes by so quickly," which after crossing the half-century mark I have validated as a veritable fact, I realized that allowing the burglar of fear to infiltrate the mind to steal the quality of life of whatever is left of this most precious and irreplaceable commodity is like committing a crime against the self. But on the other hand, what can we do to sublimate the natural anguish that seems to intensify as time speeds up toward the inevitable end while the physical vehicle breaks down piecemeal? Is it possible to extirpate the overwhelming fear of increasing deterioration, changes in social functions, a multitude of losses, and all the other setbacks intrinsic to the aging process? After spending an excessive amount of time and energy trying to ferret out the answers to these questions through intellectual investigation and complex gerontological theories, I found what I was looking for in the simplicity of Zen. The following pages relate my journey searching for the possibility of mastering the art of aging from a ZENior CitiZEN's perspective.

Just as a teenager I was haphazardly introduced to the realities of the aging process, it was in my early adult life that I came across the fascinating world of Zen Buddhism. I had just moved to Maui, Hawaii, where my desire to learn about the philosophical and attitudinal approach of Zen was awakened by my long dormant interest in Eastern culture. Perhaps I was inspired by the many Asian-Americans I befriended in Hawaii; or maybe it was the influence of an Anglo friend who was an acupuncturist and herbalist who traveled to China often and introduced me to Taoism; or more likely it was the combination of all of it that spurred my interest in exploring the wisdom of the Eastern World. In any case, before I could even notice, I'd been captured by the extraordinary depth and simplicity of Zen.

Suddenly, I started seeing both the world and myself from a different perspective, while experiencing life immersed in a mindful state that abrogated my anxieties and fears. Intellectually, I was intrigued by this approach that I could not define. Neither a religion nor a philosophy in a scholastic sense, Zen is but a way of liberation from the shackles of the dread of uncertainty; a way in which to focus on the immediacy of the present moment without being disturbed by the unforeseeable consequences of the unknown. Like life itself, Zen's complexity lies in the simplicity of its very nature.

As soon as I began delving into the subject, the first question that came up was a natural response to what I was not able to rationalize: What exactly is Zen? I found the answer in the writings of the great Japanese scholar who introduced Zen to the Western world, D.T. Suzuki, who defined it this way: "Zen is that which makes you ask the question, because the answer is where the question arises. The answerer is no other than the questioner himself... when you ask what Zen is, you are asking who you are and

❦ Introduction ❧

what your self is...Now, you know what Zen is, for it is Zen that tells you what your self is and that self is Zen."[1]

Thus, many years later when I applied a Zen approach to the challenges of the aging process, I concluded that with diligent inner work and discipline, it is possible to turn the tribulations of aging into self-empowerment. Through a method that I termed Power Aging[2], I realized that even though aging is inevitable, bleak old age is not—and neither is the anxiety about aging compulsory. The reality is that each individual going through the aging process has both the ability and the choice to experience an empowered life, or she can also choose to succumb to a Dantean purgatory of "*eldergeddon.*"[3]

As Charles Darwin concluded in his seminal study on the evolution of species, it is not the strongest or most intelligent that survives, but those who can best manage change. Since the aging process is the quintessential continuous change of a lifetime, learning how to overcome the complex transformations that take place after the half century milestone of life is imperative to Power Aging. Therefore, when it comes to growing older, the survival of the fittest depends on how well you can handle the challenges inherent to the aging process, and accept with uncompromising resilience the certainty that time will inevitably come to an end—as it does to everyone and everything that lives. It is an inescapable law of nature. And the only way to succeed in this daunting task is by mastering the art of aging, while turning the lessons that come with the passing of time into personal power. The adaptation to change is at the heart of a Darwinian evolution of aging.

But I'm not interested in the evolution of aging. I must learn about the survival of aging. And being a Zenist, I have but one path to follow. I invite you to come along, but only in accordance with *Hsin-Hsin Ming*, or the "verses of the perfect mind" by Seng-t'san, the third patriarch of Zen: "Do not seek to follow in the footsteps of the man of old; seek what he sought."[4]

Are you willing to relinquish the negative stereotypical label of "senior citizen" and replace it with the self-empowered denomination of ZENior CitiZEN? Do you want to explore the possibility of mastering the art of aging? Are you ready to embark on this adventurous journey?

Then, let's begin.

Chapter 1

The First Step of a Thousand-Mile Journey

The Starting Point

"Growing old is not for sissies," Bette Davis asserted with conviction—and she was right!

It takes an inordinate amount of chutzpah to face an indomitable foe that cannot be defeated. After all, what's a mere mortal to do in the face of the inevitable approaching death while the body gives in to the demands of nature? And to make matters worse, as the clock ticks inexorably toward the final hour, the anxiety of growing old increases with each passing year turning the present into a living nightmare of an encroaching doomed future. Alas, it seems that unless you build the inner strength necessary to cope with what's arguably the most challenging stage in human life, you are not likely to have a positive experience in your latter years. But what's a brave man or woman to do?

"I'll tell you what, man, I'm well aware that I'm growing old, but I can also tell you for sure that I'm no sissy," my burly sexagenarian workout buddy blurted out defensively when I mentioned Davis' popular quote to him.

"I'm sorry Douglas, I didn't mean to stir up your emotions," I said backing off from his unexpected reaction. "You're obviously irked about aging."

"Damn right I'm irked!" He said with anger and frustration echoing through his words. "I've been losing my stamina, I'm not as strong as I used to be, and my stiff squeaky joints have turned me into an anti-inflammatory medication junkie. But you can trust me on this, bro: I'm going to fight aging to the end." Then, he picked up a couple of 40-pound dumbbells and lifted them with abandon while growling like a menaced beast.

It was at that moment that the light bulb went on and illuminated my consciousness with a perspective that had eluded me hitherto. After hearing my friend's testosterone-infused words as he resumed his heavy weight lifting, I walked to the water fountain musing over the absurdity of what he just said. Drinking more water than I usually do, I kept thinking that fighting a natural progressive process that is impossible to evade is tantamount to attempting to halt a speeding locomotive by standing on its tracks with your hand raised with adamant determination to stop it. In both instances you will be crushed mercilessly. In fact, the surest way to self-defeat is to dare confronting a juggernaut opponent that has the upper hand on you. In the case of the aging process, it certainly has my strong macho friend by the...well, throat. That's when I realized that's got to be a better way to deal with the unconquerable adversary of old age.

Learning was the first step of my thousand-mile journey to Power Aging. After that day, I became like an alchemist in the pursuit of the Philosopher Stone of aging. I was determined to find out whether it's feasible to move forward to the latter years of life with courage and confidence in the uncompromising future of old age. Thus, in the experiential laboratory of my own life, I began exploring the possibility of turning the lead of fear of aging into the gold of a new way of embracing elderhood. My ultimate goal was to learn how to master the art of aging while turning it into inner strength and personal power. I wasn't sure exactly where to begin, but I knew that I needed to collect some basic information so I could understand the complexity of the challenging issue I decided to tackle. In a methodical auto-didactic approach, I delved into the topic of aging from an intellectual perspective, which was quite different from the observation-empirical approach that I'd learned about it in my youth when I worked at my father's nursing home. I needed to understand exactly what aging was and how it affected both individual and society. However, after reading numerous books and countless hours of research, I ended up with a substantial amount of information that augmented my knowledge of the issues of aging but did not yield the practical results I was after. In spite of compiling so much valuable data, I remained clueless as to what strategy to employ in my quest to learning how to turn the shortcomings of the aging process into personal power.

The Low Point

In a late summer afternoon, I was swinging in a hammock in my backyard feeling forlorn. Despite the pleasant sounds of blue jays and robins chirping in the trees' branches above me, I allowed myself to be hijacked by negative thoughts and concerns about getting older. As I looked back, it seemed to me that all began on the day that

Douglas, my brawny sexagenarian workout buddy, uttered the statement that turned a switch on in my awareness of aging. When he asserted with utmost conviction that he was going to "fight aging to the end," it ignited my interest in exploring a different, more effective, and realistic strategies for dealing with the challenges of the aging process. However, a few months after starting my exploratory journey to find out whether there was a way to master the art of aging, I realized that the potential hardships that come with old age were much broader and comprehensive than I'd anticipated. I was surprised to become aware of many aspects of aging that had eluded me for so long, including the socioeconomic ramifications. Because of my employment history and unsteady financial situation, suddenly the economic element of aging began concerning me more than all the other facets combined. For some reason, I'd never given a thought to the financial, emotional, existential, and all the other possible adversities in old age that were beyond the strictly biophysical transmutation. I felt dispirited not knowing what other approach to take in my pursuit of learning to cope with the challenges of the aging process.

"Damn!" I exclaimed hearing my phone ringing inside the house. Instead of feeling grateful that the sound awoke me from my daytime worrying nightmare, I climbed out of the hammock muttering unpleasant words that were in tune with my grumpy mood. Dragging my feet along the prickly brownish dry grass that stabbed my bare feet, I walked inside the house to grab the phone lying on the living-room table.

"Whass up braddah?" Jim, my good friend from Hawaii who always spoke with me in impeccable pidgin English was on the line. After a long chitchat in which we covered subjects ranging from poi to surfing, he mentioned the main reason for his calling. "Remember that hapa-haole dude Zen Master that we talked about many years ago? Well, guess what braddah? I read in the Honolulu Advertiser that he's going to be on the mainland speaking in several states; and he'll be in your necks of the wood next weekend. Since you're into this Zen stuff, I thought you might be interested in checking him out."

After hanging up the phone, I remembered when Jim mentioned to me in one of our many conversations about this Zen Master from Honolulu who was also a martial arts expert. For what I recalled, he was a hapa (half) Japanese-American born in Hawaii to a Japanese father from Kyoto and a white (haole) American mother from Oklahoma. He'd spent many years in a Japanese Zen monastery studying and practicing martial arts with one of the monks who was a renowned expert in the art of *Bushido* (the way of the warrior). Although I was impressed with his dual background in Zen Buddhism and *Bushido*, I never bothered to find out more details about this man's accomplishments. But now that my inner instability about my own aging process was assailing me, I thought it might be a good time for me to go find out what the fuss about this martial artist Zen Master was all about. Thus, I marked down the date on my calendar determined to attend the event.

The Turning Point

Since I started investigating the possibility of mastering the art of aging, I had come across some information that was anything but empowering; in fact, some were downright frightening. And as I approached the end of my

50s, I desperately needed to establish a strong mental and emotional foundation upon which to build my courage, strength, and resilience that would subdue my fears of aging. I was resolute to find the pathway leading to the Holy Grail of Power Aging; that state of being in which unwavering tranquility in the face of the challenges of the passing of time abides unperturbed. It was becoming evident to me that Zen was the only path that would lead me to such a state of equanimity as I aged.

Although it was still officially the end of summer, the signs of a wet winter to come was in the air. Despite Oregon's well-deserved reputation as a water-drenched state, the rain that was coming down the Saturday that the Zen Master from Hawaii was going to make a presentation was uncharacteristic for that time of the year. Since I wasn't feeling at my best, as it'd been an unpleasant norm lately, the weather put a damper on my interest to attend the event. All of a sudden all I wanted to do was to open a bottle of wine, cuddle up with a book, smoke my pipe, and listen to Bach's fugues with the soothing sounds of the rain drops falling on the roof in the background. However, I'm aware that the more important a call to action is to your own best interest, the more resistance intensifies to prevent what must be done. Resistance, like fear, is a thief of great opportunities, and I wasn't going to let it steal from me again. Besides, what did I have to lose but a rainy Saturday evening when I had nothing special to do anyway? (Drinking wine, reading books, smoking my pipe, listening to Bach—and even the rain drops falling on the roof—were regular routines in my life.) Thus, without giving myself too much time to reconsider, I grabbed my raincoat and headed out the door for the hour-long drive to the event.

❧ The First Step of a Thousand-Mile Journey ❧

In spite of the heavy rain fall that forced me to drive under the speed limit while the wipers moved at the fastest pace squeaking against the windshield, I arrived right on time for the beginning of the presentation. I walked in and scanned the half-filled room until I spotted a vacant chair in the front row. There were probably a couple of dozen people scattered around of what I thought it was a small space for the occasion, which was a pleasant surprise, for it would be conducive to a more intimate atmosphere. I was fidgeting on the chair eager for the event to begin when a silvery-haired woman wearing black round frame glasses stepped into the room to introduce the guest speaker. After giving the audience some inspiring information about his background, the hostess announced: "Ladies and gentlemen, it is my pleasure and honor to welcome Roshi Jesse Takanaka."

Everyone stood up in reverence as soon as he appeared. I was in awe watching the lanky shaved head old man wearing a long light burgundy robe walk in. Gazing at him without blinking, I estimated that he was probably in his late 70s or early 80s, but with the disposition and stance of someone 30 years younger. As he moved along with steady gentle steps toward the center of the room, the place seemed to be held hostage by the spellbinding presence of his being. Although only he had walked in, suddenly it felt like the room had been filled up to capacity. When he stopped a few feet away from me, I noticed how his tanned wrinkled face camouflaged the slightly slanted eyes he inherit from his father's genes. Then, he bowed to greet the audience before sitting down on a large green pillow (zafu) on the floor at the center in the front of the room.

"I spent half of my life retreated from the world in a Zen monastery located on a mountain top in a remote region of Japan," he spoke in perfect slightly accented English. "While isolated from the world for some 40-plus years, I learned more about it than during the time I participated in its chaotic ways and shared the madness with my fellowmen and women. Every morning, instead of dashing out the door for the long daily commute in snarled traffic, I sat in meditation for an hour to welcome another day of my life. During the day, while my worldly brothers and sisters were stressing over figures and facts at work, I was studying the art of being still in the midst of confusion. And when the workers of the world rejoiced the fleeting respite of a weekend they longed for after five days of drudgery labor, I spent long weekends practicing martial arts to remind me that there is no respite for those in the pursuit of knowledge and personal power."

I listened to him agape. The cadence of his words and the melodious tone of his voice flowed to me like gentle waters of wisdom cascading through the parched terrain of my mind. With my enthralled eyes fixated on him, I wondered why I had not taken my studies of Zen more seriously over the years, as well as practicing zazen (sitting meditation) with more regularity, especially when I was so fascinated with it at the time. Perhaps it was my busy and hectic schedule that deviated me from the path; or maybe it was when I went through a divorce that threw my life topsy-turvy. But the truth is that had I strived "to be Zen" uninterruptedly, I probably wouldn't be dealing with my anxieties about the aging process at this stage in my life. In any case, I could not rewind the clock, but surely I could become aware of the time that is happening now and proceed into the future accordingly.

"To practice Zen or the martial arts, you must live intensely, wholeheartedly, and without reserve, as if you might die at any moment; because in reality, you very well may. Lacking this sort of commitment, Zen becomes mere ritual and the martial arts devolve into mere sport,"[1] he continued. "This is why the Zen emphasis on simplicity and self-control, full awareness at every moment, and tranquility in the face of death set well with the samurai way of life, or *Bushido*, the way of the warrior. And even though I wouldn't associate the struggles of life with a battlefield, the practice of Zen allows for a meaningful and intimate connection with the self in an inner unity with life that unfolds independent of your will. It's by abandoning attachment to the illusion of the concept of permanence that you become free from the slavery of the fear of losing, whatever the object of your fear may be."

As I listened to him attentively, I realized that in the quiet private space of my mind I was connecting the dots of everything he was saying to my quest of mastering the art of aging. "Live intensely as you might die at any moment," shouldn't be relegated to the approach of a samurai who's constantly preparing for battle. It sounded more like a realistic motto that everyone, especially those in my age group, should apply to their way of living. And when he mentioned "abandoning attachment to the illusion of permanence," I couldn't help but think of our culture's obsession with ephemeral youth and people's adamant attachment and desperate fear of letting go of it as if it were possible to stop the passing of time. But it was when he referred to "becoming free from the slavery of the fear of losing, whatever the object of your fear may be," that his message rang in my head like an alarm clock awakening me from my self-imposed nightmarish fear of aging. Then, sitting there in the front row gawking at this old wise man, I had a Eureka moment that in the straightforward simplicity of Zen may lie the secret of mastering the art of aging that I was eagerly searching.

"As you listen to my words you may be asking yourselves a few questions: How is it possible to maintain self-control, full awareness of the moment, and tranquility in the midst of chaos and uncertainty? How is it possible to see through the veil of illusion of time and impermanence? How can you rid yourself from the attachment to everything you hold dear to your heart?" He questioned the audience whose attention he'd captured with both his words and the magnanimity of his being. "Since all these experiences can only happen inside of each one of you, both the answers and the source of strength necessary to exercise them can only be found within yourselves; each according to his and her own individual ability. However, the common path leading to this inner source of empowerment is through *dhyana*, which is a Sanskrit word for deep meaningful meditation practice that has the potential to alter consciousness. In Zen we call this practice zazen."

He paused for an abnormally long period of time leaving the audience on the edge of their seats with anticipation. Looking at him from the front row, I could tell that his speech intermission was purposeful.

"Let me make it clear that *dhyana* is not the actual experience that a person has when sitting, but the effect that meditation has on their habitual way of looking at the world. In other words, meditation is essentially a means to an end, and not an end in itself,"[2] he said followed by another brief pause. "The essential objective of meditation is neither to alleviate the stress from the mind nor to become inspired in the quietness of the transitory moment, though both happen as an effortless outcome of the sitting. The ultimate purpose of the diligent practice of zazen is to transcend our limited perceptions of the world and ourselves. It's through the eyes of *dhyana* that we can see the illusion of time and the reality of impermanence."

After the conclusion of his talk, there was no applause or fanfare. Instead, a peaceful moment filled the room with reverent silence expressing appreciation for his insights. Then, the silvery-haired hostess walked back in the room as the gentle sounds of her footsteps adjourned the stillness in the air.

"And now, ladies and gentlemen, Roshi Takanaka will take your questions," she said.

Sitting in the front row just a few feet away from Zen Master Takanaka, I raised my hand right away to ensure that I would not leave without asking questions on the topic that mattered to me the most.

"Roshi Takanaka, I would like to know your thoughts on how the Zen approach to life can alleviate the numerous challenges inherent to the aging process. Is it really possible to become unconcerned, or unattached as you put it, to the gradual deterioration of the physical body and all the diminishing functions of what once was a youthful and vibrant life experience? Is there some sort of a Zen secret to the universal human dilemma of aging?" I asked noticing that my voice was quivering by my own anxieties about the uncertainties of what may lie ahead.

The old wise man remained silent for a brief moment with his eyes anchored on mine. I felt both uncomfortable and mesmerized noticing the luminosity emanating from his stare. Then, he squinted ever so faintly and I could see his radiant slanted eyes smiling at me.

"If you could experience yourself, not as the body that you can feel and see in the mirror, but as a wandering being in a spiritual pilgrimage who needs the physical vehicle to travel through this temporal realm of existence, you wouldn't have even asked me this question. You see, unlike your selfish earthly desires or your attachment to your possessions, the aging process is not something that you should strive to be unattached, or unconcerned as you put it, for aging is a natural law of life just as the law of gravity. And in the same way that a crystal glass pulled down by the law of gravity from a higher elevation will inevitably shatter as it crashes to the ground, the aging process, be it of a person, an animal, or a celestial star, will also complete its cycle at the end of its allotted time as determined by a similar natural law."

I was about to interject to request a less philosophical and more practical answer to my question, but his steady eyes let me know that he wasn't through yet. He kept looking at me without saying a word. Suddenly, what I had felt as maternal loving eyes a moment earlier had turned paternally stern. In the meantime, my mind was racing and I couldn't stop thinking: either a natural law or a draconian edict imposed on humanity by vindictive gods, the fact is that the aging process is an undeniable challenge of the universal human experience that most everyone must endure and overcome. And I was on a life mission to find a way to assuage the drama of the denouement of the great play of life. But I needed help, and Roshi Takanaka was the one I was counting on at the time.

"As for a Zen secret regarding the aging process, if there is one, you must find it within yourself, for you are the very essence of what Zen is supposed to be; the mindfulness of your own living experience," he said. "Thus, if there is a Zen secret hiding somewhere, it must be buried within your own desire to discover it, and you are the only one who can unearth it. And who knows, you might find not only the answer to your quandary, but also a potential source of inner strength that you never imagined you possessed. But you'll find out only if you begin the process."

Motionlessly looking at him, I noticed that the loving maternal-like light was shining in his eyes again. Then, he smiled before turning his face in the direction of another attendee who had raised her hand to ask a question.

After that evening, my determination to find the secret formula for mastering the art of aging was elevated to a heightened stage. Now that I'd learned where it was buried, all I needed was to acquire the necessary tools to dig it out to the surface of my consciousness.

Chapter 2

The Reawakening of Zen

An Unorthodox Zendo

Several months after attending Roshi Jesse Takanaka's presentation, I revitalized my interest in Eastern philosophy studies and became a rededicated mindful practitioner of Zen. I went through my library and reviewed my annotations in all of the Zen books I'd read in the past, and I continued reading everything I could lay my hands on the subject. In addition, I resumed practicing zazen on a daily basis, created a Zen garden in my backyard, engaged in solitary tea ceremonies (chado), among other Zen activities that I thought would help me expand mindfulness. Determined to explore all the possibilities and inspired by Roshi Takanaka's example, I even joined a martial arts *dojo* to practice, not martial arts per se, but my ability to remain focused and tranquil in the heat of sparring battles with much younger opponents. All my efforts and dedication were fundamentally related to my unflinching pursuit of discovering how I could turn my own aging process into personal power. My ultimate goal was to use my Zen practice as the tool with which to dig out the secret of mastering the art of aging that, as Roshi Takanaka had pointed out, lay hidden inside of me. It was the only place where I would find the pathway leading to the enlightenment of aging.

"Really, this is the main reason you practice *jujitsu*?" Alan, the young man with whom I'd just finished sparring asked me with an inquisitive frown when I told him about my Zen practice.

"It seems like a very good reason to me," I replied nonchalantly. "*Jujitsu* is just one of many ways to practice Zen.[1] From brush drawing and flute playing to archery and fencing, there are many different ways to practice Zen. And by the way, what's your motivation?"

He hesitated for a moment as his eyes moved away from my gaze. "I want to learn fighting techniques that will help me defend myself against a potential aggressor."

I immediately noticed the subtle anxiety he expressed about the possibility of having to engage in hand-to-hand combat against some bully on the street. Both his words and body language revealed a suppressed fear of an impending adversary who could show up unexpectedly to challenge his skills and mettle.

"Well, in this case it seems to me that both our motivation and objectives are pretty much the same," I said.

"What do you mean?" He asked raising his chin and staring back at me right away seemingly eager to hear my answer.

"Like you, I'm also developing techniques that I can rely on to face a fast-moving opponent that I can neither defeat nor escape from. However, this adversary threatening my well-being and forcing me to prepare against, cannot be conquered with *jujitsu* techniques. Only a Zen approach will equip me with the skills I need to overcome it, even though in the end I'll be defeated," I said as Alan looked at me with a contorted face as if I spoke hodgepodge. "And our objectives are the same as well: we both want to overcome our fear of unpredictable circumstances by acquiring the skills necessary to confront the assailant whenever he shows up to challenge our resolve."

"What are you talking about, man?" He asked sounding both confused and annoyed with what he could not comprehend, yet.

"The opponent I'm preparing for is the same you and everyone else will have to deal with at some point in life. It sneaks up on you from the shadows of the passing of time; an opponent that you do not heed when you're young, until it suddenly appears to confront you to a mortal combat that wears you out piecemeal."

"Now you really lost me, man," he said displaying his frustration.

"I'm talking about the aging process, my friend; and eventually, it'll come to challenge you as well," I said noticing that the contortions in Alan's face began disentangling the confusion that had tightened it up. "As for our objectives, we both want to be ready for the moment that will call for the skills we need to meet the challenge ahead. At this stage in your life, knowing how to apply an impairing choke hold or arm lock is your goal; but mine is to develop the inner fortitude and serenity to confront, without conflict, a natural foe that I cannot subjugate. Thus, I practice *jujitsu* to improve my Zen techniques of mindfulness, tranquility, and self-control in the face of daunting situations; like when you had pinned me down ready to set up an arm bar that would have forced me to tap out."

He smiled and seemed to be smug by my comment. Then, he looked into my eye with his right eyebrow slightly raised as though he wondered who was this unorthodox middle-aged man who'd recently joined the martial arts *dojo*.

"Listen, do you think you'd have some time to talk with me more about Zen? You got me curious and I'd like to learn more about it," Alan asked in earnest.

"Sure. What about next Friday after practice? We can walk to the coffee-shop down the street and chat about it," I suggested.

His eyes lit up. "Awesome!"

Zen as the Martial Art of the Spirit

After a 90-minute practice of *jujitsu* in which I lost a couple of pounds while gaining significant self-confidence weight, my new young friend and I got together to talk about Zen.

"Since we talked last time, I did some reading about Zen so I wouldn't sound like a total dud talking with you today," Alan said chuckling through his words. "I was surprised to learn how Zen was such an integral part of the martial arts in Japan, especially in the life of the samurai. What I don't understand is how you can connect it to your 'personal battle' with aging."

"You mean, 'our personal battle' with aging. Remember, you're growing older, too," I reminded him. "As you learned, Zen is a fundamental component of martial arts, or *Budo*, the Japanese word for the way of war. But this is a very limited Western translation of the words *bu* (war) and *do* (the way). In reality, the Japanese character *bu* also means 'to cease the struggle,' which in this case the translation of the word *Budo* means 'the way to cease the struggle.' And this is exactly what I'm attempting to accomplish regarding my aging process: I want to find a way to cease the struggle against the inevitability of becoming old."

As I noticed the attentive expression in Alan's youthful face, my mind wandered to the past recollecting the day that Douglas, my burly sexagenarian workout buddy, emphatically stated that he was "going to fight aging to the end." Since I realized the absurdity of his avowal, I'd been trying to find a different approach to face the challenges of aging in a more effective and realistic fashion. In the many months since I heard Douglas' statement, I had come to the conclusion that his attitude toward aging was more like a sports activity in which the spirit of competition to trounce the opponent is the ultimate goal. In his case, however, it was an impossible task to accomplish. Me, on the other hand, I wanted to tackle my aging process in the spirit of Zen in which the struggles of everyday life was not a contest to be lost or won, but a mindful awareness of my evolutionary process at a distinct stage of my life.

"It sounds like martial arts and Zen are one and the same; it's like the very spirit of *Budo* itself," Alan observed. "But how do you go about applying it to your own personal struggles?"

"By reversing it to a non-struggle; by accepting my human condition without resisting its inevitable transformations and ultimate demise," I answered.

"I still don't understand how you can actually apply it to your daily life," he said before taking a sip of coffee.

I paused for a moment trying to clarify what I was still in the process of discovering myself. "Let's suppose that the *dojo* is the world itself and everything that happens in there within the timeframe of my practice is the only reality I know. After many years of training, the *sensei* determines that I am ready to face the most formidable opponent of all in order to test my mettle and skills. The goal is not to defeat the foe, but to overcome my own doubts and fears with unwavering spirit. In the midst of the sparring, I realize that the adversary is unconquerable and the only thing for me to do is to remain calm and resilient in the heat of a battle that I know I cannot win. It is at this moment that Zen becomes the most important skill of all; the only defense against the indefensible." Alan listened attentively and looked at me like a child enthralled with the details of a haunting story by a campfire. "Suddenly, my unbeatable opponent locks an arm bar in place and forces me to tap out or else I'll have my arm broken. But either way I cannot win the physical contest. However, in this fictitious *dojo*-world, there is another invisible clash taking place: the combat of the power of the spirit in which each individual is engaged in with and by himself. And in this conflict, granted that I remain resolute in my quest to overcome defeat itself, then, in the end, I am the ultimate winner, broken arm or not."

Alan's eyes moved side-to-side under his furrowed brow. He looked flummoxed after hearing my analogy. I decided to be more specific.

"Through the martial art of *jujitsu* you learn fighting techniques that can only help you in physical combat. Zen, on the other hand, teaches you how to overcome the most redoubtable opponent you'll ever face in your life: fear of the unknown. It trains the practitioner for a different kind of battle, the one that takes place within where the ego is snarled in the chains of fear. Thus, by letting go of the ego, the fear is carried away with it and there is nothing left but serenity of being. In my own quest to learning how to master the art of aging, I realized that I must always go with the natural flow of time and never against it, for it is a foolish attempt to achieve the impossible that will only increase my stress level without yielding any positive results. In this sense, Zen is the martial arts of the human spirit, and the only technique I know that allows me to be victorious even in defeat."

"I think I get it," Alan said as his eyes returned to a normal relaxed state. "You're symbolizing the aging process with the hypothetical opponent that you cannot defeat, and the only reasonable reaction to its overwhelming power is to surrender."

"Yes, but you're not surrendering to the opponent's dominance over you; you're surrendering to the skills you have mastered as a martial artist of Zen. As in the martial arts of *jujitsu*, you don't have to think about the technique when you need to apply it; it explodes from within whenever you need it. Through the meditative practice of zazen and the monitoring of your behavior, thoughts, and attitudes toward life's continuous changes, your mind becomes attuned with the unconscious techniques you've developed. Then, you no longer try to resist the natural flow of life or fear the inevitability of the passing of time."

"That's right! Now I remember when *sensei* talked to a group of us a couple of months ago about becoming one with *jujitsu* techniques as if they were natural elements of who we are," Alan said as his excitement reached a higher plateau.

"*Sensei* was right on. In fact, this mentality is applicable to all martial arts approaches," I said. "For instance, in *kyujutsu*, the art of archery, the bow, the arrow, the target, and the archer must all become one and the same. If you wish to be a master of an art, technical knowledge of it is not enough. You must transcend technique so that the art becomes part of you. This state of unconsciousness is realized only when, completely empty and rid of the self, you become one with the perfecting of your technical skill. As soon as you reflect, deliberate, and conceptualize, the original unconsciousness is lost and thoughts interfere with what is supposed to be an effortless action.[2] It is no different in Zen practice. When a man reaches this stage of development of the mind and spirit he can consider himself a Zen martial artist of life."

Our conversation progressed at an enthusiastic pace for another half-hour or so. After covering an array of topics related to Zen and the martial arts, Alan thanked me for sharing information with him and we bid farewell with the agreement that we'd meet again sometime in the future. As I walked home, I thought of how much our talk had benefited me, too. Not only he made some interesting observations of his own, I realized that most of the knowledge that I shared with him came from my own subconscious mind while processing my thoughts based on all the readings and research I'd done over the years. That realization inspired me to delve into my books to further my investigation of the link between Zen and the martial arts in relation to the art of aging.

❧ The Reawakening of Zen ☙

The Martial Arts and the Zen of Aging

Later that evening while smoking my pipe by the fireplace after dinner, I was mulling over the questions that I'd been obsessed with for a long time: how could I prevail against a foe that cannot be defeated? How could I overcome what is, in the case of the aging process, a seemingly insurmountable obstacle? Haphazardly, I glanced at my bookshelves and my eyes drifted toward the martial arts books section of my library. I stood up and ran my fingers through the books' spines until they stopped at Sun Tzu's classic *The Art of War*. I picked up the volume and leafed through my notes from the time I'd read it many years ago (I always highlight the text and write notes on the margins of my books, for I don't read books, I consume them like meals for my starved mind). The last four lines of page nine were highlighted: "Therefore, one hundred victories in one hundred battles is not the most skillful. Subduing the other's military without battle is the most skillful."[3] My handwritten note on the bottom margin summarized my interpretation of the message this way: "The supreme art of war is to subdue the enemy without fighting."

Mindfully gazing at the swirling smoke coming out of my pipe's bowl, I thought of the wisdom of Sun Tzu's words in relation to the aging process, which was the opposite approach that my muscular aging friend Douglas was determined to pursue. I placed a piece of paper on the page of the citation and kept leafing through the book randomly (highlighting and taking notes are a must for a studious reader, but dog-earing a book is a cardinal sin to a devout bibliophile). "If you know the enemy and know yourself, you need not fear the result of a hundred battles. If you know yourself but not the enemy, for every victory gained you will also suffer a defeat. If you know neither the enemy nor yourself, you will succumb in every battle."[4]

Even though aging is not an enemy per-se but a symbolic representation of an opposing force of nature, accepting it as inevitable is a battle already won. Furthermore, knowing yourself to be a temporal being existing within a finite scheme of life is the first step leading "not to fear the result of a hundred battles"—or years as the case may be. Suddenly, I realized that I was on to unearthing some truth from the profound simplicity of ancient oriental wisdom in relation to aging. I became utterly captivated and committed to delving into this exploratory journey of self-discovery. I was determined to find out how I could turn the aging process around and make it work for me instead of against me. In other words, I wanted to learn how I could subdue the enemy without fighting it.

I put my pipe down on the stainless steel stand and began glancing through my martial arts books collection. The books about the Japanese martial art of *jujitsu* immediately caught my attention. I grabbed one off the shelf and leafed through my highlighted notes and came across the definition and explanation of what is believed to be the oldest martial arts. It read: *"ju* means pliability, flexibility, or to give way, and *jitsu* means a fighting form or practice." I kept reading the text further as it explained how this most proficient martial art works, which is neither by aggressive action nor opposing the enemy's strength. Its effectiveness comes from turning the opponent's aggression against himself and by adjusting to his actions in battle. Its objective is not to destroy the adversary, but to incapacitate the opponent in order to render him incapable of resistance. In essence, *jujitsu*, as well as its offshoot *judo*, is the martial art of giving in to force in order to overcome it.

"Huh, as a philosophical approach, this is definitely applicable to the aging process," I mumbled holding my chin with my indicator finger and thumb. "If old age is to be perceived as the overbearing opponent that cannot be defeated, then the only way to overcome it is by incapacitating its ability to have an effect on me. In the case of aging as the opposing force, however, I'm the one who must be rendered incapable of resistance to it, for any other action will prove to be a futile effort."

I placed the *jujitsu* book back on the shelf and let my fingers guide my eyes through the titles in that section. They stopped at a yellow book spine with the title *What is Aikido?*[5] in black ink. I took the book in my hands and while perusing it I realized that the martial art of *Aikido* also focuses on fighting back by simply giving way to aggression. It is a martial art of integration founded by Morihei Ueshiba (1883–1969) who discovered that applied nonviolence is one of the most potent weapons in the human arsenal. It is a discipline that emphasizes harmony and the peaceful resolution of conflict, as well as a physical and spiritual exercise aiming to unify the body and spirit with the natural forces of the Universe.

Once again, I immediately linked the principles of this martial art to my quest of finding a way to prevail over the apprehension of aging without resistance. My first reaction after refreshing my memory about the principles of *Aikido* was the realization that the aging process is a source of inner conflict that amplifies as time goes by. Being *Aikido* a discipline that emphasizes harmony and the peaceful resolution of conflict with the natural forces of the Universe, I wondered how it could be applicable to overcoming the natural forces of aging without fighting it. At the moment the thought occurred, another *Aikido* book caught my attention. I pulled it off the shelf, opened randomly, and read: "Life is a divine gift. The divine is not something outside of us; it is right in our very center, it is our freedom. In the *dojo* we are always learning about life and death. To be victorious is to create life; to be defeated is to give up and die. Abandon petty thoughts, empty yourself, transcend life and death, and stand upright in the center of vast creation. This is the secret of *Aikido*."[6]

I paused to mull the passage over. "To be victorious is to create life; to be defeated is to give up and die...transcend life and death," I muttered as my thoughts raced through my mind. "This is how you ought to apply the principles of *Aikido* to the art of aging; this is how you can be victorious in old age," I said out loud in a more distinctive voice using the pronoun you as though I conversed with myself. "In order to create life you must feel alive and never give up your zest for living, no matter what the outside circumstances may be, otherwise you'll be defeated and die, even if your heart still beats while the air fills your lungs. You must find a purpose, both within and outside yourself if you are going to be able to transcend life and death at the latter years of your life. The past, present, and even the future are all contained in the now, the only moment when you can truly experience being alive. After all, as Einstein asserted, 'the distinction between past, present, and future is only a stubbornly persistent illusion.'"[7]

Suddenly, I noticed that I was quiet for a long time staring empty-mindedly at the ceiling with the opened book in my hand. I shook my head gently nibbling on my lower lip as I still digested the soliloquy that I just engaged in.

When I pushed the *Aikido* book back on the shelf, the volume adjacent to it demanded my attention. It was a book about the Chinese martial art of *T'ai Chi Ch'uan*. I pulled out the red cover book and browsed through it as I recalled watching a video about Chinese culture that showed elders practicing *T'ai Chi* in public parks in Beijing. I remembered marveling at the effortless fluidity in which the practitioners moved about through the empty spaces around them. The beautifully harmonious movements seemed to occur as if it were a choreographed display of unity between their bodies and the small segment of Universe they occupied. I surmised that because there was no resistance, the movements looked like a solitary dance, as though perfection danced with itself. It was at that time that I understood the meaning of "flowing with the *Tao*;" a phrase based on the principle of *Taoism* that refers to the natural flow of life without interfering with it. According to Lao Tzu, who is believed to be the writer of the *Tao Te Ching*, the "Bible" of Taoism, "the world is ruled by letting things take their course." If that's the case, then why should it be any different with the aging process?

I took the *T'ai Chi* book and sat down on my reading chair nearby. As I browsed through my notes, I refreshed my memory about how the Chinese realized more than 4,000 thousand years ago that the two *T'ai Chi* elemental powers, *Yin and Yang*, must interact and the harmonious result could bring progress and unlimited development to the practitioners of this ancient way of life. The Chinese conceived the human mind to be an unlimited dimension and the birth of what we know today as *T'ai Chi* became the invisible power. Being *Yin* the negative power (yielding) and *Yang* the positive power (action), the two equal powers oppose and yet complement each other, and in their balanced interaction lies the essence of *Chi*, or "intrinsic, internal, or ultimate energy" where individual power abides. Thus, through the practice of *T'ai Chi*, it's possible to convert *Chi* into *Nei Jing*, "the internal power," which can be cultivated through meditation and movement.[8]

Following the principle that the two *T'ai Chi* elemental powers, *Yin and Yang*, must interact and complement each other harmoniously in order to become *Chi*, the ultimate energy, I concluded that the opposite duality of youth and old age must also exhibit similar interrelation in order to generate an ultimate energy of aging. In this sense, youth would represent the element *Yin* and old age the equivalent of *Yang*; and together, they composed the *Chi* of life in its entirety. Pondering it further, I realized that if Power Aging were to take place, the *Yin* (youth) must be integrated into the *Yang* (old age) in complementary fashion in the great *Chi* of life. In other words, that youthful spirit that I experienced in the earlier stages of living has to remain present within me in the latter years of my life. What I would need to find out is how to sustain such a vibrant energy at a time in life when my physical strength was gradually dwindling. The conclusion was evident: the focus of the attention of my energy must be placed within; in the spirit that strengthens while the body weakens.

Fascinated with my musings based on the recollection of the information I'd read a long time ago, I picked up my pipe and moved back next to the fireplace where the swinging flames seemed to carry out *T'ai Chi*-like movements of their own. Listening to the crackling of the burning wood that gave off a pleasant rustic fragrance in the living-room, I began concocting the possibility of applying the principles of martial arts to the challenges of the aging process. I realized that fighting it, like my workout buddy Douglas was determined to do, would not generate any positive results, much less victory. However, if I were to yield to the natural progression of time without attempting to fight it or resist its inexorable and inevitable claim of my life, then I might be able to overcome it by default. I would become a sort of Zen martial artist capable of subduing the aging process by applying Sun Tzu's concept that "the supreme art of war is to subdue the enemy without fighting." At that moment, I became convinced that as far as the aging process is concerned, the opportunity to secure myself against defeat lay in my own hands; or as Roshi Takanaka pointed out, "if there is a Zen secret hiding somewhere, it must be buried within your own desire to discover it, and you are the only one who can ferret it out."

Suddenly, a whole new perspective of aging was opening up before my eyes. I realized that even in nature the truth about the effectiveness of *ju* (flexibility, pliability) is demonstrated in the comparison between the willow and the oak trees. In a wind storm, the sturdy and immovable oak tree will likely break, whereas the pliant and yielding willow tree will most certainly survive the ravages of the storm by giving in to its unrestrained might. Hence, the adamant oak will perish while the adaptable willow will endure the tempest unscathed. Since the latter years can be a stormy season in human life, not resisting the forces of nature is the only sure way to overcome it, and therefore survive it. Then, while puffing a billow of smoke into the dancing flames inside the fireplace, I thought that people become old when they refuse to accept aging as the natural component of the evolutionary process of humanity. Instead of flowing with the unavoidable progression of time ("flowing with the *Tao*"), they adamantly attempt to fight it in a desperate futile effort to eschew the adversary that will drub them into submission regardless of how valiantly—or rather foolishly—they resist.

At the end of the evening, I lay in bed staring at the ceiling mulling over all the information that I accumulated the entire day. Now it was crystal-clear to me that the only way to prevail in the struggle against the aging process was by yielding to it without resistance or resentment. Although it was a rational understanding based on common sense observation, the truth is that embracing such an attitude in the midst of piecemeal decline of physical stamina, psychological apprehensions, economic concerns, and diminishing social functions is an undertaking that requires an immense amount of chutzpah. It would necessitate great flexibility (*ju*); strong internal energy (*Chi*); and more importantly, learn how to turn *Chi* into personal power (*Nei Jing*).

By the time I turned off the light and rested my heavy head on the soft pillow, I was convinced that the parturition of Power Aging could only happen through the midwifery of Zen. If I were to give birth to an empowered old man in the latter years of my life, I would have to embrace the pangs of a spiritual labor and open up the entrails of my soul to allow a dynamic newborn elder into being.

Now I was convinced that I was on the right track. As I move toward the twilight of my earthly journey, I believe that the bright rays of a rising Sun is emerging in the horizon of my life as the dawn of my old age draws near. Nevertheless, much work remains to be done before this new day arrives; the day when a self-empowered elder is born.

Chapter 3

The Holy Trinity of Zen

The Gate to the Zen Path of Aging

Of all traditional religions in the world, Zen Buddhism always has been the one that made most sense to me. Unlike other organized faith groups that rely on structured doctrines, sacred deities, and strict rules that followers must conform to in order to be rightfully accepted, I identify my spiritual aspirations with Zen Buddhism's freedom to find truth within without having to observe holy dogmas or abide by austere religious laws. However, I'm more interested in the Zen element of Buddhism in a fundamentally secular way. For my individual purpose of learning how to master the art of aging, what I needed was to study and learn Zen as a tool with which to build my personal power; to discover the meaning of my human experience in the latter years of my life. To me, reaching enlightenment or *Nirvana* was only possible through self-empowerment.

Since Zen Buddhism was the route I chose to lead me to finding answers to the questions of my existence in my latter years, understanding its principles was paramount for my purpose. Thus, I decided that in my next annual trip down to The Oregon Shakespeare Festival in Ashland, Oregon, I would pay a visit to the Shasta Abbey Buddhist Monastery in nearby Mount Shasta, California, to do some homework and hoping to get some insights from the resident monks.

"Is this your first time visiting the abbey?" A young woman standing next to me in the abbey's grounds facing Mount Shasta asked me after overhearing my sighing out loud, for I was in awe with the breathtaking view.

"Yes, it is. I didn't expect it to be this beautiful," I said.

"Very likely it won't be your last visit either," she remarked with a friendly smile. "I've been driving up here all the way from the Bay Area every summer since my first visit six years ago. This place is where I recharge my spiritual batteries."

"Do you know whom I could see to ask a few questions about my personal quest?" I inquired trying to find out how I could get my investigation started. Since she was a regular visitor of the abbey, I thought she could offer me some hints.

"Well, it all depends on what you're after. If you want some in-depth information, I suggest your participating in one of the introductory retreats they offer and go from there. But if you just want a few questions answered, then you might give it a shot approaching a monk who might be available to talk with you."

I walked around with that in mind. But after a few minutes wandering about the serene arboreal environment, I realized that the few monks I saw were either engaged talking to other visitors or doing some chore that I didn't dare to interrupt. I ended up in the main building where a colossal statue of a Buddhist image I didn't recognize stood in commanding fashion. It didn't look like anything I'd ever seen before in the lore of Zen Buddhism. The imposing size of his presence was accentuated by a rope he held in his left hand and an upward sword he held in the right. But it was the stern and fierce expression in his face that verged on a wrathful appearance that surprised me to see in a Zen monastery.

"Excuse me. What does this sculpture represent?" I asked an older nun who was walking into the building.

She stopped facing it and bowed respectfully before answering my question. "This is *Fudō-myōō*; The Immovable One."

"*Fudō-myōō*?" I repeated feeling the skin in my forehead crumpling. "What does *Fudō-myōō* represent?"

"He is the protector of Buddhism," she said.

"But he looks irate, not at all the likeness of the loving peaceful Buddha," I said looking at the statue's ominous facial expression.

"*Fudō-myōō* has the ability to convert anger into salvation. His furious glaring face is meant to frighten anyone who dares to threaten those on the path of enlightenment. The sword he carries in his right hand is called a '*kurikara*' or evil-subduing sword, which represents wisdom that cuts through ignorance. See the rope in his left hand?" She asked pointing at the oversize wooden sculpture. "With it he catches and binds up demons. *Fudō*'s aureole is typically the flames of fire, which according to Buddhist tradition represent the purification of the mind by the burning away of all material desires."

The way the nun looked at me, I probably looked stupefied. Eerily, she added an explanation that indicated she read my mind somehow. "*Fudō-myōō* may look frightening to you, but he actually represents the negative polarity of power that is present everywhere in nature, and Buddhism is no exception. If you're on the path of enlightenment, he shall protect you, too."

She bowed lightly and walked away. My eyes returned to the impressive image of *Fudō-myōō* who stood there like a powerful symbol of protection. I looked at the sculpture for a very long while thinking of the polarities that seem to be present in all life: *Ying* and *Yang*; male and female; positive and negative; good and evil, among many other dualities of which youth and old age also represent. Just like *Fudō-myōō* looked somewhat repulsive to my eyes at first sight, old age has a similar disparaging reaction from most everyone. And yet, like that fearsome Buddhist deity, old age must have, not necessarily the "wisdom that cuts through ignorance," but perhaps an opportunity in time to overcome the ignorance and illusion of the temporal nature of our lives. I needed to explore the interactive dynamic of youth and old age within myself at a later date. But right then, what I needed was to find the gift shop to see if I could buy a medallion, a poster, or even a post-card; anything that had the image of *Fudō-myōō* on it.

The small gift shop that had a few scattered items on shelves and display cases, but not a sign of *Fudō-myōō* anywhere in sight. Standing behind the counter, this young monk with an impassive expression welcomed me with a silent nod. Although he seemed to me to be newly ordained, the glitter in his eyes revealed wisdom beyond his years.

"Do you happen to carry anything with the image of the *Fudō-myōō* statue you have in the shrine in the main hall? I asked not feeling very hopeful for a positive answer.

The Holy Trinity of Zen

"I don't recall anyone ever asking for it before," he replied without answering my question. "And perhaps for that reason, we don't carry anything bearing the image of 'The Immovable One.' Interesting, however, that you asked for it."

"Why?" I asked eager to hear his thoughts.

He moved slowly from behind the counter and stood right before me with his eyes darting into mine as he spoke. "Because you must be searching for truth and you need his guardianship as you proceed in your quest. It was exactly what happened to me, too. Maybe this is why you came here looking for his image. The inscrutable art of synchronicity, I suppose."

I was puzzled. I didn't know what to make of what he just said. Sure, I was searching for truth, but as far as *Fudō-myōō* was concerned, I just wanted a memento of the statue that impressed me, or so I thought.

"If my personal experience can be of any help to you, I tell you that the first time I came here I had a similar reaction when I first came face-to-face with the magnificent image of *Fudō-myōō*. Shortly afterwards, I was introduced to the great triumvirate of Zen Buddhism and I'm convinced that he was the one who guided me to that important realization. A year later I had made up my mind and requested to be accepted for monk training." He paused waiting for my replying. I had absolutely no intention whatsoever to go into monk training, for I always considered myself to be a man of the world, even though not from the world. Thus, I didn't know what to say, except ask a question based on what he said that had intrigued me.

"And what is this great triumvirate of Zen Buddhism?"

"*Dai-shinkon, Dai-gidan,* and *Dai-funshi*," he said.

"What?" I blurted out confused.

"Great Faith, Great Doubt, and Great Determination," he said waiting for another reaction of mine. As I didn't say anything, he continued. "The first of the three essentials of Zen practice is strong faith. This is much more than belief. The ideogram for *kon* in Japanese means 'root,' that for *shin* is faith. Hence, the phrase implies a faith that is firmly and deeply rooted, immovable, like 'The Immovable One' Himself, like an immense tree or a huge boulder. The second indispensable quality is a feeling of strong doubt; a doubt that leaves you no rest. It is as though you know you are a millionaire and yet inexplicably find yourself in dire need without a penny in your pockets. Strong doubt, therefore, exists in proportion to strong faith. From this feeling of doubt the third essential is strong determination, which dispels the doubt with the whole force of your energy and will."[1]

I looked at the young monk with a great deal of curiosity. There I was standing in front of someone decades my junior who was revealing to me a knowledge that was going to prove to be fundamental in my search to finding a way to master the art of aging. I began wondering about my thesis that youth and old age were as interconnected as all the other polarities that sustained the breath of life. Suddenly, it seemed to make more sense to me that youth and old age were the *Yin* and *Yang* in the spectrum of time. You can be very young and yet display characteristics of old age, such as the wisdom this young man was demonstrating to me. On the other hand, you can be very old and display a very youthful attitude toward life. And even though the popular dictum says that "youth is wasted on the young," the same can be true in reverse, since not everyone who reaches old age becomes a wise individual. Age is often wasted on the old.[2]

"Faith is the voice inside of you that reassures that all is well; that's all right to experience uncertainty in your life, especially if it leads to a greater knowledge of yourself," he continued. "The reward of faith is trust: trust in yourself and trust in life's uncanny ability to direct the right people, situations and circumstances to you. Doubt challenges you to put your preconceptions aside and reappraise your beliefs as well as the strength of your faith. Doubt compels you to face your weaknesses with courage, which leads you to develop great determination to overcome them. And it is determination that solidifies your resolve to find the answer to the questions of your life, while bestowing you with passion and will to both make and accept changes."[3]

By the time I left the Shasta Abbey Buddhist Monastery, I could not stop thinking about what I started referring to as "the holy trinity of Zen." As I walked out of this hallowed place of seclusion hearing only the chirping of birds and the sounds of my footsteps crushing dry leaves on the ground, I marveled at how I, a man in my late 50s, learned a most valuable lesson from a young man whose devotion to self-development equipped him with the tools with which to build personal power. I kept ambling toward the exit gate beholding the tall trees while thinking about both the nature and function of faith, doubt, and determination in human development, in all stages of life. It seemed to me that it doesn't matter whether you're young or old, the continuous challenges that life presents to the evolving human being will always be fraught with changes and the uncertainties of the unknown; the Great Doubt, which requires Great Faith and Great Determination to rise above them. I was convinced that even that young sensible monk living in such a consecrated environment experienced doubts and fears, albeit in a much more empowered way than the average worldly citizen like me. But that was my goal for the latter years of my life: to learn how to embrace the attitude of a Zen monk while living in the mundane world as I aged. Evidently, my first step in that direction would have to begin with a comprehensive understanding of Great Faith, Great Doubt, and Great Determination; not at the intellectual concept level, but what it means to experience it in steadfast conduct.

Driving northbound back to my home state of Oregon, I pondered over the holy trinity of Zen and how I would embrace life's tribulations at a time that is arguably the most challenging stretch in the individual human existence. Sure, uncertainty is the common denominator in the universal equation of life, and whether you're seven or seventy, the unknown is your constant companion. However, after the 50-year-old milestone, the dread of doubt is significantly magnified by the anxiety of old age and death, the latter being the most daunting unknown of all that awaits at the end of your earthly journey. It's like going through a dark tunnel that doesn't show any signs of light at the end. Perhaps, only the pious believers who desperately need some bearings in the face of the forbidding unknown can see the mirage of a heavenly home where their creator awaits in redemption. But don't we all need a sense of security when confronted by fear? Of Course we do, but I wanted my point of reference to be solidly buttressed within my own inner strength; something I could rely on instinctively rather than counting on an unverifiable intellectual reverie of numinous beings and realms that are as doubtful as doubt itself. I had to become the foundation upon which I could build my inner courage and resilience. And even if I were to explore the possibility of numinous beings and realms, I would have to experience them inside of me, not at some distant idyllic domain concocted by imagination under the negative influence of fear.

The Fourth Element

When I got home after a 5-hour drive, I decided to soak my achy body in a hot lavender bath and douse my stimulated mind in the musing of what I'd learned that day. I played my favorite Bach's violin concertos CD and inspired by my newly discovered holy trinity of Zen, I lit three colored candles on the bathroom counter: the yellow representing faith, the blue symbolizing doubt, and the red portraying the fiery action of determination. The conducive ambiance for physical relaxation and intellectual retrospection was set up. But as I'm about to step in the bathtub to immerse myself in the fragrant soothing warm water, I noticed that there was another regular white candle on the brown tile counter that demanded my attention as though it had a life of its own and griped that it had not been lit. With my right foot already in the tub, I kept looking at the white candle thinking that I should not light it because it would disturb the symbolic pattern that I was trying to create. And yet, I was unable to get the other foot in until, begrudgingly, I lit the fourth white candle without knowing why I was doing it. I spent awhile absent-mindedly staring at the flames of the four candles as they seemed to dance in synchronized fashion to the enchanting sounds of Bach's violin concerto in A minor. Then, I got into the tub and submerged myself entirely in the liquid bliss of my bath with gusto.

As soon as I came up to the surface with water dripping down my face, I dried my eyes and looked at the four wide colored candles on the counter. It was the only source of light illuminating the steamy bathroom. I gazed at the yellow candle and reflected on the meaning of Great Faith as the young monk had told me: Faith is the voice inside that reassures us that all is fine, that it is all right to have uncertainty in our lives; that the reward of faith is unwavering trust, which is very different from belief. Faith, unrestricted faith, is an experience of the heart, whereas belief is the intellectual conceptualization based on opinion and judgment. I thought of many people I'd met in my life who claimed to be true believers—in God, religion, democracy, political parties, ideologies, or even their spouses—but had very little faith in them. Thus, I surmised that Great Faith is an unconditional act of surrender to the unknown, which will never be revealed in this time and space of awareness, the now. It is the ultimate act of confidence, both in the self and the inscrutable forces of life. And whether people call it God, the Tao, the Universe, Mother Nature, or whatever nomenclature they want to attribute to this power, it doesn't really matter for it won't change it what it is. A pen is a pen whether the French call it *"stylo,"* or the Spanish *"pluma,"* or the Portuguese *"caneta."* It's just different languages referring to the same object in different words. The concept of God, the Tao, or the Universe has a very similar association; that is, distinctive terms for the same source of power. And Great Faith is deeply rooted in the confidence that this power is writing the story of life—mine and everyone else's—with utmost perfection. Thus, surrendering to the storyteller's crafty competence is the only role that the protagonist of the chronicles of my life needs to do.

Then, my eyes shifted to the blue candle and I started doubting everything I'd just ruminated about. I gazed at its swinging flame intently until it illuminated my mind with the nature of the purpose of doubt. "Of course," I mumbled through my teeth realizing that without doubt that would be no reason, purpose, or function for faith to exist at all. Like *Yin* and *Yang*, light and darkness, good and evil, male and female, and all the other essential complementary dualities that bestow meaning to life, Great Faith could only exist juxtaposed to Great Doubt. It is from their union that trust is born. I may have my fears, suspicions, and even believe there is something terribly wrong with my life or the world. But if in the midst of Great Doubt I gain the confidence to surrender to Great Faith trusting that everything is working itself out, even though I can't possibly comprehend how, then I might find myself doubting my own doubts.

I was still gazing at the blue candle's flame when I thought that Great Faith and Great Doubt were the propelling forces catapulting Great Determination. Faith is what begets the confidence to triumph over the tests of doubt, but in order to prevail, determination is imperative. I must want to achieve my goal so badly that no matter how daunting the challenges are, I'll find a way to overcome them. I must cast aside all negative thoughts, feelings, and attitudes that derail my train of confidence that will take me to my desired destination.

The fragrance of lavender seemed to have been accentuated by the steamy environment and blended in the air with Bach's violin concerto in A minor. I took a deep breath and dunked my head underwater again. Upon emerging, I immediately thought of the fourth candle and turned to the side to look at it. Why did I feel so compelled to light it when my original intent was to represent only the three essential elements of Zen that the young monk referred to earlier in the day? As I pondered about that inexplicable impulsive behavior, I thought of the meaning of the color white. It is the most complete and pure of all colors and contains an equal balance of all the colors of the spectrum. In fact, white is the color of perfection that represents purity, innocence, wholeness, completion and therefore new beginnings. I paused and mused before submerging myself underwater one more time. Suddenly, I surfaced with a sense of urgency and look at the white candle knowing what it represented in the context of my symbolic bath ritual: Great Mystery; the mystery of the unknown; of death and the completion of life that begets new beginnings. And Great Mystery is independently distinct from Great Doubt, for it is not about the unforeseeable tribulations and trials of life, but the great mystery of life itself. But what all of this had to do with my quest to find out how to master the art of aging?

Bach's music had come to the end as if it'd faded away with the delicate scent of lavender that was barely noticeable by now. The water was getting cold and the steam had evaporated leaving the bathroom ceiling and walls damp. It was time to step out of the tub and bring my thoughts to conclusion on the couch in the living-room.

Wrapped up in my bathrobe, I began dissecting the pieces of information that I'd accumulated during the day, mostly what I named the holy trinity of Zen and the unexpected fourth element that manifested itself to me through a white candle in the corner of the counter in the bathroom. Suddenly, it all made sense to me. Based on my own experience with the aging process as well as my lifelong observations of the many changes happening to people around me, I was convinced that at no other stage in human life Great Faith, Great Doubt, and Great Determination were more meaningful and important than in the latter years of life; the time when I prepare for the Great Mystery. And because of the inherently deteriorating process that occurs with the passing of time, the need to master the ability to maintain Great Faith in the face of Great Doubt with Great Determination is fundamental to overcoming, the anxiety triggered by the Great Mystery, especially the grinding psychological process associated with the apprehension about aging.

It was now clear to me that the foundation of mastering the art of aging ought to be based on the holy trinity of Zen. I was relieved that I finally had something to build on. However, Great Faith, Great Doubt, and Great Determination were theoretical principles that called for practical applicability in everyday life, which requires a very specific set of skills, discipline, and courage to deal with the constant changes that come with the passing of time. But how could I develop the strength of spirit at a time in my life when continuous physical decline and all sorts of diminishing capabilities seemed to take place?

It was late and I was getting sleepy. It was time to ensconce in my cozy queen size bed and embark on another journey into the mysterious domain of dreams; a state of being in which many answers to my questions were often revealed to me. Before turning off the bedside light, I closed my eyes and quietly intended, in a mixture of meditation and prayer, to wake up with some insights on how I could incorporate the principles of *Dai-shinkon*, *Dai-gidan*, and *Dai-funshi* into the experience of my life as I aged and moved toward the Great Mystery.

Chapter 4

Dreaming of Being Awake

The Dream

I woke up feeling motivated and inspired. Perhaps it was because of the strange dream I had. I was in a beautiful lush valley where a crystalline blue water lake stood placidly surrounded by snow-capped mountains. The Sun was right above in mid-heaven and the light reflecting from the lake was so bright that I had to squint to see the magnificent panoramic view before my eyes. I walked toward the edge of the lake and when I looked at its translucent water, I saw the image of my face submerged and occupying the entire diameter of that magical body of water.

"I'm glad you finally showed up," a soothing voice that I could not distinguish either as masculine or feminine came out of my face's image under water as it reverberated through the sprawling valley. "You're on the right track to find out what you've been looking for."

Like the legend of Narcissus, but without a narcissistic approach, I kept staring at the likeness of my semblance in the lake wondering whether I was having an auditory hallucination. Suddenly, in an impulsive reaction, I replied to the articulation utterly unaware of myself as an independent being. I wasn't sure who was speaking to whom: the me standing on the bank of the lake or the image of my submerged face. "I want to find out how to turn the frightful aging process into a courageous self-empowering experience. Is it possible at all?"

"It all depends on whether or not you want it to be possible," the inscrutable voice replied.

"Of course I do. Otherwise I wouldn't have been searching for it."

"Well, in this case all you need to do is to apply Great Faith to your Great Doubt with Great Determination, then you shall solve the Great Mystery of your quandary."

"But that's exactly the crux of my predicament. How do I go about doing it in a practical way? I need to know how to effectuate it, not theorize on the potential avenues leading there. I'm tired of philosophizing about it. I want to experience it." The tone of the voice that now sounded more like my own revealed a great deal of impatience.

There was a long moment of silence before a gentle breeze began blowing from the east. As it passed through the surface of the lake, I felt the wind gently caressing my face. "A man of wisdom who is in the pursuit of personal power must first learn to flow with the Tao, for the world is ruled by allowing things to unfold at their natural pace and in a timely fashion; without resistance or the interference of a mind overcharged with anxieties and fear. The aging process is a progressive challenge throughout the human experience, and it culminates in the ultimate test of time: old age.

"Flowing with the Tao," I repeated it softly to myself.

✎ Dreaming of Being Awake ✍

"And the only way you'll be able to surrender to the progression of life with confidence is by developing a strong *Chi*; the invisible cosmic energy of power that circulates and lies latent within every living creature. *Chi* is the soul of the Tao; the heart of God; the essence of nature, or any other denomination you may want to attribute to it. But rest assured there is absolutely nothing you can do to halt or reverse the inexorable laws of nature. However, if you work on strengthening your *Chi*, which is the life force of your soul, then the tribulations of your diminishing physical condition can actually facilitate the acquisition of personal power. In any case, if you're bold enough to even dare attempting to transform the aging process into personal power, then you must acquire the tranquil courage of a samurai who knows that he can die at any moment, because in fact, you can."

I looked around that splendid environment realizing that it represented the expansive valley of my own mind, which was reflected in the image of my face in the lake that communicate with me my ambition of becoming an empowered elder. Then, I contemplated the concept of tranquil courage without fully comprehending its meaning.

"Aging with confident resilience requires tranquility of acceptance and courageous determination. It is a spiritual aspect of valor that is evinced by composure, a calm presence of mind," the heterogeneous male-female voice of my subconscious mind spoke softly in my ears as I watched the lips of my image in the lake move. "Tranquility is courage in repose. A truly brave man is ever serene; he is never taken by surprise; nothing ruffles the equanimity of his spirit. In the heat of battle he remains cool; in the midst of catastrophes he keeps level his mind. Earthquakes do not shake him, he laughs at storms. We admire him as truly great, who, in the menacing presence of danger or even death, retains his self-possession.[1] This is the tranquil courage of a samurai; and this is what is required of you in your audacious quest to turn the most vulnerable time in the human experience into personal power before exiting this world."

I got out of bed enthused and ready to take on whatever came my way. After having that dream, I realized that my pursuit of mastering the art of aging was not something distinct from a younger person's exploration of attaining self-empowerment. The main difference, and a significant one for that matter, was that the challenges to achieve the goal happen at a stage in life when many disadvantageous circumstances are in place for the older person, though life experience often grant a beneficial edge to the mature individual. But the more I reflected on it, the more I realized that being able to achieve self-empowerment at a time when diminishing physical capacities and increasing limitations in many other aspects of living prevail, actually magnified the merit of the endeavor. Hence, Power Aging should be the final and ultimate pursuit of an individual's lifetime; and likely, the most important achievement of all.

Feeling good about myself, I decided to go for a long walk to a small picturesque park surrounded by tall evergreens a couple of miles away from my home. I thought it would be a good way to do a *kinhin* (walking meditation); and once I got to the park, I'd ponder over the holy trinity of Zen in relation to my investigation to learn how to master the art of aging. What I didn't know was that I was going to expand my understanding of *dai-shinkon, dai-gidan,* and *dai-funshi* from a most unexpected teacher.

ೀ Dreaming of Being Awake ೭

A New Day, A New Lesson

By the time I reached the park, my brow was damp and my feet sore. But beholding children having fun in the nearby playground while hearing their laughter fill the air with the sounds of mirth made it all worthwhile. I looked around trying to find the ideal bench under one of those majestic trees so I could rest and do some thinking about the holy trinity of Zen. As always, I had my leather satchel with me where I carried the important tools of my trade: a yellow notepad, writing utensils, a book, an electronic dictionary, and a tape recorder. As my eyes surveyed the park in a 360 degree angle, I noticed that not very far from where I stood, an old man sat alone with a peaceful expression of self-contentment. I observed him for a long time, and the longer I looked at him, the stronger my impulse to approach him grew. At first, I avoided the inexplicable urge to walk toward him, for neither I wanted to disturb the man's privacy nor I wanted to deprive myself of some much needed quiet solitude of my own. However, as I'm looking at him while deciding which bench to choose, he suddenly turned his head in my direction and established a steady eye contact with me. Despite the short distance between us, the strength of his gaze seemed to penetrate my soul and snared my attention as I became unable to look anywhere else. Then, he smiled and his wide blue eyes framed by deeply wrinkled skin beaconed me to approach him. I accepted his subtle physiognomic invitation and started moving toward him.

"Mind if I have a seat?" I asked looking at the white-haired man with a short well-trimmed beard who stared at me as if I were someone he recognized.

"By all means," he replied scooting over to the side leaving plenty of space for me to sit down. Although it was the sound of only three words, I was struck by both the tone of his voice and his diction. He looked and sounded as someone who was well-educated and possessed a knowledge that extended far beyond traditional schooling. I was intrigued and curious to find out about this man and the synchronicity of events that led me to him.

"You looked like you were searching for something," the old man said turning his torso sideways to face me. "Do you know what you're looking for?"

"I was just scanning the park to locate the perfect bench to do my musings," I said puzzled with the way in which he asked me if I knew what I was looking for.

"Huh, and you end up selecting a bench where an old man sits alone. It doesn't seem like a perfect spot for someone who wants to indulge in solitary musings," he remarked. "Well, you found your bench. But do you know what you're looking for?"

My body jolted slightly and I could feel the burrowing of the skin in my forehead. "Why is this man asking me the same question twice?" I thought while looking at him in the eye with a frown that my curiosity carved in my face. Suddenly, I was surprised to feel intimidated by the intense gaze of his eyes that felt like darts piercing through the protective layers of the privacy of my being.

"Do you know what you're looking for?" He asked again.

"Power!" I blurted out instinctively. "I am in the pursuit of personal power; or more specifically, how to become empowered as I age and head toward the final destination of life."

∽ Dreaming of Being Awake ∼

The old man slowly turned his head to the side and looked upwards with eyes wide open without blinking. He stayed in that motionless position for a few seconds before facing me again. "In this case, the bench you chose to do your musings might have been a good one after all," he spoke in a soothing tone that my ears translated as the voice of opportunity.

Now I was more curious than ever. I scrutinized him wondering why he pretentiously assumed he could offer me any positive perspectives on attaining personal power. After all, according to our cultural and social standards, an old man is the epitome of powerlessness. However, looking into his eyes I could see a well hidden treasure of knowledge that could offer me a wealth of benefits.

"Excuse me, but who are you, sir? I asked. I needed to know who would dare to make such a presumptuous assumption in relation to knowing about personal power.

"I'm a man who shares your ambition," he said. "But being far ahead on the path and closer to the exit door than you are, I may be able to offer some valuable insights about the journey that can facilitate your quest."

"Well, I'd like to know exactly how you think you can help me," I said. "Why don't you start by telling me something about yourself."

I'd never heard a more fascinating life story. Joseph, or Joe as he asked me to call him, was a well-educated man who graduated from a prestigious university earning a doctoral degree in Eastern philosophy. Marrying his high-school sweetheart shortly after his college graduation, he accepted a teaching job at a state university and began building his life, family, and career for some 18 years until a life-changing event turned his life topsy-turvy. While driving cross-country to spend the Thanksgiving holiday with his wife's relatives, a young man, whom investigators determined was intoxicated, crossed the center line and hit his vehicle head-on killing both his wife and two teenage children. After that tragic event, he realized how precarious, flimsy, and ephemeral life was. Emotionally devastated, which he described as being already dead while imprisoned in the physical body, he sold his house, quit his job, and went on a pilgrimage to the East in the pursuit of a superior knowledge that would help him understand the senselessness of the human condition. After spending many years traveling through India, China, and Japan, he returned to the United States older, broke, but a victorious man who overcame a crushing loss and turned his unimaginable sorrow into personal power. In spite of his wealth of knowledge, educational background, and life experience, at his older age, he was unable to secure a decent job. Thus, he had no choice but make a living doing various low-paying menial jobs until he retired and forced to live an extremely low maintenance lifestyle bordering the poverty level; akin to the Buddhist monks he encountered in his travels.

"I can't imagine being able to withstand such a heartbreaking loss," I said as my first reaction after hearing his life story. "I think the suffering would sear my heart and shred my soul into pieces."

"Grief should be the instructor of the wise, for sorrow is knowledge: they who know the most must mourn the deepest,"[2] he said without looking at me, seemingly absorbed in the emotional and mental recollection of his pain.

"I guess this is exactly why I want to learn how to acquire personal power," I replied quickly attempting to rescue the old man from his grievous memories. "Once I realized how difficult and agonizing growing old can be, I embarked on a journey to find out how to master the art of aging. But now, after hearing your life story, I wonder if it just took me a long time to become aware that my longing to master the art of aging is actually more about the art of surviving the countless losses and sorrows every human being goes through in the course of a lifetime. Perhaps it took the knowledge that comes with the passing of time for me to realize it."

"The important thing is that you realized the need to commit to finding out that you must pursue your goal. And even though it's true that mastering the art of aging is in reality mastering the art of living, there is no other time in the human experience when this skill is most needed. It takes a great deal of faith to endure life's many travails; but perhaps never more than when you're knocking on the door of the ultimate unknown."

"Great Faith!" I exclaimed remembering what I'd learned from the young monk at Shasta Abbey Buddhist Monastery. "But regardless of what source of the faith may be, faith in your own ability to carry on in the face of life's challenges is fundamental."

"Yes, without a strong faith in yourself and in life's uncanny ability to make everything work out, it's impossible to endure the trials of the journey," he said. "I'm a living testimony of the point in case."

"Someone once told me that the inherent doubt that permeates all of life is what breeds our fears, but at the same time it's also what nurtures our faith. And sometimes the doubt is so real and daunting that only deeply rooted faith can overcome it," I said feeling a tinge of fear of my own doubts about my future.

"I can vouch it based on my personal experience that the only way to overcome the long and arduous challenges of life is by living like a warrior; a spiritual warrior that is," he said and paused for awhile before continuing. "During my travels in the East, I developed the utmost respect for the traditional samurai and the way they accepted both life and death as equal partners of life; the *Ying* and *Yang* that keep the Universe expanding. I learned that the reason they were able to be fearless in the face of death was because they embraced life to the fullest. If you observe people around you carefully, you'll see that those who fear dying are the same who are fearful of living."

"What do you mean?" I asked unsure of the comparison he was making.

"Well, if you pay close attention to people you know who seem to be always worried about the inevitable life's changes, like aging for instance, or disease, accidents, losses, financial setbacks, or whatever the root cause of the fear may be, you will notice that they are also the ones most likely to be terribly afraid of death. They don't know how to live like warriors; as if they were samurais of the Great Shogun of Life."

"But becoming a warrior is not an easy undertaking. It takes much practice, commitment, and definitely courage to even want to be one, especially when you're getting older and feeble," I said. "I understand that the strength required to be a spiritual warrior has nothing to do with your physical capability, but you cannot deny that old age does affect your sense of self-confidence."

"It all hinges on your belief system. If you believe you can't, then, well...," he remarked.

"Isn't it more than just belief? Don't you have to experience this sense of empowerment with which you can overcome all obstacles, no matter what they are. Goodness, it's a very tall order for any ordinary man."

"But a warrior is no ordinary man. In fact the basic difference between a warrior and an ordinary man is that a warrior takes everything as a challenge to be overcome, while an ordinary man takes everything as either a blessing or a curse."[3] He silenced and looked intently into my eyes. "If you're committed to your pursuit of personal power and mastering the art of aging, you must first and foremost develop an unflappable warrior-like attitude, or you shall not be able to succeed in your quest. First you build the faith that you can do it, then doubt will challenge your resolve, but in the end is your determination that will ascertain the accomplishment of your lofty objective."

"But sometimes it feels unbearably overwhelming," I blurted out still thinking of his life story that he'd just shared with me.

His face hardened and I could hear the scolding cry screaming out of his eyes. I lowered my head trying to avoid his silent reprimand of my unintended display of cowardice. "Look at me," he demanded. I hesitantly raised my chin until my eyes met his with timid concern. He stared at me for a long time, then he spoke in a purposeful paced speech. "A warrior cannot be helpless, bewildered or frightened, not under any circumstances. For a warrior there is time only for his impeccability; everything else drains his power, impeccability replenishes it."[4]

I felt like I'd been jolted by a lightning bolt. The way he clinched his fist and moved his right hand upward when he said "impeccability replenishes it," left me in awe and wondering. "What do you mean by impeccability?" I asked almost sheepishly.

"Impeccability is to do your best in whatever you're engaged in. No matter how daunting the challenge may be, for a warrior it is the perpetual stage upon which he has the opportunity to shine. If you're serious about becoming empowered while learning to master the art of aging, you have to remember that a warrior cannot complain or regret anything. Life is an endless sequence of challenges and there is nothing intrinsically good or bad about them; they just set the stage for a warrior to act his power while improving himself."

After mulling over his sensible observations, I realized that impeccability was the essence of *dai-funshi*, or Great Determination. It was that necessary requirement without which you cannot overcome the obstacles of old age, even if you have Great Faith in the face of Great Doubt. But what about that fourth element that I concocted by chance in my ceremonial bath when I lit the three candles representing the holy trinity of Zen?

"And in the end it's heard no more; it's a tale told by an idiot, full of sound and fury signifying nothing," I said quoting a passage of Shakespeare's play *MacBeth*. "In the end, even the bravest warrior will pass away into the nothingness of a time that no longer exists in a spatial reality."

"But in the end there is a new beginning. And it doesn't matter where you are on life's journey, even in the expectation of an imminently approaching death, impeccability is the main duty of a warrior," he said. "Like the samurai who welcomed an honorable death in the battlefield, a warrior of life finds his honor by being impeccable. That way, even if he's heard no more, the untold tale of his passed life is a peaceful meaningful silence crowned with the glory of overcoming the final and most fearsome of all challenges."

"Aren't you afraid to die?" I asked impetuously. I thought it was a rude question to ask someone I just met. I wanted to recant it, but communication is irreversible.

"Why should I be afraid of the inevitable? I've been living my life to the fullest, and as I told you, the people who are afraid of dying are the same ones who are afraid of living," he reminded me. "The impeccability that I've developed over the course of my life gives me the inner strength and courage to march on toward the fast approaching hour of my death with enthusiastic anticipation. Besides, I believe that beyond the shadows of the unknown a bright light illuminates the rewards of a warrior who lived an impeccable life."

I took a deep breath and the fragrance of freshly cut grass passed through my nostrils nourishing my lungs with purified oxygen that enlivened my brain. Both the old man and I remained silent, while I thought over his out-of-the-ordinary observations. I looked at the distant playground where the joyful sounds of children playing merged with the cawing of crows in the branches of a nearby tree creating a pleasant symphony to my ears. Watching the kids running about with carefree mirth, I recalled the days when I was a child myself, and how fast the journey to now had happened. Then, from the corner of my eye, I took a peek at the old man sitting next to me noticing the deep crevasses that time had chiseled in his face and came to terms with myself that soon I'd be looking like that. At that moment I realized that the Great Mystery, that fourth essential of Zen that I thought about when I lit the white candle in my bathroom, was not only about the mysterious exit gate of life, but the entire temporal voyage of the embodied soul through the continuous spectrum of the unknown. Glancing at the children one more time, I thought that even at that early innocent stage of the earthly journey, the Great Mystery shrouded the experience of living. But from the milepost of the highway of life that I've reached, the Great Mystery was more like the off-ramp exit that would take me out of the road of living; and that generated some anxiety in my being. But if I managed to learn how to master the art of aging and its inevitable final outcome, then, perhaps, I'd be able to continue living and sounding almost like those children in the playground. In a strange synchronicity, as soon as I finished thinking about it, the crows erupted into a cawing cacophony as though validating my reasoning.

"Well, I guess it's time for me to get going," the old man said grabbing his walking stick. "I have to prepare my presentation for the city council meeting this evening and the first draft needs some serious revision."

"Are you a city councilor?" I asked.

"Oh hell no, I would never fit in the circus of politics at any level," he replied with derision. "I'm presenting a proposal on behalf of a nonprofit organization I chair for the development of a subsidized housing for low income elders in our community. We've earned more than half of the grant money necessary for this project; now it's up to the city and the county to come up with the balance to back up their rhetoric that they work in the best interest of their citizens. I've heard enough of their talking; now they need to back it up with some good old cash for this project."

"I have to say that I'm impressed that a man your age who could well be enjoying some untroubled leisure time chooses to commit and get involved in important humanitarian issues in our community," I complimented him in earnest.

He thudded his walking stick on the ground a couple of times as he looked deeply into my eye. "When you approached me earlier, I asked you if you knew what you're looking for. You told me that you want to find out how to master the art of aging. Well, here is my humble contribution to your investigation: the art of aging, which is nothing but the latter stage of the art of living, requires meaningful life purpose that can only be found in service. Making a difference in the quality of other people's lives makes you feel like your life is a gift to the world, as well as a retribution of gratitude for the many blessings you've received. When I look back over the years of my long life, I am stirred by emotions triggered by the recollection of the number of people whom I have to thank for what they offered me and what they meant to me. At the same time, I am haunted by an oppressive consciousness of the little gratitude I really showed them while I was younger.[5] Now that I'm on the final leg of my journey, I'm committed to serving others to honor those who have been good to me in so many ways. It is in their memory and with a heart filled with gratitude to my life's blessings that I say to you with utmost certainty: it is in service to others that lies the secret of the art of living, thereby the art of aging you want to master."

He got to his feet slowly and with some effort while leaning on his walking stick. "I wish you the best in your effort to achieve your goal. Just remember that when your mind and heart are focused on the best interest of others, you have neither the time nor the energy to indulge in the petty concerns of your ego fretting about the inevitable. Old age and death always arrive in a timely fashion. But if you stay busy living, you don't have the time to worry about dying."

I stood up to shake his hand displaying my gratitude for his contribution to my quest with my eyes and a smile. We bid farewell and he started walking away when he suddenly stopped and turned around. "Oh, yes, one more thing: make sure to explore the teachings and the life of Prince Siddhartha Gautama. They shall prove to be very useful in your quest to learn how to master the art of aging. Good luck to you, mate." He waved at me, pulled his pants up above his waistline, and treaded through the green field toward the sidewalk.

I watched him disappear in the distance thinking of the strange events of the day. It started out with a bizarre dream laden with obscure teachings of how to be a warrior of life. Then, I went for a philosophical stroll and I came across an old man who emphasized the meanings of the messages in my dream in a more realistic fashion. I guess I was right in my earlier reflections about the Great Mystery. It was much more comprehensive than my original assumption that it related to death only. It was about life itself. Now it was evident to me that life and death, like all other dualities ruling the Universe, were one and the same; connected and interdependent like yin and yang, positive and negative, male and female, good and evil, and all the others yet to be discovered. And despite all I'd already learned, I realized I still had a long way to go to figure out how to master the art of aging and establish my theory that it was possible to develop a Power Aging attitude that makes it feasible to turn aging into power.

On my way back home, I was determined to heed his suggestion to examine the life and teachings of the noble prince who would become The Buddha. Suddenly, I could feel the pangs of labor of the birth of an empowered aging man gradually coming alive.

Chapter 5

The Awakened One

The Torch Bearer

Following Joe's recommendation, the old man I met in the park, I began examining the life and teachings of Prince Siddhartha Gautama, the man who would become The Buddha. From the very beginning of my readings, I became absolutely fascinated with the fables about his birth and life story.

As it is the case with most historical events that happened centuries ago, especially the ones related to religious occurrences, they are often clouded with uncertainties due to a dearth of reliable facts. Like Jesus of Nazareth and the prophet Mohammed who lived a few centuries after the year Buddha is believed that have died in 483 B.C.E., modern scholars of both the Eastern and Western worlds are confidently assured that Siddhartha Gautama did indeed exist and his life story and teachings were carefully preserved by his disciples.[1] But regardless of what academics may say or determine about the existence of the living Buddha, it is the wisdom of his millenary teachings—and the extraordinary circumstances of his lifetime—that matter to those in the pursuit of liberating self-empowerment. Nevertheless, the legend surrounding his life is a remarkable fable worthy of his reputation.

According to the legend, the woman who was going to give birth to the one who would eventually be known as the "Enlightened One," Lady Maya Diva, was so beautiful and pure that she seemed to be of what "dreams are made on," as Shakespeare put it in the words of the character Prospero in his play *The Tempest*. The fable says her stunning physical beauty and nobility of character was the reason she was named Maya, meaning "illusion" or "illusory." It was also believed that she'd taken a vow of chastity, which her husband, the pious King Suddhodana respected because he was also married to her sister (this was not an unusual practice at the time), Lady Japiti, sometimes referred to as Mahaprajapatani. Hence, like Mary some 563 years later giving birth to Jesus of Nazareth, Lady Maya Diva (or Mayadevi) was reputably a virgin when she bore the "Enlightened One," and the "virgin birth" of The Buddha is one of the many legends surrounding his life.[2] But this sanctimonious need to disparage a dignified sexual act between a husband and his loving wife aside, the story of how the birth of prince Siddhartha Gautama came about is very fitting to the nature of The Buddha he was going to become.

Another legend reports of a mystical dream that Queen Maya Diva had one night. And since dreams were believed to be one of the ways in which gods communicate with mortals, King Suddhodana paid heed to his queen when she told him that she dreamed that a white elephant had descended from heaven and entered her womb and she was immediately filled with bliss. Puzzled, the king summoned to his palace notable mystics, astrologers, wise men, and the experts who interpreted dreams as they listened to the queen's tale in awe and wonder.

"This dream is a most revealing omen," the esoteric panel concluded. "The white elephant descending from heaven indicates that a child from Tushita Heaven, the Pure Land of Buddha Maitreya has been conceived; a child who is pure and a powerful being. We're confident that the queen is going to give birth to either a magnanimous ruler of his people or a holy child; a great sage who will exert enormous spiritual influence in the world."

The king rejoiced, for he had been longing for a son who would succeed him as a ruler of his kingdom and subjects. Thereafter, sometime around the year 563 B.C.E., prince Siddhartha Gautama was born; Siddhartha meaning "he who has achieved his goal." However, the council of wise men and mystics that the king relied on for advise issued a very important warning. "As a holy man whose purpose is the perfection of his soul, prince Siddhartha must be kept from ever seeing the signs of human suffering: old age and the decrepitude that comes with it, sickness and the way it lays waste the body, and if he witnesses the inexorable testimony of death, or abject poverty that assails so many to a life of misery, then he'll renounce the world and live an ascetic life. Should he see these signs of human suffering, he will be quite unable to ignore them and will perforce leave behind the comfortable world of kings and princes."[3]

Concerned with the potential of such outcome, the king fortified the four quarters of the palace to ensure that the prince would never come across anyone bearing these miserable signs of the human existence. Therefore, Siddhartha's childhood was sheltered and lavished in abundance, beauty, and pleasure. He would not be subjected to witness the sicknesses and poverty of the people of the kingdom. And even though his mother died shortly after childbirth, he was raised by her sister, the king's second wife, which spared him from the suffering of growing up without a mother.

Under this overly protected environment, he grew up to be a talented athlete, an intelligent and charming young man. His future as the sovereign of his father's kingdom seemed secure. Then, when Siddhartha was sixteen, he won the hand in marriage of a most beautiful young woman named Yasodhara who was considered the loveliest and most coveted girl in the entire kingdom. Legend has it that he managed to win her hand in contest by piercing seven trees with one arrow.[4]

By the age of twenty-nine, very much in love and happily married with Yasodhara who was pregnant with their child, Siddhartha continued to be walled out by the king's edict.

"I must go see what life is like beyond the palace walls, father," Siddhartha said determined to learn what life was like outside the confinements of his protected environment.

"I assure you, my son, there's nothing to see out there. It's very much the same as it is in here," King Suddhodhana lied in a desperate attempt to protect his son and successor of his kingdom from witnessing the malaises of the world. However, upon Siddhartha's adamant insistence, the king reluctantly acquiesced aware that his son needed to see the life of those he was to govern. He would make sure, however, that the infirm and old to stay indoors, and forbid all funerals or any public display of suffering.

Then it came the day, shortly after the birth of his son, Rāhula, that Siddhartha ventured out of the confinements of the palace. He summoned his servant, Channa, to ready the chariot, for they were going to explore a brave new world he knew nothing about.

"I don't know why my father was so averse to letting me come out to see the kingdom," Siddhartha remarked with glee to his charioteer while noticing that everywhere he went he saw happiness, health, and good cheer, which had been staged according to the specific instructions of the king.

Suddenly, out of one of the modest houses on the side of the road, a decrepit elderly man stumbled out on the streets. Limping along with difficulty caused by the infirmities afflicting his old warped body, Siddhartha watched in amazement the old man's shriveled skin barely covered by tattered rags. Leaning his shaky body on a staff with his right hand, he inched along the street with his left arm dangling on the side like a useless anatomic appendage to his feeble body. His vacant puffy eyes surrounded by dark circles looked like black holes in an empty human face. Then, with trembling jaws that revealed his toothless mouth, he implored: "Alms! Good hearted people, please help. I am near to death."

The frightened people on the street seeing that the unexpected apparition had defied the king's command, tried to surround the old man and rushed him back indoors in order to hide the unpleasant sight from the prince. But it was too late. Siddhartha discovered the reality of the human condition and he was as shaken as the old man himself.

Agape, he turned to Channa for an explanation. "Channa, what thing is this who seems a man, yet surely only seems, being so bowed, so miserable, so horrible, so sad? Are men born sometimes thus? What did he mean when moaning he said 'I am near to death?' Finds he no food so that his bones just forth? What woes has happened to this piteous one?"[5]

"This is nothing but an old man, dear prince! Many decades ago when he was a young man like you, his body was strong, his back upright, and his eyes were full of life. Like you, dear prince, he was vigorous, sported, made love to young mistresses, played games, sang songs, laughed with joy, and took pleasure in the simple activities of life. But then, the passing of time, the great defiler that siphons away the vitality of youth, has robbed him of his health, strength, and even joy, while making a mockery of his life through no fault of his own."

Siddhartha was overwhelmed to learn about this horrifying aspect of the human condition. Sickness, old age, and death were unimaginable sufferings that he'd never fathom possible. He remained quiet for a long time immersed in the depth of his thoughts about the nature of living and the inevitable prospect of dying.

"Tell me, Channa, can this happen to everyone?" He asked probably thinking of himself.

"Indeed, dear prince, it happens to all," Channa replied in a subdued tone of voice.

"Even to my beautiful wife Yasodhara, my darling son Rāhula, and me, too?" The prince asked, though he already seemed to know the answer.

"It is a law of nature, my lord."

Siddhartha had seen and heard enough. He told Channa to head back to the palace. As they rode along, they came across a monk in a yellow robe with shaven head and an empty bowl. The prince immediately commanded his charioteer to stop.

"And what's this vision that befuddles my mind now, Channa?"

"He is an ascetic, dear prince; someone who has renounced all worldly goods in the pursuit of an inner serenity he cannot find outside. In spite of his material poverty, this man and his kin are holy men. They search for an intangible treasure buried within themselves."

When Siddhartha thought he'd seen enough for one day, he came across the most gruesome view of all. Lying in a ditch on the side of the road, there was decomposing corpse whose stench filled the prince's nostrils with nausea. He immediately commanded the chariot to stop. Staring at the unimaginable scene while covering his nose with the sleeve of his garment, he looked at Channa and pleaded for an explanation. "And what most horrifying sight is this, my loyal companion? I'd think it to be a mirage, but the fetid air cannot delude my senses. Tell me, Channa, what horrific spectacle is this?"

"This is death, my lord. It's what happens at the end of everyone's life," Channa replied lowering his head to avoid seeing the prince's reaction.

The rest of the journey back home Siddhartha remained pensive and didn't say another word, and the days that followed were never going to be the same again. Henceforth, the veil of illusion of luxuries and ephemeral pleasures had been lifted from his eyes, and the reality of a world laden with suffering and pain transformed the awareness of the noble prince.

Going Forth

After learning about the widespread sorrows of the human experience in a life of impermanence and continuous changes, Siddhartha decided to renounce the world and go forth in the pursuit of unearthing an answer to what now troubled him the most. Attempting to transcend the suffering of daily life by indulging in trivial distractions and mundane pleasures was no longer a viable option. Neither was he going to give the blind eye of denial to the existence of the human grief he witnessed. The noble prince was confident that there ought to be a solution for coping with the misery intrinsic to the human condition and he was determined to find the answer.

"My loyal servant, Channa, settle my horse for I've decided that tonight I'm leaving the comfort of my father's palace, my beautiful wife Yasodhara, and my newborn son Rāhula. I'm leaving it all behind in order to pursue my spiritual quest. I must find an answer to the quandary of human suffering," prince Siddhartha said. "As difficult as this momentous decision is, I'm convinced that it is the attachment to things and people that bind me to an existence that seems mired by pain and sorrow; a grim cycle of suffering that begins with the trauma of birth and proceeds inexorably to aging, illness, and death."

"I shall do as you command, dear prince. I trust in thy wisdom," Channa acquiesced and rushed to settle and brittle Kantaka, Siddhartha's white steed.

Meanwhile, the prince went to his quarters to bid farewell to his wife and son. Rāhula was sound asleep and Siddhartha gently kissed the boy on the forehead before caressing the child's thick dark hair. Then, he started moving toward Yasodhara whom he thought was also asleep until her mellifluous voice filled the darkness in the room. "Aren't you happy with me anymore, my lord? Do I no longer please your fancies?"

"Nothing has changed between us, my sweet beautiful wife. It's I who have changed," he said almost in a whisper. "I realized that what I find in your loving arms is but a brief respite from the suffering that stalks my every movement. I can no longer find true and lasting happiness knowing that life's impermanence and continuous changes will bring old age, illness, and death. I'm perturbed by the awareness that our love, the rich ornaments and furnishings in this room, and even your most stunning beauty will all be swept away by the demands of the relentless time that enslaves us within its fleeting existence. Now I know that time is a merciless thief that claims our health and vitality, while slaughtering our serenity with the anxiety of old age and death."

"But death is the child of birth and the price we must pay for living," she replied raising her torso to look at him, even though she couldn't see his face in the darkness.

"And I am the birth of the child who wants to learn and grow. Leaving is the price that I must pay for living." Then, he gently touched his lips on her forehead and bid farewell without saying another word.

Like Jesus of Nazareth who told his disciples that they must leave their father, mother, wife, children, brothers, and sisters—even their own lives—if they wanted to follow him,[6] Siddhartha Gautama realized that family life fettered him to an illusion he could no longer ignore. It had become incompatible with the highest goal of his life: finding the path of liberation from human suffering. Thus, he departed and his mythological renunciation of luxuries, comfort, and domesticity became known as his "Going Forth" into a life of homelessness.[7]

And so the young prince set out to find himself. In his wanderings he met with many teachers and other truth seekers from whom he learned plenty. He practiced self-denial, meditation, self-control, yogic exercises, all for the purpose of finding a way to liberation from the shackles of sorrows of the world. Siddhartha believed the if he could transcend the self he would be able to free himself of the endless cycles of *samsāra* ("keeping going") and become enlightened and finally free from rebirth.[8] But more importantly, he reasoned that if there was birth, aging, illness, death, sorrow, and corruption in life, these suffering states must have their positive counterparts: there must be another mode of existing in the world. He concluded that such a wholly satisfactory state of being in which one can experience supreme freedom of bondage was an achievable objective. By extinguishing the passions, attachments, and all the delusions of a temporal existence that cause so much suffering in human life, one could reach an ethereal state of being: Enlightenment or *Nirvana* ("blowing out").[9]

After having practiced the principles of asceticism in an effort to achieve enlightenment, Siddhartha realized that the ascetic life did not seem to work. Depriving himself of food and enduring self-imposed hardships did not lead him to the truth he was looking for. Frustrated and disappointed, he wandered away from the ascetics and continued his journey on his own. By then he'd already learned that neither through extreme self-denial nor unfettered indulgence would he find the way to the truth of liberation from the world's sufferings. There must be another way.

Determined to achieve the goal of *Nirvana*, Siddhartha started practicing mindfulness, which helped him realize how transitory cravings were. He noticed how they appeared and vanished as he acknowledged their presences and let them go. Everything changed; everything came and passed on. Whether or not he worried about loss, loss was inescapable as change was inevitable. With change came fear, and with fear came suffering (*duhkha*).[10]

After his disappointment with the way of the ascetics and all his efforts to find out the answer to his quandary of coping with human suffering, Siddhartha sat under a bodhi tree (an Asiatic fig tree) resolute to remain immersed in *dhyana* (the Sanskrit word for deep meditation, which is the same meaning of zazen in Japanese) until he found the truth he so desperately searched for. But as every worthy goal must have its challenges necessary to create value to its achievement, the opposing force of evil that stood as the negation of everything the prince aspired to accomplish appeared to tempt and seduce him away from his quest.

"Look at their ecstatic movements and just imagine how much pleasure your body can indulge in under their gifted care," said Mara, pointing to his lustful dancing daughters whom he'd sent to arouse the prince's carnal desires. Mara, the demonic spirit and symbolic obstacle that seekers of truth must overcome, was doggedly intended to deviate him from his path to enlightenment.

Siddhartha remained serene and unmoved.

Undeterred by his indifference to the seductive maidens, Mara continued on with his persuasive strategy to snare the prince into his web of illusion. "My dear prince, you're so bright and brave; you can rule over the world if you wish to do so. I can enhance your beauty, intelligence, strength, and all the wonderful gifts nature has already bestowed upon you. If you give up this foolish spiritual pursuit that yields no tangible benefits in the only life you know and experience in the flesh now, I can offer you opportunities to become the most powerful man that ever lived. Come to me, oh gracious prince, and I'll turn you into the king of all kings and shower you with riches you'd never dreamed possible. Furthermore, I promise you that in the darkness of my world you'll be oblivious to the miseries of the world, for you'll not be able to see them. Come to me and you shall find the truth of the world of time, space, and matter."

Siddhartha was unfazed. His closed eyes and peaceful facial expression revealed his resolute commitment to accomplish his goal. In his turn, Mara was irate that his cajoling words of praise and promises aimed at arousing the prince's ego and desires had failed. If he could not kindle Siddhartha's passion for a luxurious and lascivious life lavished with the bounties of material gratification, then he would stir a whirlwind aimed at sweeping the prince out of his senses with unimaginable fear.

"Almighty powers of destruction, wars, diseases, old age, and misery, I demand your presence and command you to possess this despicable human prey who dares to ignore the authority of my temptation," Mara yelled out summoning his monstrous fiends who showed up in their horrific deformed shapes to terrify the immovable seeker. "I order you by the power in me invested by the fear of suffering and death, that you incite doubt and despair in this stubborn glob of clay and force him to submit to my wishes, lest he shall have to withstand the wretchedness of the human condition without any compensation from my domain."

In spite of Mara's horrifying army of fiends and his outburst of anger aimed at frightening Siddhartha out of his wits, the noble prince remained unperturbed and resolute in his quest to find the truth within the peaceful abode of his being. Then, reaching out with his right hand to touch the ground, he entreated the Earth to testify to his past acts of compassion. With a shattering roar, the Earth replied: "I bear you witness."[11] At that moment, Mara's phalanges of fiends were terrified and fled in fear from the power of The Great Mother.

Hence, one evening, six years after "Going Forth," he was rewarded with the ultimate achievement of his legendary life. Sitting in *dhyana* (*zazen* in Japanese) under what later came to be known as the Bhodhi tree determined not to stop meditating before reaching enlightenment (*satori* in Japanese), after 49 days immersed in meditation he became the "Awakened One;" The Buddha at the age of 35. It was at that moment of enlightenment that he experienced an intuitive knowledge of the functions and purposes of the sufferings of the human existence; he understood the cause of earthly suffering and how it could be abated in a man and woman's life's journey. He described his intuitive understanding about the root causes of suffering as The Four Noble Truths, and he established a pathway leading to the cessation of suffering that he called the Noble Eightfold Path; the Middle Way.[12] Both The Four Noble Truths and the Noble Eightfold Path comprise the essence of Buddhism.

Having decided to spread his teaching of his newly found knowledge (*dharma*), Siddhartha Gautama, now The Buddha , searched for his fellow enlightenment seekers to share what he'd discovered. Astonished by the wisdom, simplicity, and more importantly, the effectiveness of his knowledge, they formed a group of Buddhist monks that became known as *Sangha* in Sanskrit. They traveled throughout the valleys of the Ganges river spreading The Buddha 's understanding of the Middle Way; a philosophy of life that would forever alter the experience of human suffering for those who chose to follow its principles. His *dharma* became his gift to a world besieged by impermanence, change, and suffering.

After learning about the life story of the noble prince Siddhartha Gautama who became The Buddha , I realized that I, too, could reach my personal goal of discovering a pathway leading to the mastery of the art of aging. Like him, I needed to remain steadfast in my pursuit until I found the answer to the universal human dilemma of aging.

Inspired by Siddhartha's approach, I decided to sit in zazen to quiet my mind and, perhaps, in the depth of a sea of tranquility, I'd find the treasure trove containing the map that would guide me to where I wanted to go. Thus, I lit a vanilla-scented candle and a sandalwood incense noticing how the blending of fragrances pleased my olfactory sense. With no time to waste, I sat on my green zafu (meditation pillow) ready to dive into the silence of my subconscious mind hoping to hear the echoes of the answers to my quest.

After sitting for a long while, I abruptly opened my eyes knowing what I needed to do. It was the moment of my enlightenment of Power Aging; and its *dharma* was en-

❦ The Awakened One ❧

twined in The Four Noble Truths and The Eightfold Path of The Buddha .

Chapter 6

The Dharma of Power Aging

❧❧

A Moment of Reflection

"What a fascinating story!" I said while conversing with Martha, an intelligent young friend of mine who was working on her doctoral dissertation in religious studies. "The life's journey of Siddhartha Gautama from a sheltered existence of privilege and luxury to self-abandonment in the pursuit of a truth within himself is as oxymoronic as it is remarkable. It's like in order to find the self you must abandon it along the way."

"So the legend says," Martha remarked with obvious skepticism and a tinge of derision. "Sitting under a fig tree for 49 days and emerging as an enlightened being seems more like myth than fact to me."

"It certainly isn't any more farfetched than feeding thousands of people with five loaves of bread and a couple of fish as the Gospel of Mark and Mathew refer to in the Bible," I replied aware of her Christian upbringing. "The truth is that it doesn't matter whether the stories that the followers of The Buddha or Jesus described are facts or fiction. It is not the enchanting fables about their personalities or feats that give meaning to their lives. It is their teachings and the examples they demonstrated to humanity that are important."

"I guess you have a point," she said coyly.

"Of course, I do," I reasserted my position in defense of highly spiritual men who are often turned into deities by commoners because the wise experienced the human condition from an advanced perspective they could not understand. "Jesus didn't write a single word of his Gospel, and The Buddha 's teachings, the Pāli Canon, was orally preserved and probably not written down until the first century B.C.E.[1] In fact, even in literature the wisdom of teachings of knowledgeable men can be relegated to a secondary level."

"What do you mean?" She asked while scratching the top of her nose.

"I'm thinking of Carlos Castaneda's supposedly fictitious character, Don Juan," I said. "At the time when the young Castaneda was an anthropology graduate student at the University of California in Los Angeles, he traveled to the state of Sonora in Mexico to conduct some research for his thesis. It was there that he claims to have encountered a Yaqui Indian shaman by the name of Don Juan Matus whose perception and mastery of the 'non-ordinary reality' intrigued the young Castaneda. The old sorcerer initiated the seeker into a new way of seeing and experiencing life in a manner that went against the grain of the limitations of the Western worldview Castaneda was accustomed to."

Distracted by Martha's intense facial expression, I paused for a moment. Her eyes glittered with curiosity and silently besought me to proceed. She was probably wondering what in the world did some shaman in Mexico had anything to do with Jesus or The Buddha.

"Based on his experiences, Castaneda wrote several books narrating the many lessons he learned from Don Juan, which were filled with unorthodox wisdom about the mysteries of dread, clarity, and, most importantly, the possibility of acquiring personal power. And perhaps because of the unusual tales and descriptions he relates in his books, many a skeptical critic began discrediting the existence of such a sorcerer and accused Castaneda of making everything up. 'It's all fictitious,' the detractors avowed. Well, does it matter whether such a body of wisdom was concocted by the writer's ingenuity or was acquired empirically? Isn't the valuable knowledge intrinsic in the message what's really worthy of merit? You see, this is the point I'm trying to make to illustrate my comparison. The fables of miraculous occurrences and abnormal circumstances are relevant only insofar as the human imagination is concerned. In practicality, it doesn't matter whether or not The Buddha sat under the Bodhi tree for 49 days or 49 seconds; or if the Gospel of Jesus' disciples claim that he fed five thousand people with a couple of loaves, and a few fish. In the end, the only thing that matters is the meaningful relevance of their teachings to the development of human consciousness and the betterment of the world."

Martha winked at me and smiled. "Interesting observation. But since you mentioned practicality, I'm curious about how are you planning to apply this information to your quest to turn aging into personal power? I can see the Castaneda's element in there, since Don Juan's lessons spoke of personal power. But what about The Buddha 's teachings, or even, dare I mention, Jesus' Gospel? How are you going to tie it all together?"

"In the end, isn't it all about personal power? Don't they all envision the same goal?" I speculated convinced of my reasoning. "Jesus, The Buddha, and even the potentially fictitious Don Juan, they all strived for liberation through self-empowerment."

"Yes, but through very different paths," she said. "Which one are you going to take?"

I thrust out my lips while mulling over my thoughts. She looked at me with an air of anticipation as I gently shook my head in silence before speaking. "Well, from Don Juan's teachings I'll take the discipline and commitment required to persevere in the warrior's path toward self-empowerment. From the Christian faith icon I'll take the most important aspect of his life's example: love; love thy neighbor as you love thyself. And from The Buddha I'll take everything else that's necessary for self-reliance at the time in human life when the weakening of the physical body must find its strength in the power of the spirit."

"But how are you going to do it?" She insisted on my replying with a practical answer to her question. "What's your strategy in the attempt of such a lofty goal?"

Suddenly, it dawned on me that I had not given a thought about it yet. I remained mute and probably looked perplexed, for I didn't know the answer. "I'm not sure," I slurred my words out under my breath speaking to myself rather than answering her question.

Later in the day, I spent the entire evening thinking about Martha's question. I had no idea where to begin, much less how to proceed in my quest to "Go Forth" in discovering the secret of mastering the art of aging. If anything, I knew that the life story of prince Siddhartha Gautama had exerted an enormous influence on me. By the time I ensconced myself in bed for a restful night sleep, I closed my eyes and with sheer willpower I urged my subconscious mind to come up with an answer in my dreams.

When the first rays of morning pierced through the slim gap between the curtains covering my view of the outside world, I was awakened recalling the experience I had in zazen the day before. The exploratory process was simple and had already been established by The Buddha. All I had to do was to apply it to the challenges of the aging process.

The First Noble Truth of Power Aging

In old age we reach the pinnacle of the mountain of time we've been climbing with great effort and difficulty. It is from this vintage point in life that we can see and feel the finish line of our earthly journey, which in the earlier years of our existence were but a vague intellectual concept and distant mirage of an end of time that didn't seem it would ever arrive (like the experience I had at the age of eighteen when the nonagenarian lady told me that time passed by so quickly). But from the top of the mountain, the clouds of the illusion of an unchanging time dissipate in the reality of inevitable finitude. The scenery is broad and clear, and so is the image in the mirror of an aged person whose wrinkles and gray hair reveal the changes we tried to fight against so desperately—and to no avail. It is the stage in life that reassures an undeniable fact that we've known throughout a lifetime of vicissitudes: life means *duhkha* (constant changes, anxieties, and suffering). This is the first of The Buddha's Four Noble Truths.

The first of The Four Noble Truths of the *dharma* of The Buddha is a basic common fact that every human being knows so well: to live is to suffer; and suffering manifests itself in several different forms. And even though there are many positive experiences in life that we perceive as the opposite of suffering, such as joy, pleasure, comfort, and that most sought after—and elusive—feeling of happiness, because of the circumstances of human life's imperfections in a world subject to impermanence, the condition of *duhkha* always seems to prevail; like a distressful vicious cycle. In fact, even happiness itself can be a form of suffering, through the anguish of longing for it, losing it when it's happening, or the anxiety it creates once it becomes evident that sooner or later it'll be gone. What this means it that we are never able to hold on to what and whom we love, and the exhilarating feelings they bestow upon us will pass on no matter how desperately we try to hold on to them. Then, after countless experiences of sorrow and a variety of many losses (youthful fervor, happy moments, gratifying work, good friends, loved ones, etc.), we must face the certainty of the ultimate loss that awaits at the end of living as we know it: ourselves.

But before the final moment arrives (except when premature death occurs), we must cope with the challenges of aging; the gradual loss of vitality, health, social functions, among other degenerating aspects in the quality of living. Hence, the overwhelming angst that the aging process generates enhances the inherent survival instinct of the human species, as we put out a fruitless fight against a redoubtable opponent that cannot be defeated. And in the midst of this unworthy battle against the changes triggered by the passing of time, the aging man and woman risk facing a period of intense suffering in old age; arguably the most intense phase between birth and death. At this challenging stage in which people are physically and emotionally vulnerable, the many causes of human suffering are magnified by the adamant yearning to hold on to a fast-speeding time, loved ones, favorable situations, and agreeable circumstances that are all petering out. And what ensues from this futile resistance to change is the intensifying experience of suffering, which is aggravated by our clinging to a state of affairs that is disappearing piecemeal and cannot be reversed.

Although it's very difficult to do, letting go becomes the only reasonable resolution.

The Second Noble Truth of Power Aging

The Buddha's *dharma* assures that the origin of suffering is attachment to transient conditions that include not only the elements of the physical world to which we belong, but also ideas, emotions, and overall perceptions of life. When it comes to aging, however, the resistance against the loss of youthful vitality (attachment to the past) is one of the main sources of suffering and despair. Only the attachment to the fear of aging itself can be more injurious.

In addition to the natural angst that the aging process ignites in the older adult population, the detrimental influence of the media in modern industrial societies exerts a nefarious effect on people's perception of aging, which only aggravates the dread of the process. Both our youth-worshipping culture and the misrepresentation of older adults' image in the mass media create an unfavorable combination that disparages the concept of what it means to be an older citizen. Not only "the value of life" is placed on being young and beautiful—and wealthy—the negative stereotypes attributed to the more mature demographic denigrates the extraordinary potential advantages that can only be accomplished through many years of living. In other words, perceptions of older people and the views older people have of themselves are directly affected by how older people are depicted in the news media, on television, in film, and in advertising.[2]

It is no wonder most people are terrified with the prospect of growing older, and therefore do everything they can to resist and deny what they refuse to accept. However, all their useless efforts can do is to create the delusion of delaying the inevitable, while at the same time aggravating their self-imposed misery (*duhkha*) of the aging process. Their attachment to younger years and their inability to let go of them, as well as everything else they must relinquish to the past, become the source of their anguish about growing older. They fall prey to the cultural delusion of physical appearance fueled by the deceiving and profitable advertising machinery that promotes the falsehood of anti-aging miracle products that will turn back the clock of illusion. Instead of embracing the longevity revolution as an opportunity to establish a new liberating paradigm for what it means to be old; a "spiritual eldering"[3] of a conscious aging process, they transform it into a debilitating desire to hold on to the old way they were decades past.

Unfortunately, the refusal to let go becomes the chain that binds the individual to the fear of aging.

The Third Noble Truth of Power Aging

Change, which aging is the quintessential representative of the fact, is not only inevitable but it's constant. Our bodies, emotions, intellect, relationships, as well as countless life's situations, they all change like the colors of a lizard adapting to the circumstances of different environments. The main distinction, however, is that the chameleon's inherent natural intelligence understands that in order to adapt to its new surroundings, it must allow the transformation to take place without resistance, while humans, equipped with the double-edged sword of rationalization resist what we perceive to be as disadvantageous transformations. Thus, our obstinate longing to hold on to what is impossible to maintain exacerbates the suffering we experience with aging.

The Buddha's third noble truth refers to the possibility of cessation of suffering; the attainable goal of liberation through *Nirodha* (the unmaking of conceptual attachment). *Nirodha* facilitates the extinguishment of obsessive desire. It expresses the idea that suffering can be ended by attaining dispassion by removing the cause of suffering in the first place. This doesn't mean that suffering itself dissipates in thin air as if an alchemical emotional process occurred eliminating a natural and necessary human development experience. It is the reluctance to allow change to happen, either it's pleasant or uncomfortable, that is the crux of the problem. The truth of cessation—and I must reiterate that cessation does not mean the elimination, but rather the self-management of suffering—is a personal discovery, not a mystical experience. It's completely bereft of religious, psychological, or intellectual motivation. It's simply an experience that blossoms out of determination to flow with the unstoppable waves of change. Thus, cessation is not just a theoretical discovery but an experience that is very real to you; like experiencing good health when you feel fine in your physical body with no pains or aches.[4]

In essence, the self-imposed distress caused by the attachment to permanence can be overcome by removing the very cause of this suffering through acceptance, which can only be achieved through a radical attitudinal transformation of letting go. Attaining complete dispassion and attachments is what The Buddha called *Nirvana*; the state of being in which all worries, troubles, and fears are released from the enlightened mind.

Suddenly, I felt like I was getting carried away by a loftier level of speculation regarding The Buddha's precepts than I anticipated. After all, my objective was to connect Zen Buddhism's principles with the challenges of the aging process, not to aim at reaching *Nirvana* when I was still assailed with self-doubts and fears. That's when I realized that both the teachings of The Buddha and their adaptation to its Japanese mode of Zen could not be applicable to my purpose, unless I took into consideration that Zen is rooted in the Buddhist principle of transformation of the self. Attachments to people, possessions, circumstances, time, and youth must be released. After all, the ethical goal of Zen is to achieve complete security and fearlessness; to move from bondage to freedom. Zen is a matter of character and not of the intellect, which means that Zen grows out of the will as the first principle of life.[5]

Therefore, if desire, attachments, and passions are the root-cause of human suffering, then, if they can be tamed and eliminated, the anguish they generate will disappear along with them. The challenge, however, is how to develop and carry out a strategy that would bring about this experience.

The Buddha found the answer when he rose from under the Bodhi tree.

The Fourth Noble Truth of Power Aging

Although a very difficult task to accomplish, the cessation (management) of suffering in old age is possible. The third noble truth asserted that the elimination of resistance and acceptance of impermanence paved the way to the path of cessation of suffering. This was the turning point in The Buddha's resolve to work with human nature and not fight against it, therefore amplifying his state of mind that would be conducive to enlightenment.[6] But in order to enter into a state of being in which there is no attachment, no desire, and no suffering, one must follow a certain path: The Eightfold Path. This is what The Buddha determined to be the middle way between the two extremes of excessive self-indulgence (hedonism) and excessive self-mortification (asceticism). The stages of this Noble Eightfold Path are: Right View, Right Intentions, Right Speech, Right Conduct, Right Livelihood, Right Effort, Right Mindfulness, and Right Concentration. According to the "Awakened One," a well thought-out strategy of these approaches to living would lead to the cessation of suffering.

In the meantime, I, "the Sleepy One," wondered in my daydreams whether it'd be possible to apply the principles of the Eightfold Noble Path to the aging process. After all, the awareness of aging was one of the realizations that led

The Buddha to decide to leave his lavish lifestyle and family behind to pursue the truth about living.

I was determined to delve into the possibility of adapting an eightfold path approach to mastering the art of aging.

"Hello Martha," I called my friend on the phone while walking on my way to work. "I think I've figured out an approach that answers your question when we talked the other day."

"Can't wait to hear it," she replied curtly.

"Not on the phone and when I'm getting shoved off the sidewalk onto the busy street by hasty pedestrians," I said breathing the odorous fumes of a fast driving ambulance whose loud siren let her know my point." This is not going to be a quick chitchat."

"All right, then. What about getting together this Saturday, say around noon, by the water feature at the riverfront park? I can pack some bread, cheese, and fruits in a picnic basket and I'll even add a bottle of your favorite merlot to inspire the conversation. What do you say?"

"Sounds like a perfect way to start the weekend," I replied in a hurry. "Listen, I'm about to enter the office building now. I'll see you on Saturday at noon."

At the Entrance of the Path

"So, what's this epiphany that 'the Zen master of aging' encountered in the quiet temple of his mind during zazen?" Martha said sardonically while popping the cork out of the wine bottle.

"Don't joke about it. You might become one of my disciples as the years go by," I said chuckling at her friendly sarcasm while pulling off one of my own. "I think I found the gateway to the path leading to the development of my ambitious goal of establishing my Power Aging concept."

She stopped pouring the wine in the glass to look at me. Without saying a word, her eyes let me know that she was very interested in hearing about my discovery.

"I realized that the pathway to my guest has already been trail-blazed by Siddhartha Gautama; and by following on his footsteps I, too, can establish my own method to finding a solution to the challenges of the aging process. He set forth on his journey to self-empowerment when he learned about the suffering innate to the human condition. In my case, when I became aware that this inherent suffering has a distinct characteristic in the latter years of life, I embarked on my own 'Going Forth' exploration to find out how to abate the anguish that assails human beings as they grow older. And because his teachings are based on the realization of human suffering in general, I deduced that I could adapt his findings to the specific challenging phase of old age."

"Keep going forth," she said metaphorically urging me to continue.

"Everything begins with The Four Noble Truths in which The Buddha awakens to the reality of suffering as quintessential to the human condition. First he becomes aware that life involves continuous change, loss, and decay, all of which intensify with the aging process. Then, he realizes that the source of unsatisfactoriness is the desperate longing to hold on to what cannot be held, which increases with age caused by the reluctance to let go of the circumstances of younger years. In the Third Noble Truth the light bulb goes on and lightens up his mind with the conviction that *duhkha*, suffering, can be abolished by eradicating *tanha*, or craving for things and conditions that cannot be sustained on a permanent basis, which is significantly exacerbated as the aging person experiences continuous changes and losses. Finally, he becomes enlightened with the knowledge that there is an eightfold path that leads the individual out of his misery. And this is where my own enlightenment to finding a solution to the predicament of aging takes place. It is upon the foundation of The Eightfold Path that I'm going to build my concept of Power Aging."

"How exactly are you planning to do it?" Martha asked with her usual demand for details, which was one of the reasons I involved her in my investigation process. By the very nature of her inquisitive thinking, she compelled me to dig deeper into the mine of my mind until I came out with a precious stone of knowledge to show her.

"By adjusting my objective to the premises of The Eightfold Path," I replied succinctly. I knew she wanted specifics, but for the moment I still held both the pick and the coarse gem in my hands.

"Well, what part of the 'how exactly' you don't understand?" She jived.

"All right, then. Let's dive into it."

An Overview of the Eightfold Path of Power Aging

"The principal objective of the *dharma* of The Buddha is to achieve a peaceful state of being within the state of impermanence that characterizes the human existence, and the entire Universe and all life forms for that matter," I prefaced. "In order to attain this level of awareness, he envisioned The Eightfold Path, which can be divided into three different categories: wisdom, morality, and mental discipline. The first two elements of The Eightfold Path, right view and right intention, constitute wisdom. The next three, right action, right speech, and right livelihood, relate to morality. And the last three, right effort, right mindfulness, and right concentration, are the requisites of the supreme level of concentration. The movement from wisdom to morality to concentration forms an upward spiral. The aspirant starts with a glimmer of wisdom, which motivates him to morality and beginning level of concentration. Concentration, in turn, deepens the wisdom. Greater wisdom strengthens morality, which leads to higher levels of concentration. The growth spiral eventually leads to *Nirvana*.[7] Are you with me so far?"

"I think I am. But perhaps you could elaborate a little more on this spiraling connection of wisdom, morality, and concentration," she requested.

"Wisdom is made of right understanding and right thought, and these two might very well be considered the hardest practices to master on The Eightfold Path, for wisdom is achieved through empirical knowledge and insights, and not through books or the mastery of concepts. Thus, it comes into existence through the direct result of practice. Morality is the Buddhist practice that comes from a compassionate heart and mind and is expressed through the things we say and do, as well as the occupation we choose or the way we invest our time and energy. Finally, mental discipline consists of our meditation on right effort, mindfulness, and concentration,"[8] I said trying to summarize the elaboration she requested. "Shall I move on?"

She nodded affirmatively without saying a word.

"What I realized is that within the broad sphere of the state of *Nirvana*, the different stages in human life call for different approaches on how to implement The Buddha's Eightfold Path, since both the perception and experience of life is quite distinct between a child and an elder. This realization occurred when I saw a photograph of a child Buddhist monk walking next to a much older counterpart. While looking at the image and reading the caption under it, it dawned on me that if that older monk had 'entered the stream,' the Buddhist term for those who entered the path, in his middle age or beyond, his approach to The Eightfold Path had to be different from the initiate child, for he is much farther down the road of living, therefore facing specific challenges that the child is yet to find out decades later. Thus, I deduced that adapting The Eightfold Path to the aging layperson with the purpose of achieving a sort of '*Nirvana* in old age' is the ultimate goal of my proposition for 'entering the stream' of a Power Aging process that will empower the aspirant in the face of unwelcome changes at the latter years of life."

"Very well thought out," she said. "But my question remains unanswered. How are you planning to adapt the general Eightfold Path of The Buddha to a particular phase in human life when the aging person feels disempowered, distraught, and discouraged?"

"Well, everything begins with the right view," I answered ready to enter the stream of my rationalization.

Right View of Power Aging

"Right view is the forerunner of the entire path; the first step of The Eightfold Path, for it enables us to understand our starting point toward the ultimate goal of the journey," I said. "To attempt to engage in the practice without the foundation of right view is to risk getting lost in the futility of undirected movement."9

"Before you get to explaining to me how does right view apply to your concept of Power Aging, I'd like you to tell me what did The Buddha mean by right view?" Martha asked interrupting me in mid-sentence. She probably noticed that I was in a roll and wanted some clarification before I moved on.

"The Buddha knew that we all bring our own notions and preconceptions to every decision, thought, conversation, or exchange we experience. To him right view or right understanding means to see things as they are and not as we would see them through our own experience, with our own bias,"10 I replied determined to proceed to elucidating my own point of view. "In relation to Power Aging, right view means the understanding and acceptance of the aging process as a natural occurrence of living without giving in to cultural bigotry, unnecessary fears promulgated by old age niche industries, and all the media hype about the overrated values of youth. It means embodying the reality that life only happens in the present time, and not in the distant nostalgic stages of a youth long gone or in a future adumbrated by anxiety about illness, disability, and death. It is living in the moment without any judgment about it and experiencing it to the fullest of what it has to offer at this particular time. It is acknowledging the many blessings and memories of a rich life replete with experiences that helped us become who we are today; but most importantly, being aware that life is still happening right now."

"And as far as your theory goes...," she said.

"In a nutshell, the right view of Power Aging is the understanding, not merely intellectual but emotional as well, that as far as our individual development is concerned, elderhood is as valuable a stage of life as youth once was. Accepting and experiencing changed circumstances as they are and not as we wish they'd be is what defines the right view of Power Aging."

"It seems to me that the point of right view, be it of aging as you're focusing on or in the general concept of The Buddha, is to clear the path from the obstacles of fear and deluded thinking in order to gain a comprehensive understanding of reality as it is, without the illusory embellished views spoon-fed to us by the dominant culture," Martha remarked. "In that sense, the right view becomes the remover of obstacles blocking the road to liberation."

"Exactly. But once the obstacles are removed and we have a clear view of the road ahead, we must establish the right intention to move forward," I said.

Right Intention of Power Aging

"I must begin by saying that right intention is not the same as good intention, for the latter is not necessarily right or even good for that matter. As the popular dictum goes, 'the road to hell is paved with good intentions;' the road to *Nirvana*, however, is paved with right intention," I remarked to start out distinguishing the difference. "Good intention that sprouts out of ignorance can do more harm than good. Sometimes, even when the good intention is motivated by genuine love, if it's not rooted in conscientious knowledge and freedom, it can be quite deleterious."

"What do you mean?" Martha asked.

"Let me illustrate my reasoning with an analogical example. Suppose that the loving parents of an only child who makes all sorts of unreasonable demands that the parents uncompromisingly give in to. The good intention of the parents is to please the child's desires to see her happy; and yet, by allowing the child to indulge in every single whim of her fancy, the parents' good intention generates bad outcomes. They can hurt the maturity development of that child and turn her into a spoiled brat who may grow up to be an egotistic self-righteous person who expects the world to surrender to her caprices. Worse yet, the parents may impose their radical religious or political views on an innocent being who will take it all in out of love and respect for the parents, even though it may not be in the child's best interest. Thus, their good intention is not by any means the right intention."

"You just reminded me of someone I knew as a child who'd been raised by her grandmother whom she manipulated willy-nilly. She insisted on consuming an exorbitant amount of candies and sweets and the grandmother obliged in an effort to please the orphan child. It so happens that she grew up to be an obese person who lost a great number of her teeth." Martha recounted. "But children's issues aside, how do you see the role of right intention in the lives of aging adults?"

"In accordance with The Buddha's perspective of right intention, the focus is on a positive attitude toward life in a spirit of kindness and compassion with no attachments to egotistic interests. And the right attitude is to turn the mind away from the impermanence of worldly matters, which in the case of the aging person is the resolute intention to overcome the reluctance to allow time to flow unabated with all the changes it brings with it. Thus, as far as the aging process is concerned, right intention is synonymous with right determination; determination to let go and surrender to the inevitable."

"But wait a minute!" Martha interjected. "The challenges inherent in the aging process are as many as they are diverse. It's not only an issue of accepting the passing of time or attachment to youth; it's much more complex than that. Although I still have a couple of decades ahead of me before I start experiencing the effects of middle-age in the anticipation of old age, I'm convinced that what really scare folks out of their wits is the fear of illness, losing their independence or their minds, death of friends and loved ones, along with an array of daunting trials and travails that the aging process entails."

"And counteracting this anxiety is exactly what right intention 'intends' to accomplish. Having the right attitude of mind that directs it attentively to overcoming evil-mindedness, which avoids wasting precious mental and emotional energy on an undesirable outcome engineered by fear. Right intention then becomes *Dai-funshi*, or Great Determination as Zen Buddhists call it, to overcome *Dai-gidan*, or Great Doubt, with an unwavering faith, or *Dai-shinkon*. You see, right intention is but right courage," I said watching a duck waddle by a big German Sheppard as if the dog were not even there.

"So, it is the courage to ignore the possibility of imminent danger," she said after turning her head to see what I was looking at.

"No," I replied immediately. "It's the courage to surrender to what you cannot control."

"I see. The right intention to strengthen one's resolve in the face of inevitable transformations," she said.

"Inevitable yes, but not necessarily dismal," I said. "The aging process is as unique to each individual as the individuals themselves. The unknown exists only in the future that is impossible to grasp; and anticipating its arrival in a negative light only darkens the present moment, which is the only reality there is. Right intention allows for the cognitive engagement with the now without giving in to the self-destructive influence of fear."

"It seems to me that fear feeds off negative self-talk, which in turn nurtures the negative emotions people experience," Martha observed wisely.

"Indeed. And that brings our conversation to the third step of The Eightfold Path."

Right Speech of Power Aging

"Right speech, which belongs to the virtue category of The Eightfold Path, is perhaps the most straightforward and the easiest concept to grasp. It's all about verbal communication and the consequences it elicits. Although we may not always be positive about what's the right thing to say, the intention motivating the talk is often unambiguous to us. Therefore, The Buddha stipulated a basic common sense communication conduct to which practicing right speech must be observed: harsh words, lies, gossip, slander, among other rude and disrespectful speech should be monitored and avoided at all times. It's pretty much a no-brainer clear-cut approach that leaves no room for second-guessing what's the right way to talk," I said as a preamble to the point I wanted to make.

"Well, my adaptation of right speech to mastering the art of aging is equally simplistic and effective. The main difference is that both the talker and the listener are one and the same: the self."

Martha looked at me from above the rim of the wine glass she held a few inches away from her lips. She had an inquisitive expression in her eyes that entreated me to proceed. I obliged.

"Actually, my rudimentary adaptation of right speech to developing a Power Aging attitude is applicable to all stages of life, for people of all ages tend to self-sabotage through negative self-talk. However, because of the intense anxiety about growing older; an otherwise natural angst that is magnified by a culture that overvalues youth, vigor, and beauty, in the latter years of life the detrimental chatterbox implanted in the mind by fear can set out devastating consequences to well-being. In fact, even you who are still a couple of decades away from middle-age expressed concern about the haunting ghouls that can come out of the closet of old age: the horror of being afflicted with illness, the dread of losing independence or becoming senile, and all the other terrors that can appear at the end of one's time on Earth. But if we were to apply the principle of right speech that refers to speaking only words that do no harm to others, why, then, would we apply it any differently to ourselves? Why would we speak to ourselves in a way that torments the mind with words that forecast panic in a future that we cannot predict? Instead, why not speak only uplifting speech that welcomes life as it comes without reserve or resistance?"

"If it only were that easy," Martha blurted it out in a whisper.

"It's not about being easy or difficult; it's the right speech; the right thing to do. It's a matter of choice," I spoke with self-conviction. "Your mind can choose to listen to your chatterbox blabbering away all kinds of self-defeating negativity, or it can choose to listen to self-empowering statements that will help build the inner strength needed to face the countless challenges presented by the aging process. In the end, you are the one who decides whom and what to listen to."

"But you have to believe in what you're listening to, otherwise the chatterbox becomes the 'lying box' that deludes your senses," Martha pressed on challenging me as I expected.

"Then you must begin by building your beliefs; and beliefs are very powerful, therefore you must be very careful about what you choose to believe, especially about yourself," I replied looking at her in the eye. "Once you decide to embrace a positive outlook while at the same time surrendering to the flow of life you cannot control, then you begin navigating the course of your life in cruise control. The truth is that the subconscious mind believes what the conscious mind tells it whether or not it is true, or even whether you believe it or not. If you listen to the chatterbox, your experience of life is fear-producing, and you stop yourself from expanding. If you listen to your positive beliefs, your experience of life becomes devoid of fear.[11] And this, my friend, is the fundamental of right speech in the process of mastering the art of aging."

Right Action of Power Aging

"From an ethical point of view, right action or right conduct bears similarities with right speech. However, as far as my adaptation to Power Aging is concerned, right action goes far beyond codes of moral principles. Right action means getting involved in the momentous sociological, environmental, and economic crises of our time. It means engaging in community affairs in the behalf of disadvantaged citizens, like the old and poor." I was in a roll when Martha interrupted me unexpectedly.

"It sounds like rather than adapting a spiritual principle to your investigation of the aging process, you're actually politicizing it; I mean, you seem to be turning it into a social issue instead."

I looked at her with an ambivalent feeling of annoyance for her derailing my train of thought, but at the same time appreciative of the challenge she always presented to my thinking and arguments. With Martha, I always had to think on my toes. "Actually, rather than diverting from the spiritual objectives that The Buddha prescribed, this involvement in worldly affairs is precisely what the 'Awakened One' determined to be fundamental for those on the path to enlightenment. In his teachings, he was very specific that above all we must live for others; that we must live the *dharma* for the sake of the people and the welfare and happiness of the multitude, out of compassion for the whole world.[12] Hence, the way I approach right action in my pursuit of learning how to master the art of aging is that right action essentially means taking action; and in a spirit of Zen, taking action can only happen right now."

"I didn't know about this aspect of the right action principle of The Eightfold Path," she said in a subdued tone of voice. "I always thought of it as a moralistic matter, such as abstinence or diligent self-control, but it never occurred to me that right action could relate to social issues, too."

"Well, if you think of right action only in relation to the ethical conduct category of The Eightfold Path, then you have a point. My take, however, is to apply it to the self-empowerment of a vulnerable demographic but without abandoning the essence of the teachings of The Buddha. In fact, Buddhists realize that action is twofold: it is made up of which we do and that which we refrain from doing, or do not do at all.[13] And considering the gravity of the world situation in the twenty-first century, not taking action is, indeed, the wrong action."

"But why place this burden on the feeble shoulders of the aging men and women who are on their way out of this world anyway? Why not leave it up to the young who will have to deal with it in their still blossoming lifetime? After all, they're the ones who will have to deal with the mess in the first place." Martha's questions and observations made me realize that she didn't understand where I was coming from. I had some explaining to do.

"Even though the mess left behind has been going on for many generations, there is a sense of responsibility that I and many other conscientious older citizens have toward the future. Speaking strictly for myself, I harbor a feeling of guilt for not aggressively pushing the agenda of what I call 'the rebirth of civilization;' a new socioeconomic order that is sustainable and more humane. But political views aside, the importance of getting older citizens engaged in worldly affairs is manifold. Firstly, their active participation in the collective challenges of our times makes them feel useful and alive, which also deviates their attention from individual concerns about their health, finances, loneliness, and all the other distress-causing apprehensions of their aging selves. What people don't seem to realize is that one of the most critical aspects of aging is the fear of being cast aside from society as a useless citizen, and this is particularly true of my generation."

I paused to take a sip of wine and collect my thoughts before continuing.

"The youth of the 1960s heralded the coming of a new era of older folks whom they have become today. At that time they were fighting for civil rights and in the best interest of minorities and oppressed segments of society. Ironically, as the older citizens of today, they're joining the ranks of an obscured discriminated class. And if the mind-altering experiments they did back then were not enough to transform their consciousness, their aging process will, for nothing changes consciousness more effectively than growing older, especially when we reach the last few decades of life.[14] It would be a wasteful shame to let all the experience and passion of what is arguably the most socially-active generation in history to fade away into the sunset without taking action."

I noticed that Martha was looking at me in a quasi-reverential manner. Perhaps she was seeing me as the quintessential revolutionary Boomer who participated in the Free Speech Movement at U.C. Berkeley or some of the many other momentous events of the 1960s that brought about significant social transformations during the Counter-Culture Revolution. But that is not the case. I'm a member of the latter lot of the Baby Boomer generation, therefore I was a child in the 1960s. But as an aging member of this remarkable generation whose consciousness has been changed by the potent effects of the passing of time, I knew that there has never been a better time for right action than right now.

Right Livelihood of Power Aging

"I can't help but wonder how are you going to apply right livelihood to your Power Aging concept when most older citizens are actually retired?" Martha asked breaking the long silent that her gazing at me had created.

"Just as right action bears similarities with right speech, so does right livelihood connects with the two other elements of the ethical conduct category of The Eightfold Path. Now, because making a living is not applicable to a retiree, then right action takes on a modified version of its original intent as the action turns into the doing of what would be equivalent to a professional occupation. Thus, what you do with your time becomes the right livelihood, except that your earnings are of a different nature: good karma credits that yield excellent returns."

"Like the way a retiree would choose to volunteer her time?" She asked.

"Exactly. At that stage in life, time, which is the most valuable commodity temporal beings have in their lifetime account, becomes the currency of life that can be spent or invested as one wishes. So, within the context of The Buddha's teachings in The Eightfold Path, someone who no longer needs to work for a living must still face the predicament of right livelihood. The choice he makes regarding what to do with his time becomes all that matters. He has the option to spend his currency of life in trivial activities that entertains and distracts his worried mind, or he can choose to invest it in selfless worthy causes that will generate most benefit to people and the world as whole." I paused to toss a grape into my mouth, then continued while still chewing on it. "Of course that does not mean giving up the jubilations of retirement altogether. It's about the balanced middle way, and by doing so, the retiree can practice right livelihood in accordance with The Buddha's *dharma*. But it takes commitment and effort to dedicate the last years of life to service."

Right Effort of Power Aging

Probably noticing how quickly I was shoving grapes into my mouth, Martha realized that I was hungry. She grabbed a paper plate from the sturdy hemp picnic basket and filled it with a slice of sourdough bread, three different kinds of cheese, and more grapes before handing it to me with a smile. I picked up the bottle of wine and refilled our glasses getting ready to resume our conversation.

"Without right effort there's not much you can accomplish in your life. Along with right mindfulness and right concentration, right effort belongs to the three mental disciplines categories of The Eightfold Path. It is the starting point of the mental development necessary to carry out whatever you're committed to achieving. It is the foundation upon which a positive attitude that nurtures productive thoughts and feelings is based on. When you have a positive attitude and constantly strive toward your goal with unwavering effort, then you have applied The Buddha's approach of right effort to your life." I stopped talking to take a bite of bread smeared with brie cheese that I washed down with a couple of consecutive sips of wine.

"But how does right effort apply to your Power Aging concept in practical terms?" Martha asked, always pushing the envelope and challenging me to dig deeper into my own thoughts.

"The Buddha taught that there are four great efforts: the effort to avoid, the effort to overcome, the effort to develop, and the effort to maintain,"[15] I said while wiping off some cheese from my mustache with a paper napkin. "As we age, the effort to avoid that is most important is the negative thoughts that engender fear of the challenges of old age. They are, undoubtedly, the most deleterious act we can commit against ourselves. Therefore, we must apply the effort to overcome this self-defeating anxiety, for it'll only aggravate what cannot be changed. Then, the effort to develop kicks in and motivates us to strengthen our will and move forward with determination to overcome whatever challenges comes ahead. Once this is accomplished, then it's just a matter of making the effort to maintain a salubrious state of mind that is conducive to self-empowerment."

Martha was about to say something but I interrupted her before she could get started. "Oh, yes, and what can we do to foster the development of the four great efforts?" I said anticipating her questioning. "By practicing right mindfulness."

Right Mindfulness of Power Aging

"In a sense, right mindfulness is the spouse of right effort and they progress hand-in-hand as an inseparable couple. Without right effort right mindfulness does not come into being because mindfulness requires a significant amount of effort, particularly in the beginning of the practice. Conversely, without mindfulness, effort would be wasted and futile.[16] When we are mindful of our thoughts, we're constantly observing ourselves, and therefore we become aware of both our feelings and actions," I said. "I consider right mindfulness to be the backbone of Zen Buddhism."

"It makes me think of Shakespeare's many references to our daily experiences, as though we lived in a world of dreams; a reality enmeshed in an illusory perception," Martha said. "Like his character Prospero's famous statement: 'We are such stuff as dreams are made on, and our little life is rounded in a sleep.'"

"From the Buddhist perspective, our ordinary state of consciousness is seen as being severely limited and limiting, resembling in many respects an extended dream rather than wakefulness.[17] And this view has been backed up by many prominent thinkers, like the Russian P.D. Ouspensky who asserted that there is nothing permanently subconscious in us because there is no conscious mind in the first place. He claimed that people live in a sleep-like state of being, do everything in sleep, and worse yet, do not know that they are asleep. They are neither aware of their limitations nor their possibilities.[18] Within this dismal context of lack of self-awareness, the purpose of cultivating right mindfulness is to awaken the individual from the dream of this illusory perception engendered by the limitations of time and space. But developing mindfulness requires great effort and discipline."

"Which must be hard for aging folks," she remarked, incorrectly.

"Not anymore than in any other stage of life. The time to decide to cultivate mindfulness exists only in the moment, and whether the moment takes place in childhood or in the eighth decade of your life is inconsequential. Some people start earlier in life without investing the necessary effort and discipline to endure and give up along the way. Others realize how critical mindfulness is to an empowered existence later in life and they stick to it until they master the ability to live in the now," I said looking at Martha holding my half-full glass of wine. "Mindfulness, like enlightenment, can happen at any stage of life. The only requirement is the determination to pursue it and not give up until it's been conquered; until you feel present at every moment in your life. But again, it's not an easy task to accomplish. It takes a lot of practice."

"That's why I mentioned that it must be hard for older folks to achieve it," she said defensively. "I mean, constantly monitoring your thoughts and your reactions to them, man, that's exhausting. Besides, it can be frustrating to have those moments like 'oops, I missed it again' all the time. I guess it goes back to the issue of living in a sleep state of mind in which we're constantly awaking from the dream of being mindful of the here and now that we seem to be seldom aware of."

"It is the mindless of the automaton that is programmed to think the same negative thoughts over and over again, while triggering all sorts of unwelcome emotions. It's the ignorance of the 'dream within a dream' in which the mind either rewinds to the comfort of a known past or fast-forward to the anxiety of an unknown future. In the meantime, the mindfulness of living, which can only happen in the now, is stolen by a mechanical way of being that causes continuous anxiety and suffering."

"And what's the antidote for such a self-destructive behavior? She asked.

"The practice of meditation certainly helps in the practice of mindfulness. It helps reminding us that life is always unfolding moment by moment in a concatenation of events that moves naturally toward the future without our having to think about it. Meditation, then, is the antithesis of mechanical thinking and paves the way to mindfulness."

"For some reason I always thought of meditation as a laser-focused concentration," she said.

"Sure, concentration on the present moment; on the breathing," I said.

"So, is it what the right concentration aspect of The Eightfold Path is about?" She asked.

"Let's say that meditation is the technique that allows right concentration to evolve," I said pouring some more wine in her glass and mine. "Well, I guess we finally made it to the last aspect of The Eightfold Path."

Right Concentration of Power Aging

"Right concentration is the pathway to right mindfulness; the cornerstone of the practice. It is the means through which to focus the attention on awareness that allows you to see beyond the veil of Maya, the veil of illusion," I said. "In Sanskrit, concentration is called *samadhi*, or 'one-pointed meditation,' which is the ultimate stage of meditation at the highest level of concentration. With regular practice, the mind develops a stillness that gives way to unperturbed peacefulness in the face of whatever comes your way. It leads to a courageous state of being that the Japanese scholar, Inazo Nitobe, refers to as 'tranquility is courage in repose.'"

"Huh, that resonates with what Paul Tillich called 'the courage of confidence.' He claims that the wise man that courageously conquers desire, suffering, and anxiety, surpasses God himself,"[19] Martha said. "I interpret it in a similar line to the Buddhist concept of *Nirvana*."

"In my estimation, this is the ultimate purpose of right concentration when it reaches the *samadhi* level," I said. "That level of tranquility as courage in repose is the outcome of Great Faith and self-confidence, which banishes the anxieties about the unknown. When you reach that level of concentration that breeds both bravery and serenity, that's when you become a truly empowered individual. And that, my friend, is what I'm after: I want to apply the principles of Power Aging into a pragmatic approach for daily living. There is great need for developing inner strength to face the challenges of aging in an uncertain time."

"People of all ages are searching for a sense of purpose and wanting to find meaning in a world in chaos," she said. "It's not only the older adult population that is in need of building inner strength, though I understand they face a unique challenge that the rest of us younger folks will only experience at a later date. But in any case, self-empowerment is something that everyone should be after."

"Sure, but attaining it when you're at a most disadvantageous condition makes it much more difficult to accomplish," I said. "Add to it the cultural bias and the negative stereotypes that people have about aging, now you have a serious obstacle to overcome."

Martha looked at me in silence for a long while. "So, how are you going to go about teaching your Power Aging *Dharma* to a flock of vulnerable partisans?"

"I don't know. Maybe I'm going to have to sit under a Bodhi tree for a long time to figure it out," I replied in good jest. "But before I even attempt to spread a *dharma* that I'm yet to determine how to effectuate, I have a lot of learning to do about my own aging process and how it's been changing me. Then, I want to find out how it's been affecting new generations as well."

The Sun was beginning to set behind the western mountains and the crimson sky announced that it was time to go. We bid farewell after Martha wished me good luck and asked me to keep her abreast of my project's progress. She climbed on her bicycle and rode away as I started my long walk back home. While ambling along the riverfront park mesmerized by the breathtaking hues that changed colors gradually as I moved westward, I began outlining a strategy through which I'd be able to apply my concept of Power Aging into an empirical reality.

Now that I had decided to implement Zen Buddhist principles to my quest, I needed to verify the feasibility of my approach to the realities of the aging process and what it means to be an old adult in the twenty-first century.

Chapter 7

The Myths of Aging

The Evolution of Aging

There was a time when old age was exalted and venerated. Although some cultures still regard their elders with utmost respect and even hearken their input in individual and social affairs, the youth-crazed focus of modern industrial Western societies have done away with what has become an archaic cultural tradition. However, as Baby Boomers, which are the most educated, socially conscientious and politically savvy older generation in human history comes of (second) age, the possibility for a renaissance of the values of seniority is unfolding. Furthermore, scientific and technological developments have dramatically expanded human life span to unprecedented levels.

Longevity is a phenomenon of the second-half of the twentieth century. In 1800, the average life expectancy was less than 40 years. By 1900, when one in five babies didn't make it to their fifth birthday, life expectancy at birth was just 47 years. Today, the average lifetime has extended to more than 77 years in all of the modernized nations of the world.[1] And this upward trend is escalating at a rapid pace with the population age 65 and over and age 85 and over projected to grow exponentially from 2010-2050.[2] In essence, people are living longer and growing old later in life than any previous generation. Consequently, at no other time in human history has it been more critical to transform the mindset of what aging is supposed to be. Just as the early twentieth century marked a renewed interest in the study and understanding of old age, much progress is expected to occur in the twenty-first century regarding both the quality of life and the experience of living of elders; not only at the individual level but collectively as well.

Perhaps foreseeing that the advancement in medicine and technological developments would transform the demography of the world in the twentieth century, Ilya Ilyich Mechnikov, a Russian scientist who pioneered research into the immune system and received the Nobel Prize in medicine in 1908, coined the term gerontology in 1903 for the emerging study of aging and longevity. The word gerontology, which derives from the Greek *geron* (old man) and *logy* (study of) is the study of social, psychological, and biological aspects of aging. This is not to be confused with geriatrics, which is the branch of medicine that studies the diseases of older adults, whereas gerontology is a multidisciplinary study. Gerontologists view aging in terms of four distinct processes: chronological aging, biological aging, psychological aging and social aging.[3]

Since my probing into the possibility of transmuting the vulnerability of old age into personal power lies not on the medical aspects of aging, I focused my interest in finding out how the four distinct processes of gerontology could be readjusted to favor the aging process instead of its perceived disempowering beliefs. But as soon as I set forth in my investigation, I ran into seemingly insurmountable myths and stereotypes about aging. That's when I decided to summon the assistance of an expert.

Looking for a Second Opinion

"The foundation sustaining the myths and stereotypes of old age is gerontophobia; the fear and negative attitude toward the aged," said Jeff, a friend of mine who's an academic in the field of public health and human sciences when I went to visit with him at his university office. "Since phobia is by definition an illogical fear, you can assume with certainty that the myths and stereotypes are illogical as well."

"And how did gerontophilia get lost in this process?" I questioned referring to the old-fashioned and rapidly disappearing respect and reverence for the aged in modern societies.

He looked at me and chuckled shaking his head. "Gerontophilia has long been on the endangered list of social values. Most stereotypes of old age are negative at best and insulting at worst. In fact, the many outdated concepts, myths, and prejudices toward older adults are so prevalent that it requires an inordinate amount of fortitude from the individual to look forward to the future with optimism and confidence, especially after the fiftieth birthday milestone."

"Gee, you make it sound like we're culturally conditioned to think of old age as though it were a sort of a boogeyman that suddenly creeps out of the shadows of time to haunt us in the latter stages of life," I remarked tongue-in-cheek.

"Well, if that's the case, then it's time to exorcise the ghoul by debunking the myths, while acknowledging the realities of the transformations that take place with the passing of time," he replied following on my off-beat analogy.

"So where do you begin this process?" I asked.

"Firstly, as a society we have to acknowledge that the aging process is not something that happens overnight. It starts at the dawn of conception and continues unabated until the sunset of life. It is a natural universal progression that can be observed in all life forms; even the Sun is aging and will die in approximately 2.3 billion years," he said. "Thus, aging is not only a natural process and a necessary requirement of human development, but it should be also a welcome adventurous journey. Unfortunately, our culture places all the emphasis on the youthful years while disregarding the fact that youth is but a milepost on the road to old age."

"Point in case," I said. "But that does not change the common misconceptions about aging."

"True. Only debunking the myths will," he concluded.

I left his office thinking about the many myths of aging, both the negative and the few positive ones as well. Yes, there are quite a few embellished misconceptions of old age, which the quintessential is the notion of "golden age" when happy-go-lucky retirees bask in the glory of their retirement years. Actually, it is rather bizarre that juxtaposed to the terrifying prospect of debilitating old age lies the equally deceptive myth of an idyllic golden age. But neither the horrors of physical decrepitude in institutional confinement nor the imagery of happily retired seniors sunbathing somewhere between the Tropics of Cancer and Capricorn is realistic. The truth is that the average older adult longs for a modest retirement years with a modicum of financial stability and some active participation in social life. What they do not want is to become invisible and disposable. Alas, with the negative stereotypes attributed to old age by our youth-worshipping society, older adults have their work cut out for them. Perhaps my academic friend was right: we must debunk the myths of old age.

"Hey, Jeff, would you be able to get together some time this weekend to talk about the myths of old age with me?" I asked on the phone. "I'll treat you for lunch at your favorite Thai food restaurant downtown. What do you say?"

"Oh brother, you do know how to entice me through my appetite weakness, don't you?" He replied laughing through his words. "How can I say no to it? What about on Saturday at noon?"

Old Age and Senility

"Fortunately, both the aging process and the attitude toward it have changed significantly since the mid-twentieth century," Jeff said after I inquired about the evolution of aging in recent years. "In addition to the extraordinary advancements in medicine, nutrition, lifestyle, economic development, among other factors that have greatly contributed to what is commonly referred to as 'successful aging,' there has been a significant change in the outlook of the aging process."

"Sure, but it seems to me that the mental health forecast of the modern aging population is bleaker than it's ever been," I remarked thinking of Alzheimer's disease in particular.

Jeff looked at me while placing the menu he held in his hands on the table. "Generalizing the mental health forecast of the aging population at large is a myopic perception. After all, anticipating what will happen in old age without taking into consideration the many variables that distinguish different individuals such as genetic makeup, education, lifestyle, attitude toward aging, just to name a few, is a fallacious myth that disfavors every aging citizen by infusing fear in the unknown future."

"But it's more than mere generalization, Jeff; it's a fact of nature," I said convinced of what I was talking about. "Let's face it, as you get older, both your mind and body do not function as well as they used to. And the number of old folks losing their mental marbles these days is very high; and the future outlook doesn't bode optimism either. Not too long ago, I read a brochure from the Alzheimer's Association stating that someone develops Alzheimer's every 68 seconds. That's an astounding pace!"

"Although it's true that many older adults will succumb to senility, the same can be said about the many people who will develop cancer, and a large number at much younger age," he remarked as a prelude to his argument. "The truth is that becoming senile is not an ungodly draconian edict imposed on all humankind at the end of life; just as cancer is not a general fatality either, even though it's a widespread disease. Some people will acquire it but many more won't. Oxymoronically speaking, it is the luck of the draw, and it's always been this way."

"I guess you have a point," I said picking up the menu at the sound of my rumbling stomach.

"I most certainly do," he asserted with utter disregard to hypocritical humility. "Mozart fell ill and died at the age of 35, while Verdi composed the opera *Falstaff* in his eightieth year and *Ave Maria* at 85-years-old. Now, how is that for debunking generalization?"

Old Age and Isolation

"As you know, I have a special interest in the sociological aspect of aging. To me, the social and psychological changes that take place as you age are issues of great concern, both at the individual and societal level," I said. "And the withdrawal from the workforce aside, I think the most pervasive and damaging consequence of aging is the isolation and loneliness that come with the aging process."

"Although many older adults end up living in solitude, though not necessarily lonely or isolated, this trend can be attributed to several sociological factors ranging from economic circumstances to changes in marital or social status caused by retirement, divorce, widowhood, and, of course, relatives who move far away to pursue better economic opportunities. Whatever the situation may be, the reality is that with the passing of time a multitude of losses take place in everyone's lives, until the ultimate loss of life itself arrives uncompromisingly." Jeff spoke of such grave matters so casually that it disturbed my equanimity, which I noticed when I swallowed dry air.

"Sure, whatever the situation may be, you're still dealing with loss, loneliness, and potential isolation," I said with a quivery voice that revealed my subtle fear of that happening to me sometime in the future.

"But rather than a depressing realization, loss is a natural consequence of growing older at any stage of the aging process," he replied seemingly unmoved by the tone of my voice. "Take for instance the child of a military father who has to move constantly in the course of her childhood. She will experience many losses of friends, teachers, neighbors, among many other people and places that she must accept to leaving behind while adapting to new sociological circumstances. Indeed, loss is an intrinsic factor to the experience of living that often begins at an early age and continues on throughout the course of a lifetime."

"But at any age, how do you go about learning to cope with loss and continuous change, especially as you grow older?" I asked expecting a hint of hope.

"As far as I can tell, the only way to handle the challenges of loss and changes is by learning to develop a salubrious relationship with yourself," he said without giving too much thought to it. "This way, loneliness is unlikely to become a haunting prospect later in life. Of course, humans are social creatures and therefore need interaction with friends and peers. This is why the role of the community is critical to mollifying the effects of elder isolation. When communities become responsibly engaged in the welfare of their older fellow-citizens, then this generalized myth of the lonely and isolated elder will no longer be a noticeable factor; certainly not any more than the millions of young lonesome city dwellers."

Old Age and Poor Health

The popular restaurant was busy as usual and it took awhile until the waiter finally showed up to take our order. After he left dashing back to the kitchen trying to keep up with the rush weekend lunch hour, Jeff and I resumed our conversation.

"What about the health issue, Jeff? It seems obvious that health deteriorates as the years go by," I said eager to hear his response.

"Poor health is not by any means a trademark of old age. In fact, the majority of older adults 65 years of age and beyond maintain very active healthy lifestyles and remain fairly healthy in old age," he said. Then, the pulled out a professional journal out of his briefcase and handed it to me. "Take a look at this."

I held it in my hand at the opened page as he gave it to me. It read: "According to the National Center for Health Statistics, about two-thirds of those 65 years of age and older report their health status in positive terms (good, very good, or excellent). Although the proportion of older adults who rate their health in positive terms seems to decline with age, more than 60 percent of the oldest-old (those 85 years of age and older) continue to evaluate their health status positively."[4]

"This is very interesting," I remarked.

"But that's not all," he replied pulling out a book that he handed it to me. "Check this out and tell me what you think."

I leafed through the book and I was stunned with the photographs of elder citizens in superb physical condition. The book was a collection of images by photographer Etta Clark in which she displayed photos of older athletes in extraordinary health and magnificent physical form.[5] Even though the images of those poster men and women for athletic shape in later life did not represent the norm as you're conditioned to perceive elders to be, they inspired me and sent a visual message that for those who take good care of themselves—physically, mentally, emotionally, and spiritually—it is possible to live a long healthy life.

"Absolutely amazing!" I exclaimed.

"Inspiring, isn't it? And this has become a new trend in aging since the mid-twentieth century," he said. "Actually, Clark's portraits of older adult athletes are but a selective illustration of numerous examples of a growing number of healthy elders, some of whom are excelling at record-breaking levels of endurance at older age."

"That's right! Now I remember reading about Diana Nyad who at the age of 64 swam the 110-mile journey from Cuba to Florida in her fifth attempt and 35 years after she first tried the remarkable feat," I said recollecting how impressed I was when I found out about her extraordinary determination to succeed in her self-imposed challenge.

"And not to be outshined, there is also the case of Olga Kotelko, a retired school teacher who at 77-years-old entered her first 'masters' track and field competition and at 94 she was still competing. She was the only woman in the world over 90 still long-jumping and high jumping competitively,"[6] Jeff added another example to astonish me even more. "Of course, elders like Diana Nyad and Olga Kotelko are exceptional examples of superior athleticism and good health in old age. Nonetheless, there is a growing number of older citizens who are diligently striving to improve on and prolong physical fitness as they age. Oh yes, and there is that dude who completed the Ironman race; the 140.6 mile of biking, swimming, and running at the age of 70.[7] It's a brave new world of aging out there, man."

~ The Myths of Aging ~

Old Age and Victimization

Some 15 minutes after taking our order, the waiter finally showed up dexterously holding my eggplant basil with shrimp dish in one hand and Jeff's *prik khing* calamari in the other. In a polite and yet hasty fashion, he made sure we didn't need anything else before hurrying away to meet the needs of other customers at crunch lunch time. As soon as he walked away, I engaged my friend in conversation again.

"What do you think about elder abuse and victimization, Jeff? Is it a myth or a fact?"

"Although it's true that a large number of older citizens are subjected to victimization by abuse or neglect, being a target of crime is definitely not idiosyncratic to this particular demographic. The reality is that all vulnerable populations, be it children, women, the poor, or the uneducated, they are all sought-after preys by unscrupulous and opportunistic people who are always prowling after their next target. In fact, national and local surveys show that the elderly are actually less likely to be victimized than are younger persons, in all crime categories.[8] Unfortunately, the various forms of abuse that vulnerable older adults endure are often carried out by close relatives or those entrusted to care for them."

Old Age and Poverty

"And then there is the economics of aging," I said. "For many and various reasons, there seems to be so much poverty among older citizens. Once their ability to work decreases, so does their income."

"Poverty, at any level of consideration, has never been an exclusively demographic issue, but a broad socioeconomic malady that affects millions of people who are often condemned to live through it for a lifetime," Jeff observed with reason. "Social inequities have deep roots that spread through the grounds of lack of educational opportunities, unavailable health care, inadequate housing, insufficient nutrition, volatile job market, and the list goes on. It is not by any means an old age issue, but a calamity of socioeconomic inequality."

"Are you trying to say that this myth is based on the large number of older citizens who depend on their meager Social Security benefits and limited Medicare for their health care needs?" I asked.

"Somewhat. But ironically, while certain subgroups among the elderly continue to show relatively high rates of impoverishment, Baby Boomers earn more than $2 trillion in annual income and own more than 77% of all financial assets in the United States; not to mention the fact that they spend approximately $157 billion on leisure and travel each year.[9] Based on this and other economic statistics about the financial wherewithal of the Boomer Generation, the myth of widespread poverty among older citizens is debatable. Having said that, so is the impression that the economic situation of the average older citizen has greatly improved since President Lyndon Johnson's War on Poverty legislation of 1964."

Old Age and Religion

Half way through our succulent meals, I broached the subject of religion and the seemingly increased religiosity among older citizens.

"It seems to me that most houses of worship are filled primarily with older folks. What's your take on the assumption that people tend to become more religious as they get older?"

"Being death the greatest mystery of life, the closer you get to it the more you need a sense of comfort and reassurance in the face of the unknown," Jeff pointed out wisely. "But in reality, however, death has been always hovering around you from the moment you are born."

"Sure, theoretically you're at the risk of dying from the time of conception," I said. "But what does it have to do with becoming more religious in old age?"

"Through accumulation of knowledge and life experiences, aging tends to change consciousness and incites a deep desire to understand the purpose of your life as you approach the end of the journey. Since growing older brings continuous loss, so it's only natural that older citizens develop a proclivity to become, not necessarily more religious, but more concerned with spiritual matters," he said.

"I guess it makes sense," I agreed.

"It certainly does. But what often goes unnoticed is that traditional religious services provide opportunities for socialization for many disaffiliated older people. In this sense, the pursuit of organized religion fulfills a twofold purpose: it provides spiritual support for coping with the mystery of death, while fulfilling the need for communal connection at a time in life characterized by recurrent loss."

Old Age and Productivity

As soon as Jeff mentioned recurrent loss, my mind immediately drifted to the subject of work and how it affects older professionals in the current competitive job-market climate. I had one particular case in mind.

"A friend of mine was laid off in his late fifties and he could not find work anywhere. He told me that someone had hinted to him that older workers are less productive and that's why he couldn't convince any employer to hire him," I said working on the final bite of my almost empty plate. "Do you think there is any validity to this claim? Personally, I think it's absurd!"

Jeff looked at me holding the fork close to his mouth before putting it down on the plate to reply. "As a gross generalization, the myth that older workers are less productive is pathetic and it's the quintessential ageism; not to mention that's an affront to the Age Discrimination in Employment Act of 1967. Of course, like the other myths we've discussed so far, there are many variables that will determine the truth of sweeping statements regarding productivity in the workplace. However, granted that similar educational and training levels are in place, older adults actually should have an edge over younger professionals, though it's often not revealed as being the case."

"Sure, but in spite of their abilities, professional experience, and age discrimination laws, older workers seem to have far more difficulty securing employment than their younger competitors on the job-market," I said letting out my not-so-subtle indignation.

"Unfortunately, that seems to be true. An Associate Press-NORC Center for Public Affairs Research poll finds many people over 50 reporting great difficulty securing employment and feeling that their age is a factor.[10] Although surveys show that older people believe they experience age discrimination on the job-market, research also found that older workers outpace younger ones in nearly every metric, except for jobs in which there is high physical demand.[11] And yet, as a general rule, employers tend to favor the hiring of younger workers," Jeff concurred with my comment backing it up with some research evidence he knew so well.

"Despite the illegality of age discrimination in the workplace, which is virtually undetectable and nearly impossible to prove, there is no denying that older capable workers' knowledge and experience can be a great asset to any organization," he continued. "If the business world can overcome the narrow-mindedness of ageism, it will realize that older workers often yearn for making meaningful contributions in the final stretch of their careers."

Old Age, Retirement, and Declining Health

The waiter, who was huffing and puffing and looked spent, stopped by our table to pick up the empty plates before dashing out probably eager for his shift to be over soon. Noticing how exhausted he looked, it reminded me of the myth of declining health in old age; a subject I had to broach.

"I guess there is no getting around the issue of deteriorating health that comes with the passing of time," I said looking at the waiter maneuvering his way around tables with a mountainous tray of dirty plates he carried above his head. "I've heard several times people say that older retirees tend to suffer decline in health when they no longer participate in the workforce."

"Well, I can certainly agree with the fact that older people are at a greater risk of falling ill than younger individuals do," Jeff said. "After all, like an older motor vehicle, the more mileage you add to it the more likely it is to develop mechanical problems. Nevertheless, assuming that this natural biological progression is an indirect consequence of retirement is ludicrous. But having said that, the lack of mental and physical activity can be detrimental to anyone's health regardless of age. The obesity epidemic and the widespread attention deficit disorders among the youth come to mind. Presumably, this myth grew out of a misperceived assumption that most retired citizens spend their idle time sitting in rocking-chairs flipping through television channels all day long, and therefore experience a decline in health due to physical and mental inactivity."

"But isn't the decline in activity a fact in most retirement cases?" I asked.

"Not really. In a gerontology study entitled *Retirement in American Society*, the conclusion was evident: retired people were no more likely to be sick than were people of the same age who remained on the job.[12] Besides, older retirees today are much more socially active and involved in productive activities than previous older generations. This new aging demographic known as Boomers is a new breed of old people. Many of them are interested and engaged in turning the final stage of life into new possibilities for change."

"Perhaps, retirement offers them an opportunity to continue on the incomplete tasks of changing the world they set it out in their youth in the 1960s," I said thinking of my own intentions.

"Exactly! Retirement offers the Baby Boomer generation the most precious gift of all: time. Considering that in modern industrial societies most people don't seem to have enough time, having the luxury to engage in activities that contribute to worthy social causes can only be good for one's overall health; and I mean not only physical and mental, but social as well."

Old Age and Sex

Suddenly, at the table next to ours, a young couple stood up getting ready to leave the establishment. I couldn't help but notice the attractive beautiful woman acting amorously toward her handsome companion. At that moment, the topic of sexual relations came to my mind and I had to ask Jeff his opinion on the matter in relation to older people.

"Hey Jeff, what's your take on sexagenarian sex?" I asked with purposeful alliteration while watching the young couple walk out of the restaurant canoodling in an affectionate embrace.

"Why not octogenarian sex?" He replied right away with a question of his own. "Our culture is inherently laden with taboos, prejudices, guilt, shame, and, of course, myths of all sorts. So, it's not surprising that sexual activity in old age falls into a few of those discriminatory cultural misconceptions."

"Really, sex in your 80s?" I retorted with a furrowed brow. I wanted to sound and look cool with my progressive scholarly friend, but the idea of having sex that late in life with a woman in the same age group left my stomach churning.

Probably noticing the contorted expression in my face, Jeff smiled looking at me as if I were dim-witted. "Even open-minded adults can feel quite uncomfortable just with the thought of their parents having sex, so you can only imagine how they might feel about the idea of the grandparents indulging their naked old bodies in lascivious acts. Well, they may remain that way only until they get old themselves and engage in salacious exploits with their 80 plus-year-old sexual partners."

I didn't say anything this time, though I believe the expression in my face still conveyed my disturbance. I felt like one of the many trivial-minded citizens whom I discounted as culturally retrogrades, which it didn't make me feel good about myself.

"As numerous studies have demonstrated, including the renowned Masters and Johnson's research on human sexuality, sexual activity was never supposed to have an expiration date; and neither was it meant to be sinful, filthy, nor any other slight brought about by inane Puritanism," he continued. "One of the culprits for some decline in sexual activity among the old is the undue acceptance of stereotypes about the sexless older years. The truth, however, is that healthy older men and women can and should have satisfying sex lives regardless of their age. But of course, before becoming able to experience a satisfying sex life, at any age for that matter, you have to believe you can have it."

"You mentioned Masters and Johnson's studies," I said with renewed interest in the subject matter. "I remember watching a television show inspired on their work in which an older couple in their late 70s were having loud ecstatic sex in a hotel room. At that time, I couldn't help but wonder about the fictitious aspect of that particular episode."

"Trust me, there's nothing fictitious about having sex in your 70s or 80s. The problem is that in America sex is generally regarded as something for the young and attractive," Jeff said. "Masters and Johnson mentioned in their studies that thinking of an elderly couple engaging in sexual activity usually provokes discomfort. In fact, the idea of sexual partners in a nursing home seems shocking and immoral to most people. But despite these cultural myths, the psychological need for intimacy, excitement, and pleasure does not disappear in old age, and there is nothing in the biology of aging that automatically shuts down sexual function."[13]

"Really? I always thought that the hormonal changes that take place in middle-age ought to have an impact, not only on the libido but on the ability to perform sexually as well," I remarked with skepticism. "Isn't it true that both men and women lose their sexual mojo as they age?"

"I guess those erectile dysfunction meds commercials on TV are more effective than I thought," he said with a grin. "Sure, there are many men who for medical reasons may be afflicted with impotence and need an extra chemical help. However, granted that good health is in place, the decline in hormone production have but a minor effect on sexual activity, as Masters and Johnson's studies concluded."

"What about women? It has to affect them, too!" I pointed out.

"Certainly, but not at the level our culture leads us to believe," he said. "In the highly regarded nationwide study of female sexuality, Shere Hite posed the following question to the older women subjects of her study: 'How does age affect sex? Does desire for sex increase or decrease, or neither, with age? What about enjoyment of sex?' Well, guess what? Most women who answered these questions felt that their sexual pleasure had increased with age. One subject who was 66-years-old responded that her sexual desire had not diminished at all; in fact, her sexual enjoyment was as great as ever!"[14]

"You've got to be kidding!" I exclaimed astonished with the information.

"I kid you not. You'd be amazed of how many older women are having satisfying sexual experiences," he said looking at my startled face. "I once participated in a study at the university in which I interviewed a 61-year-old divorcee who shared with me that after 33 years in a sexually unfulfilled marriage, she was finally having the best sex of her life. I remember her words clearly when she said: 'If someone had told me in my younger years that I'd be having the best sex of my life in my 60s, I'd have thought it to be absolutely crazy and ridiculous; and yet, that's the absolute truth.'"[15]

While I mulled over—with a great deal of skepticism—the prospect of enjoying sex in my 70s and beyond, Jeff interrupted my musings with an off-the-cuff observation that made me wonder whether he was reading my mind.

↭ The Myths of Aging ↭

"Incidentally, I'd like to point out that Charles Chaplin fathered his eighth child at the age of 73 with his fourth wife, Oona O'Neill, who happened to be 36 years his junior and with whom he was married for 34 years."

Old Age and Long-Term Care

Jeff and I left the restaurant and I walked with him to the nearby college campus where he worked and I'd parked my car. As we chatted about sports and other trivial subjects, a mini bus with a logo of a memory care facility stopped in front of a shopping area and a wheelchair lift lowered a very old lady to the sidewalk. Suddenly, I halted my steps and lost interest in the fumbled football in the 3-yard line in the last minute of the game that Jeff was talking about. He noticed my reaction and stopped to face me.

"That's another myth right there," he said nodding his chin in the direction of the lady in the wheelchair. "Contrary to misled public opinion, most old people do not end up in nursing homes, especially among the so-called young old, which are people between the ages of 65 and 74. Actually, a relatively small percentage of the 65 plus population live in institutional settings. It is true that the percentage does increase significantly with age; approximately 3.5% for persons between 75 and 84 and 13% for people over 85-years-old."[16]

"Huh, that's not a frightening percentile at all," I replied looking at the old lady being rolled in the store by a white-clad assistant.

"These numbers are indicative that, in reality, a minority of even the old-old adults end up in long-term care institutions," Jeff remarked. "Now, can I finish my story about that clumsy fumble that cost my team the game?"

Chapter 8

The Facts of Aging

The Tarnished Image of The Golden Age

"We're moving to Florida," my next door neighbor, Chuck, said when I was outside checking my mailbox and noticed the large moving truck parked on his driveway.

"Well, that's exciting!" I exclaimed happy for my mid-sexagenarian neighbor I'd known for many years. "I bet Lois and you must be thrilled about spending your retirement years where the Sun shines year round."

"Retirement? Oh, hell no! I don't think we'll ever be able to enjoy such a luxury," he said as his eyelids drooped to the weight of his despondency. "We feel very fortunate to have found a job as live-in caretakers of a motel in Orlando. We've been unable to find work around here for a long time, so we have to go wherever we can make a living."

I walked back into my home realizing that I was holding the mail in my hands but had left my mind outside. I could not have fathomed in a million years that my next door neighbor, who like me, lived in a nice house in a middle-class neighborhood, was in such a financial strain that he had to move cross-country to secure an income to make a living at that stage in his life. I tossed the electric bill, credit card statement, and a slew of junk mail on the kitchen table and walked to the living-room pensive and suddenly preoccupied with my own future. After all, being in my 50s and with a measly 401-k retirement account that would barely keep me afloat for a couple of years, Chuck's reality had an unwelcome impact on the perspective of my own future. Besides, I'd been laid off twice in the last twelve years from jobs that I felt very "secure," and I remember how difficult it was to find employment again. All of a sudden, my quest to finding out how to turn aging into power took on an unexpected economic detour. Now I had to explore an important aspect of growing older that I had not given any thought about.

After my friend Jeff clarified many stereotypical misconceptions about aging, neither he nor I thought of talking about the deceptive myth of the so-called "golden age" in which retirees sail into the glorious sunset of rest and leisure. Suddenly, my neighbor Chuck made me realize that the idea of guaranteed retirement, much less the enjoyment of it, was as misleading as all the negative myths Jeff and I talked about. Apparently, it did not represent the reality of millions of older citizens. Like the negative myth generalizing the assumption that most old people end up in long-term care institutions, the myth of the "golden age" when retirees enjoy a carefree lifestyle of travel, entertainment, and fun-in-the-Sun seemed more like a concoction of injudicious marketers in the profitable industry of aging and longevity. I needed to uncover some facts about it.

Retirement Myopia

The next morning, I went to my local public library to carry out some research that would help me better understand retirement in the twenty-first century. I walked straight to the reference desk to solicit assistance for my research project where a grey-haired clerk greeted me with a welcoming smile.

"Oh my, you are the fourth person to ask me about it in the last couple days," the friendly lady said after I asked where I could find materials about retirement. "In fact, I spent so much time helping a young social worker collect data for her work with senior clients that I've learned quite a bit about the subject myself."

"Then, perhaps all I need to do is ask you questions," I said bantering with her.

"I'm afraid I haven't learned that much, but I'll be glad to share with you the little I know. In the meantime, let me walk you to the section where these resources are located." She asked a colleague to take over the desk and led me to through the wonderful maze of bookshelves where bibliophiles like me love to get lost.

Walking next to a librarian surrounded by thousands of books is to a bibliophile what a candy store is to a child. The lure of learning exuded from the distinct scent of old books in the quiet studious environment. But as we moved through the aisles of bookshelves that temporarily distracted me from the focus of my visit, the lady, whose name tag read "Elizabeth," captured my attention. I thought I was standing right next to a living example of what I'd come to the library to find out. An older woman whom I surmised was in her early to mid-70s, working at a stage in her life she could very well be enjoying retirement. However, she seemed to be very content with her work, which made me wonder whether she worked by choice or necessity. Although I didn't want to pry into her personal life, I was on a research mission and I needed to gather as much information as I could.

"Have you been working here for a long time?" I asked as though placing a crowbar on the lock that would open the box of information I was after.

"Oh, no, I don't work here; I'm a volunteer," she replied while stopping at the retirement books section. "I've been doing it since I retired from my accounting career some ten years ago. Having worked with numbers all my life left me starved for my love of books that I neglected in order to pursue what my parents called 'a real job.' Well, now that I've inherited their estate and have the means to do as I please, I'm fulfilling my lifelong dream of being around books all day. But as you'll learn in some of these books, I'm one of the few lucky ones. I work because I want to be useful doing something I like, but many people my age work because they must. Let me show you something."

She pulled a book off the shelf and opened it at a specific page and started reading out loud to me: "The socioeconomic reality of a growing number of older Americans does not reflect the misleading idyllic image of retirees basking in the Sun. In fact, many Americans cannot afford to even think about retirement and fear that they'll have to work well into their 80s, granted that they'll be healthy enough to do so. A survey released by Wells Fargo & Company found that nearly three-quarters of Americans expect to continue working into what long has been considered traditional retirement age (early to late 60s) because they do not have the minimum financial resources for self-sustenance. The poll found that 37 percent of people have no retirement savings at all and three in 10 people in their 60s have less than $25,000, suggesting that they will have no choice but to live on Social Security,[1] which is mathematically impossible to cover the basic needs of housing, utilities, food, medication, etc."

"Goodness, considering the unprecedented growing number of older citizens in our society, it sounds like we have a serious socioeconomic crisis at hand," I remarked while contrasting Elizabeth's reading with Jeff's observations on Baby Boomers' wealth. "I guess the economic situation of the average older citizen is not as rosy as I've been led to believe."

"Rosy? For many of my generation cohorts their economic situation is pitch-black," she said and for the first time her friendly smile faded away as her countenance took on a somber expression. "According to the AARP Foundation, one in four seniors struggles with poverty in the United States.[2] This means that every day nearly 25% of Americans age 65 and above are faced with heartbreaking choices, like having to determine the priority between paying rent or heating the home; buying food or medication, among other disheartening options."

At that moment I was feeling very disconcerted. Suddenly, I realized that on the opposite side of the spectrum of the deceiving myth of blissful golden age years lies the possibility of destitution in old age; a time when adults are more vulnerable than ever and may need as much care and protection as children do. Looking at me in the eye, Elizabeth seemed to be able to tell that I, albeit in an unpleasant way, was getting what I came in for. And since the pursuit of knowledge can often times be a painful experience (there is some truth to the popular dictum that "ignorance is bliss"), she grabbed another volume from the shelf and handed it open to me with her indicator finger pointing at a bottom of the page paragraph. I read it in silence: "According to a survey conducted by the University of Kentucky Center for Poverty Research, the number of U.S. senior citizens facing hunger risk rose from 700,000 to 3,000,000 between 2001 and 2007."[3] I closed the book and shook my head in disbelief.

"Now you understand why I consider myself to be one of the few lucky ones," she said looking right into my eye. "With a growing number of seniors on limited fixed incomes and the sheer mass of Baby Boomers coming of age, food insecurity, among other basic necessities of life will likely grow at alarming rates in years to come."

After showing me how the books were indexed and organized, Elizabeth returned to the reference desk. Watching her as she walked through the corridor of bookshelves, I experienced mixed feelings of apprehension about the looming demographic-economic crisis and hoped that, like Elizabeth, I'd be one of the few lucky ones enjoying my latter years doing what I love without worrying about my next meal.

I selected a few volumes and moved to a study desk from where I could look out and see the distant rolling green hills in the horizon. Then, I pulled out a yellow pad from my backpack and took copious notes; not only citations from the books, but my own observations as well. After a couple of hours that seemed to have gone by faster than I realized, I began reviewing my annotations and I was surprised to read what I had written down based on the information I compiled: "While millions of older citizens struggle to make ends meet, the hucksters of golden age bliss advertise products and services to the few privileged senior citizens who control more than 77% of all financial assets in the United States (with a reminder that 20% of the people own a remarkable 89% of all wealth in the U.S., leaving only 11% for the bottom 80%), the prospect of a stable old age for most Americans is quite dismal, indeed."

A Challenge of International Proportions

The loud roaring in my stomach reminded me that it was mid-afternoon and I was starved. I put the books on a nearby reshelf cart, bid farewell to "lucky" Elizabeth, and left the library thinking that I'd just found out about a very important element of the aging process equation that I was attempting to solve: the economic common denominator. It was a critical piece of the puzzle without which I could not form a vision of empowered aging. After all, how can financially deprived older citizens become empowered when their basic needs are not met on a daily basis? I thought of the words of a maligned philosopher, economist, and sociologist who claimed that "it is not the consciousness of men that determine their existence, but their existence determine their consciousness." I definitely had some serious investigating to pursue further.

Sitting at a corner table by the window of a popular local eatery renowned for its lunch specials, I was about to finish munching on my scrumptious double-decked grilled chicken and Swiss cheese sandwich when the headline of an article in the newspaper I was reading almost made me gag: "Elderly Japanese turning to crime." As I chewed on the last bite of my lunch, I read the piece with great interest. It reported that criminal offenses by those 65 or older in Japan have doubled in the last ten years, with shoplifting accounting to 59% of the cases. It mentioned the case of a citizen named Fumio Kageyama, a 67-year-old man who is described as one of the many growing number of "silver shoplifters" who are struggling to make ends meet in one of the most affluent nations in the world. Mr. Kageyama worked as a construction worker for 40 years. After he became too old to work, he wound up on the streets and turned to petty theft to survive. After being caught several times for stealing a bowl of rice and pork from a supermarket, hot-dog buns, fried noodles, among other basic staples, he was sentenced to prison for two years. He was quoted as saying: "It wasn't great to get caught, but I just didn't give a damn…I never did this when I had a job."[4]

For some reason the last bite of my sandwich didn't taste as good when I swallowed it along with my reading. I put the newspaper down on the table before I could finish the article. I gazed outside the window half-mindedly trying to make sense of the plight of older people who cannot care for themselves. When I picked up the paper again to continue reading, the facts baffled me even more. Considering that Japan's plans to cut welfare further in order to balance the skyrocketing national debt, and the fact that some 4.47 million people are set to join the ranks of retirees in the next 10 years, the senior citizens crime wave is but a foretaste of the challenges ahead in a country with a rapidly aging population. Unfortunately, in the United States we are in a very similar demographic collision course—and we shouldn't expect very different results.

As for the few privileged golden age citizens planning their next getaway to some exotic sunny place on Earth, don't expect to come across the likes of Mr. Kageyama wherever you go—nor Mr. Jones, the grey-haired produce clerk in your neighborhood supermarket who always greets you with a friendly smile, for without helping you with your groceries, he wouldn't be able to keep food on his table either, much less a roof over his head.

Aging as a Socioeconomic Issue

Suddenly, I was sailing in uncharted waters, for the winds of awareness had blown my aging process research vessel off course. When I embarked on this investigative journey, all I could think of was how to become self-empowered to face the many challenges of old age. However, what I had in mind was the basic four gerontological perspectives of aging: chronological, biological, psychological, and social aging. Evidently, there was the economic element inherent in the latter category that evaded me. Until then, I considered social aging only in terms of the changes in social relations such as the impact of retirement, divorce or widowhood, loss of friends, etc. But there was another fundamental component sustaining social aging that had its own center pillar: the economics of aging.

After spending an inordinate amount of time thinking about the story of Mr. Kageyama in Japan, a highly developed nation with a solid economic infrastructure, I realized that there must be millions of other old age survivalists around the world, especially in underdeveloped countries. It became evident to me that the challenges of aging are not limited to individual travails, but it is a sociological issue of great concern to communities and societies around the globe. I needed to collect more information to uphold the inference of my common sense. The first logical step was to find out what the most reliable international data-gathering organization in the world had to say about this matter. Thus, I resumed my researching process.

On October 1, 2013 the United Nations released a report on the far-reaching implications of an aging world population. The report's startling conclusion is that the world is aging so quickly that most countries won't be ready to support the growing numbers of elderly. According to the report, by the year 2050—for the first time in human history—people over the age of 60 worldwide will outnumber children under the age of 15. At the same time in the United States, more than a quarter of the U.S. population (26.6% to be exact), will be 60 and older, compared to 19.1% in 2014.[5] At the international level, the problem is magnified by the fact that the fastest-growing populations of the elderly are in developing nations (note that the term "developing nations" has long been an euphemism for poor countries.)

Probing it further, I came across the case of Truong Tien Thao, who runs a small tea shop on the sidewalk near his home in Hanoi, Vietnam. He is 65-years-old and plunging into old age without a safety net. He wishes he could retire, but he and his 61-year-old wife depend on the $50 a month they earn from their small street business operation. He expressed his legitimate concerns this way: "People my age should have a rest, but I still have to work to make ends meet…My wife and I have no pension, no health insurance. I'm scared to think of being sick. I don't know how I can pay for the medical care."[6]

Because population growth, not aging, has drawn the lion's share of public attention, the warning sirens for the "grey tsunami" that is about to crash on the shores of nations worldwide never went off. Unfortunately, unlike the tsunamis triggered by geological activity, this demographic tidal wave hits the shores piecemeal. Hence, by the time one realizes its presence, the socioeconomic infrastructures have been already inundated: health care systems, pensions, economic safety nets, transformations in the job market caused by delaying retirement, either by choice or necessity, among other serious consequences to a world whose population of 2 billion people over the age of 60 is growing five times as quickly as the population as a whole.[7]

An Eye Opening Awareness

In my lofty aspiration (some would call it presumptuous) of wanting to learn how to master the art of aging, I found out unexpectedly that, besides the individual purpose to overcome the challenges of the aging process, there is a collective element that intermingles with the personal effort to prevail in the impossible-to-win struggle against the passing of time. It was a potent realization that had escaped me when I first embarked on my investigative journey. Now it was clear to me that when it comes to aging, it is not only the individual who must be the focus of attention, but also the collective aging society and all the inherent sociological repercussions that affect the quality of life of all elders—and the following generations who will become elders one day. This was a pivotal moment in my quest and a lesson that would pave the way for my continuing investigation: mastering the art of aging may begin with the individual but it definitely doesn't end there.

Since my gaining awareness of the collective element of aging, I'd been thinking about the great Chinese sage, Kung Tzu (Confucius) who deemed that the highest ideal was that of a world government that he called *Ta Tung* (Grand Common Wealth). In his vision, the ruler of state is not concerned about lack of wealth; he is concerned about fair distribution of wealth. He is not concerned about poverty, but also about insecurity; and when there is fair distribution of wealth, there will be no poverty. Of course, poverty at any age is a formidable foe to overcome; but in old age and without assistance, it is an insurmountable economic behemoth.

Perhaps moved by my outrage with economic injustices that affect the most vulnerable citizens, I started reading *Hagakure*, one of the most renowned treatises in Eastern literature and a manual of the samurai class. I think I was unconsciously searching for a combative, even retaliatory response to protecting the interests of the elders that I would likely become one day. However, what a surprise to find that even in a classic manual of a fearsome warrior class, the answer is revealed as compassion. I learned it when I came across the following passage: "Seen from the eye of compassion, there is no one to be disliked...There is no limit to the breadth and depth of one's heart...The foundation for ruling the country in peace is compassion."[8]

Apparently, even fierce warriors can embrace the wisdom of the ancient Chinese sage, Kung Tzu. Then, why can't we?

❦ The Facts of Aging ❦

Aging as a Collective Predicament

Fascinated by my newly acquired enlightenment of the aging process at a collective level, I registered to participate in a gerontology conference titled "The Aging Individual in Aging Societies." When I first saw the advertisement for this event in my local newspaper, I was stoked with the serendipity of the timing of this opportunity that was going to happen in a convenient location not very far from where I live. Thus, I didn't hesitate to submit my application and enrollment fees a couple of months in advance.

Walking in the lobby area of the posh hotel where the event was taking place, I headed to the conference rooms area eager to collect more information that could contribute to my quest to discover how to master the art of aging. Following the tantalizing fragrance of freshly brewed coffee, I found my way to the foyer where the sight of mouth-watering pastries on a large platter wetted my appetite. I grabbed a cup of coffee and a chocolate croissant and settled myself on a comfortable black leather couch with a white marble coffee-table in front of it. I looked around the jam-packed place and the cacophony of voices engaged in conversations filled the air creating an ebullient atmosphere. Between bites of croissants that dropped buttery flakes on my silk silver jacket and sips of coffee that burned the roof of my mouth, I perused through the conference program trying to decide which session to attend first. Among the many options available in the schedule of the day-long conference, there was one whose title caught my eye: "The Human and Financial Cost of Caregiving." Although it was not a matter that affected my life directly, I thought it would be important information to understanding a critical widespread issue of the aging process.

The Human and Financial Cost of Caregiving

"According to data from the 2000 U.S. Census Bureau, 80% of all care provided to older people in the United States is provided by family members; and 73% of caregivers are employed either full or part-time," the presenter, a respected official from the local city's public health department stated. "In all, 70% of older adults rely on the assistance of informal (non-paid) caregivers such as spouses and adult children. More than one in five workers ages 45 to 64 is a caregiver, typically for a parent. If you're not currently playing that role, chances are you either have done this or will be doing someday. In economic terms, unpaid caregiving is a hidden part of the United States' economy. A study showed that in 2009 the roughly 42 million unpaid caregivers in the United States provided and estimated $450 billion worth of care, which is equivalent to Walmart's total annual sales that year."[9]

Between taking notes and listening to the presenter's words, I paused to mull over such staggering economic data while wondering about the human cost for those caring for their older loved ones who depend on them. I couldn't imagine being able to take care of my already busy and sometimes nearly chaotic life, while having the responsibility to look after and nurse an elder parent. And without the financial means to hire outside help, how could anyone manage such a daunting task? It was not until the presenter resumed speaking that I released the pen that was pressed between my teeth and relaxed my tight facial muscles.

❧ The Facts of Aging ☙

"But statistical data and dollar amounts aside, there is the overbearing emotional cost of dedicating so much time and energy to a dependent loved one. And as the longevity revolution continues on unabated, it seems necessary to revisit the role of society in the nurturing of communities, which involves allocation of resources and citizenry allegiance to the commitment of caring for our elders with respect and dignity." The presenter turned quiet as he paced silently for a few seconds before resuming. "Unfortunately, we're a long way away from making significant strides in taking collective responsibility of caring for society's elders; and the problem is definitely going to become magnified in the decades ahead."

When the presenter invited the participants to ask questions, he was inundated with inquiries from people who were clearly overwhelmed by the burden of caregiving; not only the emotional stress in their lives, but likely a great financial strain on their family budgets, too. I sat in quiet anticipation to hearing the concerns and testimonials of those who deal with this challenge on a daily basis feeling thankful that it was not my case; at least not yet.

"Yes, ma'am, the lady there in the back," the presenter said pointing to a middle-aged woman way back in the room. The event's assistant rushed in her direction to hand her the microphone.

"Thank you for taking my question," she said immediately after standing up. "My husband developed Alzheimer's disease four years ago at the early age of 61 and I've been caring for him ever since. We don't have children and I work full-time to keep a roof over our heads and food on the table. As his condition is deteriorating, it's becoming impossible to care for him without help that I cannot afford; and neither can I afford to stop working. What can someone in my situation do? Are there any resources available for people going through similar dilemma?"

With my neck twisted backwards so I could see the tall and thin woman whose voice echoed a distress call of her daily living, I felt a wave of compassion wash over me. Looking at her, I wondered how many hundreds of thousands, more likely millions of people like her, had to endure such an emotional and financial ordeal—every day! As soon as the presenter started answering her question, I grabbed my yellow pad and pen and began jotting down notes in a continuous flow of uninterrupted writing.

"There are a few community-based initiatives, mostly sponsored by religious and nonprofit organizations, but they offer minimum basic assistance to those receiving care and some respite for the caregivers themselves," he said. "As for monetary support, public financial assistance is mostly non-existent, unless you fall below the threshold of the poverty level, which is the rock-bottom low income bracket. Therefore, a large and growing number of people in desperate need of help do not qualify."

Hasting to write down as much information as possible, I accidentally dropped my pen on the floor and watched it roll under the seat in front of me. I was bent over trying to reach for it when the presenter started reading a passage from a book to help illustrate the questioner's case.

"There is certainly a real crisis in caregiving that our society is failing to address, as opposed to an irremediable power imbalance between caregivers and care receivers. The true villain, especially in the United States, is not biomedicine but inhumane and just plain stupid social and health policies that amount to 'it's your lookout' when faced with chronic, incurable age-related diseases. More than two-thirds of Alzheimer's patients are cared for at home, usually by a spouse...Medicare doesn't pay for any of the help that home caretakers of Alzheimer's patients need. If you don't have enough money to pay for home health care aides, you're on your own. Nor does Medicare pay for long-term care...Private long-term care insurance, which generally does pay some of the cost of home health aides, is an unaffordable joke for the vast majority of older Americans."[10]

As soon as he finished reading, he continued making his own comments about the passage, but I wasn't listening anymore. At that moment, I was absorbed in my own thoughts reflecting on my realization of how critical the role of the community is in the collective aging process of society. I remained pensive for awhile until I remembered that I was yet to recover my pen. After several attempts stretching my arm under the seat, I managed to get it back. Then, I placed the yellow pad in my lap and wrote: "If it takes a village to raise a child, as the old African proverb says, then it must take a nation to care for its elders."

The Holes in the Safety Nets

When that session was over, I skipped the coffee break and went straight to the next presentation I wanted to attend so I could get a front seat. Now that I'd become aware of its existence, I was more interested than ever in learning as much as I could about the economics of aging. Thus, I selected a session titled "The Holes in the Safety Nets."

ZENior CitiZEN

"As regrettable as it is, history has shown that the development of a major crisis is what's often needed to prompt a new movement for change," the attractive 40-something lady wearing an elegant navy-blue suit began her presentation. She was the executive director of a NGO that advocates for governments' financial support of older citizens. "This was certainly the case during the Great Depression of the 1930s in the United States when the Social Security Act of 1935 was implemented. With its passage, the United States became one of the last industrial nations to establish a federal old-age pension program. Thirty years later, in 1965, the Social Security Act was amended to provide health insurance for the elderly. Today, both programs are in dire straits and perhaps even in jeopardy of becoming unavailable to the massive number of senior citizens in the next few decades."

Taking notes at the speed of light of both the data provided and my own thoughts about the issues, at one moment I stopped my pen's motion in mid-sentence recalling some related information I'd read awhile back. It was about the astounding cost of Social Security and Medicare, which along with the escalating mammoth national debts, these vital safety nets for the elder population were at serious risk of being reduced or even eliminated altogether. It was hard to imagine it ever happening, but as I listened to the presenter, it sounded more probable that I wanted to believe.

"When the American Social Security system was first implemented in 1935, there were about 40 wage earners supporting each retiree with their tax contributions. By 1990 there were only 3.3 workers for each recipient.[11] As this discrepancy continues to augment through the twenty-first century when massive number of citizens are aging, the prospect for sustainability of the American safety net system is in dire straits; and of course, so are the future of our low income elderly population."

In the face of this dismal economic scenario, I surmised that citizens' involvement at the grassroots level was the only strategy that could yield effective long-term results. I kept writing my thoughts down as quickly as I could: budget priorities will have to be reevaluated; the taxation system must be reformed to balance the blatant inequities in the distribution of wealth, among other remarks related to fiscal responsibility in relation to human needs. At a time when globalization and technology tend to wipe out middle-income jobs and favor those at the very top of the socioeconomic ladder (the top 1% took 95% of all new wealth created in the United States from 2009 to 2012)[12], I had no doubt that as a nation we have the responsibility to ensure that the minimum requirements for a dignified living in old age will be in place for our elder citizens when they need it the most. And considering that aging is a universal human experience, it would behoove us all to support and promote the rights of older citizens. After all, one day most everyone will need that encouragement, too.

It's just a matter of time.

Chapter 9

It's About TIME

Ticking Away

"And you run and you run to catch up with the sun but it's sinking, racing around to come behind you again. The sun is the same in a relative way but you're older, shorter of breath one day closer to death. Every year is getting shorter never seems to find the time."[1] The music blasted in the steamed up bathroom as I took a shower while singing along.

I'd be listening to the song, *Time*, since I was 16-years-old—and that's a long time! There is something about it that has fascinated me since the first time I listened to it; and there's no other song that I've listened to more times in my life than, well, *Time*. The song starts with clocks ticking with interspersed loud clamors, as though to remind the listener that time is passing by at that very moment. And even though I've been listening to it for more than forty years, I experience it much more differently now than I did when I was sixteen. Perhaps it's because my perception of time has changed significantly as I got older. When I was a teenager, I had a limited understanding of the concept of finitude of time, for I could not fathom that my existence as I knew it was ruled by such an enigmatic and relentless measurement standard. Nevertheless, as I've been listening to it over the years, *Time* has been awakening me to the reality of my ephemeral existence that one day will expire. It has made me realize that in the temporal nature of my life, time is my most valuable asset. And unlike other tangible commodities, time cannot be stored, contained, formed, controlled, or preserved for future use. It must be spent wisely because once it's gone there's no recovering it. I became aware that I can't stop the flow of time any more than I can stop the flow of a river. But I could stop the water running from the shower head, and it was time for me to get out of the shower and get ready to go to the party at my friend Tina's house.

Because I was judicious with my time management, I arrived at the party on time. As soon as I stepped in the crowded living-room, I could feel the place teeming with excitement. Since it was a book launch party for Tina's third novel, there were many fellow-writers, intellectuals, and some members of the local media that Tina managed to wheedle them to come. I was excited to be there.

"I'm so glad you made it," Tina said greeting me with her customary friendly smile as soon as she spotted me from across the room. "Come, let me introduce you to some of my friends."

She took my arm, enlaced it in hers, and walked me around introducing me to small groups of people chatting with the sound of John Coltrane's saxophone in the background. As a waiter was slithering along making his way through the crowd with a tray with champagne flutes on it,

I snatched one without his even noticing it as Tina and I passed through the French doors leading to the veranda in the backyard.

"I want to introduce you to those guys," she said leading me toward a small group of three gentlemen standing by the built-in brick grill next to the oval-shaped swimming pool. "I think you're going to enjoy talking with them. They're very smart and interesting people."

After introducing me to Paul, a white-bearded man in his early seventies who was a professor emeritus of philosophy at the local university; Charlie, a young graduate student in Fine Arts; and Richard, a physicist around my age wearing large square black frame glasses supporting thick lenses, the lovely hostess left after gentling kissing me on the cheek.

"Oh, my, what I walked myself into," I said in good jest after realizing that they were smack-dab in the middle of some serious philosophical and scientific discussion. "I might need some additional champagne just to pretend to keep up with this conversation. I'm afraid that quantum physics is not what I'd consider to be up my alley."

"It all depends on your perspective," Richard retorted. "Paul has a proclivity to argue about everything he cannot understand by creating more confusion with his philosophical inquiries. Charlie, on the other hand, sees the Universe with an artist's eyes as if it were a canvas where God creates His magnum opus. And I, well, I'm a scientist, I observe and analyze the world from a strictly pragmatic point of view. So, how are you going to contribute to our collective folly of trying to understand the nature of time?"

"Time? Really? Is it the underlying subject of the conversation?" I asked stunned with the strange coincidence of having had an urge to listen to one of my favorite albums before coming to the party—and I replayed the track *Time* a couple of times.

"Yes, we've been talking about time. You just happened to arrive at the moment that Richard was ranting about Einstein's theory of relativity, while attempting to explain a phenomenon that even Einstein himself believed to be an illusion of perception," Charlie said gently patting Richard on the shoulder.

Richard turned to look at me. "Well, now that you are up to speed..."

"Please, Richard, not the speed of light again," Charlie interrupted with a chuckle before Richard could finish his sentence.

"Now that you're up to speed," Richard resumed smiling slyly at his friend. "What perspective are you going to bring to the discussion: a philosophical, artistic, or scientific approach?"

I paused and looked at each one of them in the eye before replying. "What about a Zen approach?"

Time Zone and Time Zen

"You don't have to be an astute scientist like Einstein to figure out that time is definitely an illusion," Paul spoke out for the first time. "The only reason we can keep track of it is because of the sophisticated atomic clocks that work as the primary reference for all scientific timing. In fact, the world's time-keeping network involves atomic clocks in more than 26 countries contributing to the hub located at the International Bureau of Weights and Measures in Sèvres, France."[2]

❧ It's About TIME ☙

"At least I am glad to hear your acknowledging the scientific element of it," Richard said.

"Yes, the scientific element of illusion," Paul replied almost in tandem.

"Something you can determine with verifiable measurements cannot possibly be an illusion," Richard ignited his scientific rocket-thinking mind and took off. "Let me go back to the subject of the speed of light, which is a whopper-fast speed of 186,291 miles per second; per second for crying out loud! Conversely, there is the nanosecond, which is an infinitesimally small amount of time that light travels only a foot of it. In all, there are unimaginable large distances and inconceivably small ones that can only be determined with the measuring tape of time. Now, Paul, the philosopher, may conjure up images of an endless Universe without beginning or end. In his turn, Charlie , the artist, hears the symphony of life that whispers in the wind whizzing by his ears. But I, I'm a man of science, and I believe in the rationalization of the Universe, including the existence of time in a mathematical conception." Then he paused, turned toward me, and asked point blank as though he challenged me to a gentlemen's intellectual duel. "What do you think?"

I looked into his eye acknowledging and welcoming the challenge. "I think I live in a different time zone of perception. I recognize that time is important to scientific observation because the events that scientists attempt to measure and explain all occur within a timeframe. However, we know from Einstein's Theory of Relativity that there is no standard or absolute timeframe, because time can be defined only by measurements. The measurement of time is based on reoccurring natural phenomena. For example, a year is defined by the amount of time it takes for the Earth to make one complete revolution around the Sun. A day is defined as the amount of time it takes for the Earth to make one complete revolution on its axis. The year and the day are then broken down into more arbitrary units—months, hours, seconds, and so on.[3] But the utilitarian function of measuring time aside, in my time Zen of perception the only focus of my mindful experience of living is happening right now. The days, months, and years that have preceded this moment and all the others that are yet to come, either they are measurable or not, they do not exist in my experience of time, which can only happen in the eternity of now. In this case, I suspect that Paul's assessment of time as an illusion makes total sense to me."

Paul smiled in smug self-gratification. It seemed that he felt validated.

"This concept of 'nowness' is so woo-woo!" Richard lashed out his derision.

"I guess it all depends on what time Zen you exist. For you and me, a lifespan of, say, ninety years, is a fairly long life. But compared to the billions of years in the life of the Sun, it is an infinitesimally small nanosecond existence. And on the other end of the spectrum of time as you define it, human lifespan would seem endless to a fly whose life allotment is a mere 48-hour period. Therefore, the only relevant element of time lies in the now. Whether the lifetime is of billions of years or a couple of days, it can only be experienced once at a time; and all time is now."

It's About TIME

Zen Time

"Father Time!" Richard exclaimed in dismay. "Oh, please, Paul, what a juvenile concept."

"Not in a Santa Claus kind of way, you analytical baboon, but as an element of fatherhood of our human existence; a godly component of life as we know it," Paul explained his philosophical take while venting out his frustration with Richard's scientific-oriented mind.

"I get it and I agree with you, Paul," Charlie chimed in. "Whether time in an illusion of our perception or the measurement of a temporary reality, there is a fatherly element to it; even godly in a sense of creation. The evidence is in the art of music that could not be created without the observance of time. In fact, even the music term tempo, which is fundamental to the cadence of music, means time. Tempo determines the pace of musical notes and how the composition plays out. Therefore it's essential to the creation of the most noble of all arts."

"In the kingdom of art, music is the queen," I blurted out instinctively.

"Yes, but even in music the science of mathematics is dominant and determines how and when the tempo will fulfill its function in the process of creation," Richard said. "It is the mathematics of time that allows us to calculate astronomical distances and the creation of masterpieces such as Bach's *St. Matthew's Passion*. I suppose I could say that in the kingdom of science, mathematics is the king."

"It seems to me that all of you speak of time as either a philosophical concept, an artistic element, or a scientific endeavor," I said addressing all of them. "While acknowledging each individual reasoning, from my Zen standpoint, time, like love, is not something to be conceptualized but experienced. In fact, even talking about it is a waste of time. And worse yet, thinking about the finitude of time, which can only engender fear and anxiety about an uncertain future. But the truth is that we humans are very fortune to not know what and when things will happen in the future. And as for ending, even a magnum opus like Bach's *St. Matthew's Passion* eventually comes to an end, and the creative genius behind it ended as well."

"What do you mean we're fortunate not to know the future?" Paul asked abruptly as though what I said had rubbed him the wrong way. "I'm not sure that is the case. I for one would love to take a peek into the future."

"Well, the unknown is actually a blessing in disguise that compels you to remain focused on the here and now, for you don't know when or what the future brings, or ends for that matter," I said. "If the unknown were non-existent, you'd be aware of how many days you have left in your allotted time; how many special moments you'll spend with your loved ones. And every time you made love with your wife, you'd know exactly the countdown number of those loving encounters left in the balance sheet of time. The anxiety of knowing would be unbearably higher in intensity than the exciting trepidation of not knowing what the next moment will bring. But perhaps worst of all, such an undesirable knowledge would compromise the quality of the present moment. In the end, the unknown allows you the possibility to experience life without rationalization."

"How can you experience life without rationalizing the experience?" Richard blurted out as his excessive analytical mind demanded an intellectual explanation for the simple act of experiencing the present moment. "I don't buy into this new age gobbledygook."

"I think, therefore I am," Paul, the philosopher, joined the rationalization bandwagon by quoting the infamous mantra of Rene Descartes, the mathematician-philosopher who reduced the experience of living to an intellectual interpretation.

I turned to look at Charlie as he remained silent. At that moment I realized that the artist is the one most capable of understanding the emotional experience of being human.

"So, how does your Zen mentality explain the qualitative experience of time?" Richard asked me in quasi-defiant fashion, again.

"Time never was before I was born, and never will be when I'm no longer. Therefore, time exists only insofar as I do. I am time; my time," I replied looking into his eye as if he were a Zen initiate troubled by the incomprehensibility of a koan, the inscrutable question that cannot be answered with the cognitive mind. "Perhaps, in genuine Zen fashion, I should give you a more simplistic answer based on scientific logic: put your hands on a hot stove for a minute, and it seems like an hour. Sit with a pretty girl for an hour, and it seems like a minute. That's relativity explained in accordance with the qualitative Zen experience of time."

Richard's furrowed brow revealed that he was stumped. His befuddled mind finally caught up with him.

After exhausting my tolerance with Richard's scientific rationalizations of the unknowable, I politely excused myself and walked away repeating in my head the words of Isabella, the character in William Shakespeare's *Measure for Measure*: "Man, proud man! Dressed in a little brief authority—most ignorant of what he's most assured. His glassy essence, like an angry ape, plays such fantastic tricks before high heaven, as make the angels weep."[4]

I passed through the beautiful white frame French doors again back inside the house. As soon as I walked in the living-room, I noticed how the cacophony of multiple conversations competed for air space with the solitary melodious sounds of Miles Davis' trumpet that had replaced Coltrane's saxophone. With my empty flute in hand, my eyes scanned the room like a thirsty eagle on the hunt for a wandering waiter. Suddenly, a gentle hand grabbed my bicep just when I spotted my prey across the room.

"Are you having fun?" Tina said flashing her joyful pearly smile. "Oh, Lord, look at your glass! It's empty! Let's go refill this puppy."

She took my arm in hers and we walked toward the waiter who wiggled his way through the crowd dexterously balancing a tray with champagne flutes above his head. At the request of the hostess, the waiter handed each of us a glass as she led me to the bay window in her library. We sat down on the fluffy purple pillows and after catching up with mutual updates of our lives, she asked me about the men she'd just introduced me to.

"Time? Is that all you guys talked about? She asked.

"Pretty much," I replied without much else to say.

"It must be a guy thing," she said turning to look outside through the window. "Does it really matter when time began or when it's going to end? Even if we managed to figure it out, it wouldn't change in the least our experience of it. In the end, it's all about the process of living."

"What did you say?" I asked abruptly raising my upper body and leaning toward her. All of a sudden, I felt a very similar sensation I did when I heard Douglas say that he was going "to fight aging to the end." It was as though a light bulb had just been turned on in the darkness of the tunnel of the unknown.

"What's the matter?" She asked looking surprised with my reaction. "I just said that in the end, it's all about the process of living. Isn't it what time is all about?"

"The Living Process," I whispered through my breath realizing that I'd found the answer I'd been looking for.

To Be or To Become: That is the Question

Indecision can be a deadly hesitation—or it can become an opportunity to rise to the occasion. Had Hamlet not vacillated about whether to be or not to be was the real question of his dilemma to mete out revenge for his father's assassination, Shakespeare's famous drama would have ended with a completely different denouement; and who knows, maybe it would have turned into a comedy instead of a tragedy. But had Hamlet been aware that he was always in a process of becoming, then, despite his fears and doubts, he might have made up his mind and carried out what he intended to do. Fortunately, for the world of the dramatic arts, the character's self-questioning of "to be or not to be," led to his demise and turned the play *Hamlet* into one of the most revered works of art in all literature. However, real life is an entirely different kind of drama.

I was having this thought while sitting in my armchair shortly after arriving home from Tina's book launch party. Since she casually referred to time as nothing but a unit of measurement of the process of living, I couldn't stop thinking about it with my own interpretation of what it meant in a broader perspective. The more I thought about it, the more I realized that process was the key word in my quest to mastering the art of aging. And as my mind sped through the runway of curiosity ready to take off and eager to arrive at the destination of conclusion, the tragedy of Hamlet's quandary made me aware, not only of the important distinction between the verbs to be and to become (the former invokes a permanent state, whereas the latter implies continuity), but also the connection of the verb to become with my random discovery that process is the definitive element in the development of self-empowerment. What a revelation to learn that "IS" is always becoming something else through the continuous unfolding of process.

By dictionary definition, process means to progress, advance; a natural phenomenon marked by gradual changes that lead toward a particular result.[5] It's characterized by continuous motion and transformation, as it flows in a perennial movement of "gradual changes that lead toward a particular result." In this sense, process has an inherent relationship with time, since it takes time for it to unfold. And process is ubiquitous in countless aspects of life: the aging process, the evolutionary process, the democratic process, the developmental process, and the list goes on *ad infinitum*. Process is what life is made of—and time keeps track of it.

Although it was late, and in spite of the amount of champagne I drank at the party, I was not feeling sleepy. I realized that my..., well, of all things, mental process, was keeping me awake as I thought about process itself. Suddenly, I experienced an emotional recollection of my response to Tina's words when she referred to the role of time in the process of living. It seemed to me that it was at that moment that I realized, albeit subconsciously, the negative perception and resistant avoidance our culture dedicates to the aging process. Somehow there seems to be an unspoken correlation of the aging process with the nature of permanence of the verb to be, for no one wants to be old—and conversely, everyone wants to be young. It is an unwelcome stage of life that people fret about, sometimes even when they are very young. There has been documented cases of people as young as in their teens who suffer from gerascophobia, or fear of getting old.[6] But if we were to regard the aging process as the natural and unavoidable process that it is, then we would likely not mind it at all, as Mark Twain suggested in his popular practical joke about it: "Age is an issue of mind over matter. If you don't mind, it doesn't matter."

But how can we possibly not mind what matters so much? After all, it's about quality of life. And yet, quality of life is not necessarily determined by the age of a person. Someone young who suffers from a chronic painful illness or is afflicted by abject poverty doesn't have a clue of what quality of life is. On the other hand, an octogenarian who is in fairly good health and is financially independent has the opportunity to enjoy excellent quality of life. Therefore, in spite of all the hardships intrinsic to the aging process, old age does not automatically preclude good living. It just makes it a bit more challenging to achieve.

The real issue, then, is not the aging process per se, but the attitude we espouse toward it as we either embrace it courageously or let our fears struggle attempting to eschew it to no avail. If we choose to focus our attention on the anxieties of the aging process, then there is a killing-of-the-present that takes place by the fear that the prospect of getting old generates. In this case, the aging process becomes a torturous self-defeating progression that both aggravates and expedites the inevitable changes resulting from the passing of time.

There must be a better alternative to experience aging; a way of growing older without feeling intimidated by the challenges of the process. Something along the lines of Chuang Tzu's concept of *wu wei*, or active inaction, which is the course of action that is not founded upon any purposeful motives of gain or striving. In such a state, all human actions become as spontaneous and mindless as those of the natural world. In Chuang Tzu's view, the man who has freed himself from conventional standards of judgment can no longer be made to suffer, for he refuses to recognize death as any less desirable than life. He becomes one with Nature, or Heaven, as Chuang Tzu calls it, and merges himself with the Tao, or the Way.[7] If this spiritual liberty of *wu wei* were to be applied to the aging process and become a spontaneous and mindless development, then the anxiety of aging would be sublimated and the source of suffering channeled into self-empowerment. In essence, mindfulness would become solidly rooted in being alive—in the Living Process, instead of the aging process.

This is the reason that when Tina casually mentioned that in the end time was all about the process of living, I felt as if a lightning bolt had struck my consciousness altering my understanding of the relationship between time and aging. It was a truly Zen moment that showed me how consciousness can change in a nanosecond, which made me realize the importance of time even in its infinitesimal measurements. It also made me recognize that it is in the Living Process that the verbs to be and to become reconcile into the yin and yang of harmonious aging, because its ultimate goal is to remain mindful of being alive in the here and now, regardless of the time zone of life it occupies. Thus, with the dominant Living Process approach in place, the aging process becomes both secondary and merely circumstantial; a necessary and unavoidable aspect of life that is not to be feared but embraced. After all, in the latter years of life, the primary objective of living should not be limited to personal gratifications of a temporal existence, but the empowerment of the individual human spirit whose nature is as mysterious as life itself.

After a long time mulling over the two opposing attitudes toward aging, I realized that the fundamental distinction between the Living Process and the aging process is that the former makes me feel empowered to be still developing and growing, regardless of my age. The latter, however, is laden with trepidations about future circumstances that are far beyond my control. Surely, old age is a significant setback to physical vitality, among many other losses that cannot be recuperated. However, for as long as I'm still alive, the opportunities for personal growth are as available to me now as they were in my younger years—and maybe even more so. But if I am to spend my limited fast-dwindling time focusing on the apprehension of growing older, I'd be committing chronocide (from the Greek khronos, meaning time, and the Latin cide meaning killing). In other words, I'd be murdering my own time by omission. I certainly have no intention of experiencing death while I'm still alive; and for that reason, my mindfulness must lie on the Living Process, not in the consternation about the aging process that leads to the fated end of my time. At that moment I became aware that there are two alternatives to being an older citizen: the senior citizen, the one who focuses on the drawbacks of the aging process; and the ZENior CitiZEN, the one who is committed to the Living Process and sees the opportunities for self-empowerment even at a time when he seems to be most vulnerable.

Suddenly, I glanced at the clock on the wall and I was surprised to realize that it was already 3:45 am. With a slated professional engagement at noon, I'd better hurry up and ensconce myself in bed to get some rest. After I was done with my nightly toilet, I had an urge to listen to *Time*, one more time, before going to sleep. Unable to fall asleep, I ended up listening to the entire album while lying in bed staring at the ceiling while ruminating my conversations and thoughts about time that day. It was not until the final lines of the last song entitled *Eclipse* that I took notice the time that had passed. And the very moment that I became mindful of it, I heeded the closing lyrics of the song that helped me understand how misperception can create the illusion of reality: "All that is now, all that's gone, all that's to come, and everything under the Sun is in tune, but the Sun is eclipsed by the moon."[8] I could feel the furrows in my brow as I thought about the absurdity of an inconspicuously small piece of rock covering the sight of a magnificent star. And yet, from the visual vantage point of the Earth, the optical illusion seems undeniably real. "And so it must be with time," I mumbled lowly in a succinct solitary soliloquy. "The present, past, and future are all part of a continuous linear stream that is eclipsed by my limited experience of it. Like a solar eclipse, time itself must be a chronological illusion."

I turned off the light to go to sleep. I closed my eyes convinced that I am a time traveler—and so are the billions of people who came before me and the billions more that are yet to come. I imagined the limited lifespan of my life, say eighty years, as a microscopic dot in a continuous linear stream of time where millions of years have already passed and millions more are yet to come, and I realized how insignificantly fleeting what I experience as a long life actually is. The chronological illusion syndrome, I guess. Furthermore, the dot that my individual life occupies in the endless spectrum of past and future is crowded by millions of people who share that particular era. They are my contemporaries, my generation, and the population with whom I age with.

By the time I dozed off into dreamland, I was determined to investigate the nature and roles of collective aging in different historical times. But above all, I wanted to understand the responsibilities of my generation within the context of the challenges of our time.

The Collective Experience of Time and Aging

It had been three months since I met Charlie at Tina's book party when he contacted me. Apparently, he needed someone to make a presentation on the topic of aging to one of the classes he taught as a graduate student teaching assistant; and as he casually mentioned it to Tina, she suggested contacting me. At the time he called me, I'd been spending a significant amount of time investigating the repercussions of the cultural environment on the aging process; the collective zeitgeist of aging. Thus, I welcomed the opportunity to process all the knowledge I'd accumulated by speaking it all out to a young intelligent audience.

"The history of a nation, especially the ones in the so-called New World, is in fact the history of a succession of generations adapting to, as well as transforming, the circumstances of their historical time,"[9] I said in the earlier moments of my presentation to a group of a couple of dozen students crammed in the small classroom. "Simplistically speaking, the generation cohorts share the same 'aging location' in time and history, as well as a generation's collective mind-set according to the ethos of their specific region. They share socioeconomic conditions, political circumstances, cultural dominance, and environmental changes, among other traits that define a generational era."

I looked around the room and noticed that the students were still in the "sizing-this-dude-up mode." Not wanting to lose them along the way, I jumped straight to what mattered most to them: their generation.

"But when a generation is challenged with unprecedented problems, its cohorts must respond in equally unprecedented fashion. This is when a new chapter in the history of generations is written. And considering the circumstances of your historical time, this might be the most important chapter ever written; or else it could be the last," I said noticing that I'd just harnessed their attention. "The generational inheritance that you've received and the trail blazing path you're setting up for the next ones is an enormous collective responsibility."

"Considering what we've inherited, it doesn't seem like the Baby Boomers did a very good job. Did they?" Remarked a dark long-haired young man with a defying look in his eyes that reverberated in his voice when he spoke. As

I looked at him, I recalled the events in the 1960s' version of the Wild West at UC Berkeley, the Civil Rights movement, the blossoming of the ecological movement, and all the many efforts that my cohorts put out to impart positive social change and I thought that his was not a fair judgment. Ironically, he was wearing a black T-shirt with a stamped photo of Jim Morrison on it, and his personal image could have come straight out of the infamous Summer of Love. But my role was to be helpful, not defensive.

"Perhaps, it's the same reason the Baby Boomers failed to change the world: they got a bad inheritance from their predecessors. But if that's the case, the only thing that matters is that at some point a new demographic group is going to sever this pernicious complacence pattern and make meaningful and lasting changes. And the way things are going in this fledgling new century, we'd better join forces and reestablish the state of urgency for change that the Baby Boomers initiated. Time is running out; and for the individuals of my generation, it is literally."

The young man straightened himself up from his slouching position, put his elbows on the desk and looked at me as though to say that I got his attention because I earned his respect. My eyes scanned the room and I could tell I had conquered the audience.

"The truth is that both individuals and generations are transformed by the experience of their historical time," I resumed talking. "If we take a look back to the beginning of the twentieth century all the way to now, we see the common thread stitching through the fabric of our collective identity. Starting with the GI Generation, the folks born between 1900 and 1924, who grew up in an era of great strife enduring the adversities of the Great Depression, which led to one of the most horrific armed conflicts in history: World War II. Having had the resilience to undergo extreme economic hardships and the bravery in the face of war, this generation has been regarded by some as 'the Greatest Generation.'[10] The GI generation has been characterized as a civic-minded generation with a reputation of toughness and strength. Among the valuable contributions this generation passed on to the next was the inspiration of valor in the face of vicissitudes in life; a lesson we can very much use today."

"I can only imagine that the next generation turned out to be very resilient," a young woman sitting in the front row pointed out.

"Perhaps, it was the generation that needed to inhere this resolve the most, but instead, it was one of the most terrified generations ever," I said watching her excitement transform into disappointment before my eyes. "It was the first generation to be prepared for the terror of thermonuclear war. The children grew up practicing drills and instructions on how to proceed during a nuclear attack. Fear was the dominant experience of the youth of this generation: fear of war; fear of a nuclear holocaust; and even fear of thinking of what might happen anytime."

"That surely brightened up my day," a guy with a nasal voice spoke from the back of the room making the students laugh on what sounded like sarcasm. "Seriously, I mean it, these folks got such a bad hand from the deck of time that makes me feel like the challenges of my generation are not that bad after all."

In an effort to not witness enthusiasm transmute into disenchantment again, I decided not to remind him that the risks, anxieties, and fears the Silent Generation (1925 –

1945) experienced only have been magnified throughout the twentieth century. Instead, I chose to put the spotlight on what I really wanted them to see: how one generation influences the other.

"Even with a bad hand, you can still bluff your way to winning, granted that you know how to play the game," I said beginning to pace around. "Perhaps because there was so much apprehension about the post World War II situation, the Silent Generation began to make some noise that would reverberate like drums of rebellion in the ears of the ensuing demographic. Since the late cohorts of this generation, the ones born in the early 1940s, blended with the upcoming Baby Boomers, their influence was evident, important, and necessary. By the early to mid-1950s when the Baby Boomers kids were still playing in sandboxes with their scattered toys, the latter batch of the Silent Generation, now adolescents and young adults, were playing guitars in a unique musical style that conveyed their contempt for archaic social norms they would be determined to transform."

"Rock n' roll!" Someone exclaimed while I was taking a sip of water.

"Yes, but no sex and drugs yet," I quipped eliciting laughter from the young audience. "The notorious 'sex, drugs, and rock n' roll' slogan would be introduced by the youth of the Baby Boomers. But rock n' roll as an art form derived mostly from the rhythm and blues music of the 1940s, erupted into the social scene not only as an unprecedented musical style, but also as vehicle with which to revolutionize stale social norms. Suddenly, a young southern boy by the name of Elvis Presley emerged as a symbol of a youth renaissance culture. He was like a demigod who embodied the spirits of the Greek gods Eros and Apollo into one young man. He was an out-of-the-closet sex symbol at a time of silent sexual repression. He epitomized the ultimate renegade; the harbinger of things to come."

At that moment the room was silent; like the epithet of the generation I was talking about. They looked at me displaying curiosity and anticipation; seemingly eager to hear what I was going to say next. All of a sudden, it occurred to me that I was storytelling the recent history of collective human journeys through the spectrum of time within a century; and perhaps, the most determining century in the history of Western civilization.

"By the time the Baby Boomers were coming of age, they exploded into the social scene like an atomic bomb had been dropped smack center of long established cultural values that they viewed, not only as archaic, but a detrimental and dangerous way of living. Therefore, they ignited a Counter-Culture Revolution that set the world on emotional fire; a revolution like no other in history."

"With all due respect, sir, your last statement sounds like an extrapolation," a young man with a conservative look wearing a swanky grey jacket objected.

"Perhaps not," I replied right away. "When you analyze the nature of the main revolutions in history, you can see that the Counter-Culture Revolution is unique and with a very broad objective scope. The French Revolution put an end to the abuses of tyrannical aristocracy and gave birth to the imperialistic Napoleonic era. The Bolshevik Revolution overthrew a despotic government, and replaced it with another. And even our own American Revolution gave birth to a new nation at the cost of eliminating many indigenous nations. But the Counter-Culture Revolution was unique in the way that it became a desperate call for radical social transformation at the global level. Those young rebels acknowledged that the economic and cultural values of greed, selfishness, and unfettered consumption of superfluous stuff must be snuffed out before life on the planet is smothered to the point of no repair. As you can see, the Counter-Culture Revolution, even though it was carried out in immature fashion, was both comprehensive and widespread like no other revolution in history. In fact, I would argue that it's also the longest ongoing revolution in human history, for it's still happening today, even though it has been restrained by the dominant authorities that resist change."

"That's right. I remember seeing video footages of the protests on the streets of Seattle in 1999 against the World Trade Organization," a female student sitting in the front row blurted out. "Those images looked like they could have come out of a newsreel of the 1960s."

"No kidding. And what about the anti-globalization movement? The Arab Spring Revolution? The Occupy Wall Street Movement? The ongoing activism to save the Earth? All of them seem to bear similarities with what happened in the Counter-Culture Revolution!" A brunette with a long ponytail sitting right next to the first one to comment remarked.

"Yes, but the most important thing to you should be what you are you going to do with your generational inheritance. What will Generation X, the ones born between 1965 and 1979; the Generation Y, who came to Earth between 1980 and the year 2000; and how we'll all prepare for the coming of age of Generation Z who's been arriving in the twenty-first century? And that, you may rest assured, is the only thing that really matters at this critical turning point in time."

At the end of my presentation, many students came to talk with me to ask me questions and even advice about what to do to reignite or recreate a new Counter-Culture Revolution. As I spoke with them noticing the mix of fervor for change and fear of an unstable future in their eyes, it dawned on me that my generation's role in the history of social transformation did not end in the 1960s and 70s; to the contrary, it'd reached the apex at the pinnacle of our own individual time as we became the elders of society.

"I appreciate your coming to talk to my students," Charlie said as I was packing my briefcase. "I never thought about collective aging before, and how one generation influences the other. Very interesting."

"I know, it makes me wonder about the role of the individuals of my generation at this stage in our lives," I said getting ready to walk out the door. "We've become the elders of the tribe now; and yet, sometimes it seems to me that most of my cohorts are neither interested nor concerned about the current situation of the world we'll be leaving behind. I think most people are so obsessed with their own aging process that they forget about the generational responsibility we all share. Perhaps, like the yuppies of the 1980s, we have sold out to the values of greed and selfishness to a point of no return. After all, we won't be around to witness a decimated world inhabited by some 10 billion people in the next few decades. Shame on us for giving up the values we fought for in our youth."

"Well, what could a bunch of old folks do anyway?" The twenty-something Charlie asked nonchalantly.

"A lot!" I said halting my steps by the door way immediately turning around to look at him in the eye. "Most of us 'older folks' have what's needed to lead the way: time, resources, and the accumulated experience of the years. Personally, I believe that active participation in social affairs is the greatest antidote to aging; if not physical aging, the aging of the mind that's expedited by inertia and a feeling of uselessness. 'Older folks' certainly have one final shot at making meaningful contributions to generations yet to come. When we were young we tried to influence the old. Now that we are old we should be trying to influence the young."

"You mean, leaving a legacy?" He asked.

"Not in an egotistical way of wanting to be remembered for good deeds done, but by doing it because it is the right thing to do," I said. "We make a living by what we get, but we make a life by what we give, so Winston Churchill said. And granted that he is right, is there a better way to feel alive as you age?"

By the time I was in my car driving home, I realized how important that presentation was to me. In addition to the opportunity to process the learning I'd acquired in the past few months, I now understood the role of collective aging as generations replace one another through the life cycle of time. It occurred to me that, from a Zen Buddhist point of view, generations were like chronological *Sanghas* (the collective term for those who are followers of The Buddha) traveling through time, each attempting to improve on the development of humankind until the species could reach the *Nirvana* of a higher consciousness. However, after evaluating my own assessment of generational exchange through the twentieth century, I concluded that these

Sanghas of contemporary time travelers seemed doomed by an endless cycle of repetition of mistakes. In reality, it resembled a *Samsara* (the term used to describe the ordinary world dominated by the endless cycle of life and death) in which the same shortcomings are revealed over and over again in every generational *Sangha*. But according to Mahayana Buddhism, *Nirvana* and *Samsara* are not two different worlds or different locations, but one and the same world experienced in two different ways.[11] To the ignorant, it's the continuous recurrence of missteps. To the enlightened it's the consistent experience of attainment.

But concerning the aging process, my role as a member of my generational *Sangha* should be to act as though I were a sort of *Bodhisattva*; someone who's committed to making a contribution to the collective development of the next demographic *Sangha*. Instead of focusing on my personal limitations and the many trials of growing older, if I were to serve the common good, maybe I'd accomplish two goals simultaneously: take my mind away from self-absorption while doing some good, therefore leaving my own anonymous legacy as I aged in peace.

Alas, the individual challenges of aging can be imposing hurdles to jump over. However, I'm well aware that self-empowerment can only be achieved through personal trials. Personal growth demands the overcoming of obstacles, and there is no way around it.

As the maxim of medieval alchemy says, "For the branches of a tree to reach out to the bright blue sky, its roots must go deep into the darkness of the Earth."[12]

Chapter 10

The Obstacles to Power Aging

❧

The Aging Process Itself

"How's it going Brad?" I asked the septuagenarian friend of mine. At the time, we both volunteered our time serving on the board of directors of a nonprofit organization striving to assuage the countless needs of homelessness.

"I guess I'm so-so," he answered my pro-forma question in doubly dubious fashion, which made me raise an eyebrow of curiosity and concern. Although the question was merely the casual manner in which we greet in our culture, Brad's answer carried a dual message of uncertainty with well-being. Since we were both hurrying to get into the conference room for the beginning of the board meeting, I took a mental note to catch up with him at the end. I just smiled and patted him gently on the right shoulder as we walked in the already filled up room.

Throughout the meeting, I discreetly—and meticulously—observed my old friend's mannerisms, facial expressions, the sound of his voice, even his breathing pattern that were punctuated with occasional sighs. He seemed uncomfortable and tense; perhaps even in physical pain, for he was constantly moving and adjusting his posture on the chair. And at the time when there was a heated discussion about the growing number of elder clients procuring the services of the agency, I noticed his forehead muscles tightening up while his protruding Adam's apple indicated he was swallowing dry.

"But how the hell are they supposed to survive on Social Security allowance alone?" Said Tony, a fired up Latin board member who'd always been passionately vociferous on behalf of disadvantaged populations. "Besides, in an anemic economy with a very crowded job-marketplace where millions of younger workers fresh out of college are being hired at entry level salaries, who's going to give a decent job to a willing and competent sexagenarian? I'll tell you who. No one! No wonder one in four seniors struggles with poverty in the United States."

At that moment I couldn't help but notice how tensed up Brad became; even small globs of sweat began forming in the wrinkles delineating in his pale cheeks.

"Even those who do have either a good paying job or a reliable retirement plan are struggling to keep up with the rising cost of health care," said Mary, the head nurse in the oncology department of our local hospital. "It's getting to be very expensive to be sick and old."

As soon as the meeting was adjourned and people started walking out of the room, I approached Brad as we headed out side by side toward the long hallway.

"Well, it sounds like perhaps you're so-so or maybe getting-by O,K., if I'm guessing it right, though I suspect that perchance things might get better," I said bantering with him as I related to his answer when I greeted him earlier.

He halted his steps and turned around to face me. Although his eyes smiled at me, both his words and the tone of his voice communicated the unspoken anxiety of his being. "This business of aging is getting to be old and overwhelming. My back and my knees ache all the time; my blood pressure and cholesterol are in stiff competition for higher numbers, which is the opposite direction my financial situation has been heading these days since I had triple bypass heart surgery, which was caused by the high blood pressure and cholesterol in the first place. I've been living alone since my wife passed away five years ago and my social life has been reduced to this once a month board meeting and the Monday night reading club I attend at the public library. All things considered, I guess I'm so-so is not a bad answer after all."

We resumed walking out of the building and all of a sudden I noticed that I was the one feeling antsy about the prospect of my own future. Listening to our footsteps interspersed by the internal sounds of my own deep breathing, I observed how Brad hobbled favoring his left knee. My first instinctual reaction was to suggest his considering the use of a cane, but I realized that verbalizing it would only exasperate his already distraught state of mind. Instead, I decided to perk things up by broaching some uplifting aspects of the aging process in modern times.

"I hear you, Brad. I'm lagging some two decades behind you and I'm already feeling the effects of what's probably the most challenging period in human life. However, I realized that being older person is not what it used to be. People are aging much better these days."

"That's not what my body tells me every day," he replied sardonically.

"But you're so much more than just your body," I contested his lighthearted self-mockery. "Inside this aching aging body lives an intelligent and sensitive man with some half-million hours logged in this earthly journey, which can give you an extraordinary perspective of the reality of the illusion of time."

"Whatever, but my back and knees still ache every day," he retorted sounding like a stubborn curmudgeon who refused to give in to a positive way of thinking.

"I hear you, but is it where you're going to focus your attention for the rest of your days? Remember, there is only so much time left and you'd better make the most out of it. Of course, getting older is a challenging universal trial that tests our resilience and mettle, but many people continue living extraordinary lives at their latter years," I said.

He stopped and turned to look at me in the eye. "Really? And who are they?"

"You, for starters," I said right away intending to infuse him with some positive energy he seemed to be lacking at the moment. "In spite of all your bitching about aches and pains, you've been a major contributing force on the board of directors of this organization we both serve. And with your experience and professional background, you could be helping many, many more groups and individuals who could benefit from your talents. Instead, you spend so much time moping about your physical ailments that you lose your concentration, mindfulness, and neglect the effort you could be making to improve both your life and that of others," I said thinking of the last three elements of The Eightfold Path.

❦ The Obstacles to Power Aging ❦

"Who else?" the adamant curmudgeon insisted on getting some real people and not only a pep talk about his own situation.

"All right, my fuddy-duddy friend, I'll give you a laundry list to assuage your ill-will. Let me start with someone I respect dearly, the former President of the United States, Jimmy Carter, who at the age of 90 was still in the trenches of domestic and international affairs, writing books, and traveling the world in various diplomatic missions," I said noticing that Brad had slowed down his walking pace in what seemed to me an effort to be mindful of his concentration on my words. "Of course you remember when you told me that John Glenn, the former astronaut who became a U.S. Senator from Ohio completed a 10-day research mission in orbit aboard the space shuttle Discovery. Well, he was 77-years-old at the time of that mission. And then there is the famous English philosopher and writer, Bertrand Russell, who was deeply committed to the cause of anti-nuclear proliferation efforts at the age of 89. And in the area of entertainment there is the pianist and composer, Irving Fields, who at the age of 99 performed a show dubbed '90 and Going Strong.' Joining him in the performance were Emmy-winning entertainer Fyvush Finkel and clarinetist Sol Yaged, both 91.[1] And of course there are the more popular ones, like the Spanish painter Pablo Picasso who was still creating masterpieces at the age of 90. And the 88-year-old crooner Tony Bennett who still tours and entertains full-houses with his charming singing. And the 85-year-old academy award-winning actor and director Clint Eastwood, not to mention the nonagenarian actress Betty White, and the list goes on. The point I'm trying to make it is that you, we, don't have to settle for the waiting room of death while we're still alive. For as long as we breathe there is opportunity for growth, regardless of the physical disadvantages of our aging bodies."

By the time we reached the street corner, there was not an opportunity for Brad to reply. He was going to the right and I to the left in the direction of our destinations. We stopped, looked at each other somewhat wistfully, and bid farewell with silent smiles as I patted him on the shoulder. Then, my brain set the mechanism of body movement in motion and I started walking faster as though I was running away from something. I felt anxious. Fearful, even. All of a sudden I realized that I'd just given an inspiring pep talk to my old friend Brad, as I tried to dissuade him from falling into the angst of lonesomeness and the pangs of aging, but now I was the one feeling uneasy about it. Ironically, at that moment I was the one feeling frightened. It was standing there in the middle of the street that I confirmed that the most challenging aspect of the aging process is being intellectually and empirically aware of its existence. It is the greatest obstacle to the Power Aging approach I so desperately wanted to achieve.

At that point, I was shuffling my feet through the sidewalk while mulling over the countless trials and travails intrinsic to the aging process. I noticed the sweat drops forming on my forehead and I knew that they were not happening because of my walking pace. I felt apprehensive about my future, worried about my health, losing my job because of my age, losing those I cherish, losing my mind, losing my independence, losing my life. Surely, there were the likes of countless examples of famous personalities, not to mention the numerous unknown elders around the world, who live and lived rich, productive, and fulfilling

The Obstacles to Power Aging

good lives well beyond their eighth decade of living. But in hindsight, what good did it do to Brad my mentioning the good examples of the so-called successful aging? After all, like me, he is experiencing it at a deep personal level in which only the individual herself can know.

By the time I got home I was feeling exhausted. The weight of my unexpected apprehension with the potential vicissitudes of old age made the eight-block walk feel like a marathon. It was a full-blown mental and emotional fatigue. I kept trying to withdraw from the intellectual Zen principles I'd deposited in my memory bank, but at that moment there seemed to be no pipeline pumping the empowering juices of my intellectual knowledge to the parching grounds of my insecurities. If only I could become the principles themselves, I wouldn't have to reach out for it whenever an imminent need occurred, for I'd be self-empowered by default of being.

Lying in bed looking at the ceiling empty-minded, I became mindful of a noble truth of my own: there is no amount of intellectual learning that can appease the angst of the aging process. I realized that in spite of all my studies and readings, I succumbed to the anxiety of what is a natural process of life in which I have no control, except monitoring my thoughts and managing my emotional reactions to them. The only way that I would be able to overcome my own thought-generated fears (the mind is the factory where emotions are manufactured), was to become the internalization of the principles of Zen manifested in my daily living. And for that to take place, I'd have to be mindful at all times; mindful that I must pave the way to becoming an empowered elder who is impervious to outside circumstances I cannot control. I had to become Zen itself. I had to become a ZENior CitiZEN.

"To be or not to be. That is the question," I slurred the words of Hamlet out lout in a sleepy sound. "Whether 'tis nobler in the mind to suffer, the slings and arrows of outrageous fortune, or to take arms against a sea of troubles, and by opposing end them? To die, to sleep no more; and by a sleep to say we end, the heartache and the thousand natural shocks."[2] I paused nibbling on my lower lip while reflecting on the words of The Bard. "Well, the legacy of Hamlet is that of a character who paid the ultimate price because he could not make up his mind," I continued my end of the day soliloquy. "Perhaps what is the question is not 'to be or not to be,' but to become or not to become. To be is static, complete, done, whereas to become is a continuous changing process that can be nurtured into self-empowerment."

But becoming is neither an easy nor ending endeavor, especially in regards to the aging process. Sometimes the hurdles on the track of becoming older are so high that the risk of tripping and tumbling are equally high, and so is the potential for getting hurt. The good news is that with the challenges come the opportunities. The bad news is that the opportunities can be fraught with *duhkha*.

Becoming a caregiver

It had been a very busy day at work. I needed to take a break and decided to walk to the kitchen to get some hot water for my afternoon green tea time when I stopped suddenly and looked down the hallway. A good looking early sexagenarian couple was walking toward me. By the loving and attentive manner in which she attended to the man's erratic motion, I could tell right away who was going to be the newest client of the adult day care facility I administered. I stood motionless and greeted them with a welcoming smile as they approached me. When they got closer, I noticed that behind the friendly smile she reciprocated, the glitter in her eyes revealed an exhausted woman whose husband wavered by her side as he treaded in the thick fog of dementia.

"Welcome Bill," I said after we introduced ourselves. "I'm going to make sure you have a good time here with us."

By the time I finished my sentence, he had already wandered off without replying either with words or even a subtle change in physiognomic expression. His wife, Janet, looked at me with raised eyebrows and a disconcerted smile shrugging her shoulders at the same time. I called the head nurse and asked her to carry out the preliminary evaluation and registration procedures while I walked Janet to my office.

"It's been a struggle; a big multifaceted struggle ranging from financial hardship to quality of life," she said following her statement with an accentuated sigh that disclosed her pent-up emotions. "We don't have children and our closest relatives live thousands of miles away, so I'm pretty much on my own carrying for him while doing my utmost to keep my very much needed part-time job. In the beginning it was possible to live him alone for a few hours, but it has reached a point in which I cannot leave him by himself even for a moment. I'm here because I'm in desperate need help."

I placed my elbows on the desk and touched my fingertips under my chin. In an instinctive motion, both my torso and my compassion leaned in her direction as I listened attentively to her story.

"Looking at him now you wouldn't be able to tell, but Bill was a very vivacious and hardworking man," she continued. "He took great pride in his work as an electronic engineer for a multinational corporation where he'd been working for almost thirty years. Then, when the economy hit the skids and went south, so did his job and he was dismissed unceremoniously with only a modest severance package to assuage his disappointment. After losing his job, I began noticing gradual changes in his demeanor. He became more introverted and even morose at times. I'm convinced that was the triggering point of the subsequent heart attack he suffered. No longer employed and without health insurance coverage, and not old or poor enough to qualify for public assistance, the unexpected hefty medical expenses consumed our life's savings and then some. We were on the brink of filing for bankruptcy, but luckily we managed to turn around the corner when I got a meager income part-time job to supplement his Social Security benefit, both of which are vital to our budget. But now that his condition has deteriorated to the point that he barely recognizes me, I'm in a catch-22 situation in which I cannot continue working without help to care for him, and I can't care for him unless I continue working."

"How long it's been since he reached this advanced stage of dementia?" I asked trying to understand the progression of the illness in relation to the events of his life, for I've always wondered about the theories of French psychiatrist Jean Maisondieu who has no hesitation suggesting that Alzheimer's may be a "cry, a refusal, a sort of social and intellectual suicide."[3]

She paused and lowered her head with eyes briefly fixated on the floor. "Oh, it was about six months after his open heart surgery; a year and half since he lost his job. I remember exactly the day when I first noticed something wasn't right with him. We were on an airplane on the way back home from visiting family in Michigan and he looked aloof and unresponsive to the conversations I tried to engage him. His eyes looked vacant and devoid of any signs of enthusiasm. I recall thinking that for the first time as far as I could remember, his beautiful blue eyes were turning grey from the inside. After that day, it has been a gradual downhill motion toward the unrecognizable stage he is at now. Altogether, it's been about three years."

After explaining to me the details of his condition and her delicate predicament, I realized that I was the one who suddenly found myself in a catch-22 situation. Although the organization I was entrusted to managing held a nonprofit status, which is a misnomer because nonprofit organizations are and must be run as viable businesses, I was conflicted with not accepting Bill as a client because of their inability to pay. Because they were above the ludicrously low poverty level guidelines, they didn't qualify for public assistance through the Medicaid program. On the other hand, if she couldn't get help caring for her husband, they'd not only fall head first into the abyss of poverty, but also her own health would deteriorate probably even faster than his. Looking at the apprehensive and dejected woman sitting across my desk, I didn't have the nerve to send her away without giving her what she came for. I made a temporary arrangement with her to have Bill come in twice a week until I procured a grant or community support to finance the cost of the service she could not afford.

As I watched them walk out through the same hallway they came in, I thought of the millions of people going through similar situations as Janet's; and I say hers rather than theirs because the brunt of the load lies on the shoulder of the caregiver. For all practical purposes, Bill was not present any more and he might not even be aware that he once was. What distinguishes humankind from all other members of the animal kingdom, his mind, was hijacked by a nefarious disease that's been growing to epidemic proportions. According to the Alzheimer's Association, by 2025 the number of people age 65 and older with Alzheimer's disease in the United States will grow to 7.1 million, a 40 percent increase from the approximately 5 million diagnosis a decade earlier[4] (and there are many other types of dementia-causing illnesses). Not only it is a growing health problem of great concern, but also of extraordinary economic consequences, for elder care cost is escalating at a pace that only a small financially privileged segment of society can afford. With the median bill for a private room in a nursing home costing above $91,000 a year—and increasing at 4 percent a year—the staggering rise expenses pose an enormous burden on individuals, families, communities, and governments.[5]

I went back to my office and sat at my desk thinking about the magnitude of the challenges of an aging society. At the individual level, there was the pain of witnessing the health of loved ones deteriorate piecemeal and the mounting emotional and financial stress the situation creates. And from a societal standpoint, it is an unprecedented socioeconomic problem that is rapidly growing around the

The Obstacles to Power Aging

globe; a problem so imminent that has become an urgency. Contrary to the debauched individualistic and selfish ethos of Western societies, the manifold problems of aging is as much an individual challenge as it is a collective dilemma. Because we all age and most of us will live to be old, we have all become caregivers—and potential receivers of care. In fact, some 40 million Americans dedicate an estimated 37 billion hours of collective unpaid caregiving worth some $470 billion in labor value, and a large number of them will carry out the essential voluntary work for five or ten years.[6]

Suddenly, my parched throat and sleepy eyes reminded me that I never got the hot water for my green tea. I walked back to the kitchen thinking about Janet's situation. How could someone like her have the time to even consider pursuing enlightenment, or any spiritual endeavor for that matter, when her entire being was consumed by the daunting task of caring for her husband without any support system in place? As I walked back to my office bobbing the tea bag in my mug and leaving a water drops trail on the floor, it dawned on me that, like the difference between the verbs to be and to become, there is a meaningful distinction between an enlightened and an empowered spirit. To be enlightened is to reach a serene state of being in which a profound sense of inner peace coexists with and in spite of the trials of living. To become empowered, however, is a continuous self-development process that charges up the individual with a high dosage of personal power that allows her to face the challenges of life with unfazed courage. But is there a sufficient amount of self-empowerment that would help alleviate the daily ordeal of Janet's caregiving obligations? The question lingered on my mind for a few minutes without an answer. It was not until I burned the roof of my mouth with hot tea that I realized that only the emotional burden could benefit from becoming empowered. However, there was very little self-empowerment could do to meet her practical daily needs to deliver care for her ailing husband, make a living, do housekeeping, among many other tasks, not to mention taking time for herself. At that moment I realized that only a self-empowered community—at the neighborhood, city, county, state, and at the national government level—can fulfill those individual needs of a rapidly growing number of citizens who are becoming caregivers or receivers of care.

By the time I took the last sip of my tea that had already turned cold, I was convinced that while it's an utopian aspiration to be an enlightened society, to become an empowered community is not only feasible but a growing necessity of our challenging historical time. But since communities are composed of individual citizens, they must become empowered themselves, and the best way to reach this level is through education and practice.

Indeed, becoming empowered is like turning into the caregiver of your own self. And while enlightenment may offer the inner peace to accept the inevitable, self-empowerment is the source of energy from which to draw from when the unexpected, unimaginable, and unrelenting misadventures of living come in the winds of change.

If enlightenment is the pair of wings that allows us to fly to a higher level of consciousness, self-empowerment is the solid rock upon which we are able to stand when the world around us falls apart.

ഌ The Obstacles to Power Aging ര

Love Losses

It was a rough start. My mother died within a couple of months after giving birth to me. From the get-go I learned about loss of love; and it began with what is undoubtedly the greatest and most important love of all. It wasn't an easy lesson for the infant whose loving maternal bosom vanished without warning. Later in my young adulthood, I thought that the ill-fated loss of my mother at such a young age had exerted a beneficial effect on me; something like an inoculation against *duhkha*, the pain of the world. Unfortunately, my gullible wishful thinking dissipated as quickly as my mother disappeared. Soon I began experiencing all sorts of disappointments, frustrations, separations, and a slew of inconvenient and unwelcome events that generated very unpleasant feelings, albeit I could feel that the hardhearted experiences strengthened my spirit (as Friedrich Nietzsche asserted, "what doesn't destroy you strengthens your spirit"). But as far as the conscious loss of love is concerned, this most poignant pain that seems to shred the ethereal heart into pieces, I first experienced it vicariously during the many conversations I shared with my father.

"I can't even imagine the grief," I said after witnessing the anguish exuding from my father's melancholic eyes as he narrated that tragic day in his and my life. The distinct difference in our shared sorrow is that I was under the protective barrier of unawareness of what was going on, even though I could feel the absence of my mother's love replaced by the emotional vacuum that permeated the environment. But for my father, a 32-year-old man with three children ranging in age from three months to 4-years-old, he lived the experience at a high turned up intensity level. Yes, an emotional intensity knob that sometimes can be turned up to 359 degrees pushing a person to the edge of the abyss of despair. And unless we develop the self-empowerment shield that protects against the "slings and arrows of outrageous fortune," we risk hearing the echo of our own panic-stricken voice reverberating in the valley below as we fall to a temporary death of the being. However, those who cultivate inner strength, eventually come back to life, though the scars will remain as indelible badges of honor of the evolving individual.

And the losses go on and on. They don't seem to end. Every moment of happiness must pass; and so does every fun weekend, blissful holidays, delightful birthdays, special events, pleasant celebrations, even the casual daily joys of living; all of them must pass away into the realm of memory. Then, the more pernicious types of losses come to remind us that the minor ones are not as bad as we made them out to be. After all, what's the passing of a memorable month-long vacation compared to the passing of a life partner with whom we journeyed with for decades? What's the true value of a special event, whatever it may be, measured up against a vital organ in the body threatened by a devastating disease that may compromise our lives? And how does a birthday celebration contrasts with the mourning that death entails? *Duhkha, duhkha* everywhere!

But *duhkha* also brings new beginnings and possibilities for compensating what we lost. It bestows power, too; or at least for those who pursue it through diligent self-development. *Duhkha* is not characterized only by anxieties, distress, suffering, and continuous change. Like yin and yang—or more like mother and father in the sense of giving birth to an empowered self—*duhkha* is well balanced in its nature of pain and growth; of joy and sadness; of light and darkness; of love and the absence of it. In fact, in the play of life where all the world is a stage, as Shakespeare proclaimed, *duhkha* is like a stage manager that makes sure the timing and synchronicity of the scenes assist the actor to deliver her emotional performance as determined by the script, no matter how charged it may be. D*uhkha* is a dagger and a gift. It can perforate the heart with a vengeance, but at the same time, from the depth of the anguish of the human experience, it sows the seed of the lotus of self-empowerment to bloom.

After giving much and long consideration to the function of *duhkha* in life, I realized there is an underlying educational attribute to it that can be easily by-passed by the self-absorbed individual. Because people tend to think of education as an exclusive intellectual activity, they seem utterly oblivious to the importance of the education of the heart, the emotions, the soul. And suffering is the sharpest tool with which to chisel the spirit; the chalk that writes on the blackboard of time the rules of the game of life. But when it comes to losing a close loved one, like a spouse, a lover, a friend, or a mother at a young age, the pain can be so searing that makes us forget to learn.

Once I learned that Siddhartha Gautama lost his mother at a very young age, I developed an unusual sense of kinship with him, for I shared similar experience with the one who was going to become the Awakened One. I wondered whether losing maternal love in infancy paved the way to a strong determination (*dai-funshi*) to going forth. Perhaps it functioned as a primer for developing self-reliance, resilience, and inner strength. I know that in my case it did. And because I developed such a strong sense of individual independence, the prospect of losing it was as terrifying to the adult as the departure of the mother was to the child.

Loss of Independence

For the older aging person, one of the most dreadful losses that *duhkha* can impart on her is the loss of independence. Everything we take for granted in everyday activities; something that seems as banal as walking can suddenly become as vital as breathing. And it doesn't take much to realize the importance of this seemingly simple physical function. All it takes is losing it. But nothing, absolutely nothing can compare with losing the mind, for that surrenders the perception of life from the very center of loving and learning. It relinquishes the autonomy of the being to total dependence and care of others; a responsibility that falls mostly on the shoulders of close loved ones who can also lose their own minds in the process of caregiving while juggling numerous other responsibilities.

"All the world's a stage, and all the men and women merely players. They have their exits and their entrances; and one man in his time plays many parts. His acts being seven ages."[7] This is how Shakespeare, through the lines of his character Jacques in Act II Scene VII of his play *As You Like It*, refers to the different ages of the human experience. Jacques reveals that it is in the sixth age that everything shifts and life becomes more challenging than ever before. It's the time when "his big manly voice turning again toward childish treble" heralds the dreadful sounds of the upcoming end of "this strange eventful history."

The Obstacles to Power Aging

However, it is not the end that we fear the most, but the journey leading to the final destination. We fret about the weakening of the body and the disempowerment associated with continual deterioration of our physical capabilities. Then, at the top of the pyramid of our worries, sits the anxiety of losing our mind or independence, "sans teeth, sans eyes, sans taste, sans everything." And independence for most of us is an essential element of quality living.

But the decline of physical condition does not necessarily lead to destabilization. In fact, counteracting the side-effects of the aging process by diligently working on self-development can compensate the bodily disadvantaged with an empowered mindset. Even the loss of independence does not automatically eliminate the zest for living; sometimes it even exacerbates it, no matter how old you are.

"Hey, Mat, may I talk with you for a moment?" I asked my colleague on the aging and disabilities services advisory council of the local chapter of the Area Agency on Aging we served. Mat, a good-looking man in his early 50s, was afflicted with a neurological condition that rendered his physical body useless, though his mind was sharp as a blade. He could not move any part of his body from the neck down. Harnessed to a mechanized wheelchair with a device protruding close to his mouth that allowed him to verbalize in slow slurred statements his thoughts, ideas, and the many valuable contributions he made to the council.

"Maaary...would...you...please...let...us...be...alone?" Mat's request to his round-the-clock personal care assistant stumbled out of his mouth with great difficulty. The young woman excused herself and walked away. I was temporarily distracted by the gentle clacking of her high-heel shoe steps dwindling along with her silhouette down the hallway when I noticed Mat staring at me. He seemed to be in anticipation mode, as though eager to find out the reason of my wanting to speak with him. There was neither slurring nor any misunderstandings in the language his eyes spoke. They spoke loud and clear.

"It's been a long time coming that I've been wanting to thank you very much," I said seeing the frowning in his eyes that his brow would have expressed if the brain could communicate with the facial muscles. "A long time ago, I was feeling totally bummed out because of some personal issues that were not going my way. I was sliding down a path of self-pity and despondence when you suddenly came to my mind and I immediately started experiencing shame and guilt instead."

His eyelids twitched as his eyes disclosed a great deal of curiosity. I'd gotten his attention.

"Ever since that day, I've been thinking a lot about how courageously you live your life; how you overcome every day the unimaginable challenge of having your vibrant and intelligent being trapped in a body unworthy of the magnanimity of your soul. And yet, you carry on with great determination, not only to be alive, but to make a positive difference in the lives of others. I want you to know how much I admire you; how much of an inspiration you are to me in my pursuit of self-empowerment. But above all, I want you to know how much I respect the strength of your spirit." Then, I slightly bowed my head in a reverential act to someone whom I considered to be a Zen master in his own right.

✌ The Obstacles to Power Aging ✌

As I slowly moved my head upright, my eyes met his in a deep emotional bond of mutual appreciation. At that moment, watching his eyes well up until a solitary tear drop cascaded down his immobile countenance, I learned that loss of independence is not by any means the loss of self. To the contrary, people like Mat were living testimonies that an empowered spirit can withstand and overcome all the trials and travails of the temporal human journey. They can continue to be productive citizens and sources of inspiration to many people like me. Furthermore, they prove that a truly self-empowered person cannot be restrained by physical limitations, for their power is rooted in the solid grounds of a stalwart spirit.

At the end of the day that I shared my thoughts and feelings with Mat, I was still thinking about the many other similar cases I'd witnessed in my life. I remembered Ken, a man of 38 years of age who'd become paralyzed in a car accident since he was twelve. I met him at a self-empowerment workshop I attended and I'll never forget his clever sense of humor and remarkable zest for living. Thinking of Ken reminded me of a former co-worker of many years past, a beautiful young woman who shared a similar misfortune as Ken's. In spite of her wheelchair bound future, she lived joyfully in the present like very few healthy people live in the fictitious "good old days" of the past.

Perhaps the only loss of independence we ought to be concerned about is the independence of a mind committed to the pursuit of self-empowerment, which paves the way for the enlightenment of living and the *Nirvana* of being, regardless of how old the being happens to be.

The Invisibility Element

A fascinating aspect about growing older is that we become invisible. It's not like we literally disappear defying all the natural laws in the books. We just become someone that no one notices anymore, and this is particularly hard for women whom our culture infuse with the pseudo-value of physical attractiveness as one of their primary assets. Once they lose this spurious aspect of their gender identification, they become ignored by the eyes of attraction, almost as though they ceased being women by an irreverent edict of time. They transmute from the uniqueness of being female humans to the generalized perception of old humans, which encompasses everyone of a certain age. And once we cross the Rubicon of latter years, we seem to become invisible to the younger viewers on the other bank of the river.

    I once observed this phenomenon on a Saturday afternoon at my local supermarket. The place was teeming with hurried and harried shoppers getting ready for the three-day weekend sponsored by a national holiday on Monday. With shopping carts at a premium, I looked around hoping I'd be lucky to catch sight of an available cart, or perhaps an already shopped customer relinquishing one at the exit door. No such a luck. What my eyes spotted instead was something I'd never noticed before at the supermarket: a frail-looking elder woman probably looking for the same thing I was. Forget about shopping carts, now she became the object of my interest. I observed her from afar and she looked frazzled by the speedy commotion happening around her. People walked in, out, and by seemingly oblivious that the much older fellow-citizen could use some help.

The Obstacles to Power Aging

Suddenly, my fixation with her was disturbed when I saw a young couple with two small kids in tow letting go of their shopping carts. I rushed ahead of the competition and snatched the coveted item before walking back toward the old lady flashing a "I'm going to help you" smile.

"Here, ma'am, this cart is for you," I said gently pushing it in her direction.

She looked at me and her face was illuminated. "Well, don't you need this cart, too?"

"I'll get the next one. This one is yours," I said.

"Well, what if we share it?" She suggested.

At first I wondered how we would go about sharing a shopping cart in a jammed-packed-busy supermarket. But it didn't matter; the magic of the moment rested on the words she spoke last: "what if we share it?" Of course, we'll share it, but not only a utilitarian shopping cart.

"Good, so let's get going," she said immediately after I agreed. "It's very busy here today."

We walked in side by side exchanging small talk until we entered the congested aisles. It didn't take long for her already slow moving pace to come to a complete standstill; like an unspoken call for a time-out. I realized that here it was my opportunity to learn about this old stranger who just crossed my path; someone who had been journeying on this Earth for a long time—and became invisible along the way.

"It's not as easy as it was five years ago," she mumbled trying to catch up her breath. "One of these days I might not be able to do my own grocery shopping anymore."

Ever since the day that I met Ms. Porter, an octogenarian African American widow who lived alone on a Social Security benefit allowance, every time I went to the supermarket I stopped at some people's watching vantage point to observe how many elders walked in and out of the supermarket. The first time I did it, I was stunned to realize that I'd never noticed how many old adults were out there that I'd neglected to see before. I wondered how it happens that as we get older we gradually disappear from the public view; or at least we're no longer counted for. I came up with a few theories: firstly, we lose some of our utilitarian function in society. For women, they lose their physical attractiveness and sex-appeal. And for everyone else, we all look slow and weak for the fast-moving and competitive artificial nature of modern living. Therefore, albeit unwittingly, younger people become indifferent to older citizens who are no longer perceived as integral parts of our fast-paced society. From a coarse physiological standpoint, the elders become the excrement of a consumerist and superficial society that has used them up and now dumps them in the W.C. of obscurity.

However, of all the theories that I concocted about the invisibility element of old age, there was one that seemed to be closer to the truth than any other: Fear. Yes, fear of old people for what they represent and reveal what awaits everyone in the future. Looking at their feeble and unattractive appearance is a terrifying reminder that The First Noble Truth cannot be avoided, even when we make extraordinary efforts to not acknowledge it. *Duhkha* is real and as inevitable as it is necessary; and old age is a major component of this reality of living—and dying.

But how can the elder become visible again? Well, she can't, not as long as utilitarian socioeconomic values remain the same. The unspoken cultural discrimination against older citizens nudges them off to the side until they fall into the void of anonymity where no one can be reminded of a simple truth that has been considered a noble one by the enlightened few. What the older citizen can become, however, is self-empowered to face the challenge of defying his own debility that has ironically become his strongest and most daunting opponent ever.

Whether or not we become invisible as we age, we must go forth into a truly invisible future that, like time itself, cannot be seen but only experienced. And like time that moves toward the invisible and unknown future in uninterrupted sequences of brief moments, we have no choice but flow with the current of life, lest we intensify the effects of *duhkha* through anxiety and fear. We must flow with the Tao (the Way of Life), for it is the only approach that does not allow any effort to resistance. Flowing with the Tao is like floating on a river whose strong and directional currents take you right to the ocean, effortlessly; and the ocean is the only destination that we want to reach. And time shares many similarities with water. It cannot be contained, controlled, shaped, and its passing cannot be stopped. We cannot prevent the flow of time any more than we can stop the flow of the river; and any foolish attempt to resisting it may cause our drowning, either in water or anguish, whatever the case may be.

There was a time when I questioned whether it was feasible to embrace such a stalwart attitude in the face of the challenges of a most vulnerable stage in human life. After much reading and thinking, I realized that it has been done successfully in the past, although in different—and more demanding—circumstances. The Japanese samurai is the quintessential example of a redoubtable attitude, which is detailed in the work of the eighteenth century samurai veteran, Yamamoto Tsunetomo. He said that above all, the Way of the Samurai should be in being aware that you do not know what is going to happen next. Therefore, thinking of victory or defeat was an irrelevant waste of time, for the only thing that matters is plunging into the unknown with courageous abandon. Tsunetomo stresses that your life advance daily, becoming more skillful than yesterday and more skillful than today; and this is a never ending occurrence. And no matter if the enemy has thousands of men, there is fulfillment in simply standing them off and being determined.[8] Because in the end, you are the only one who matters to see the invisible person you may have become.

Regardless of the undeclared demographic apartheid taking place in modern industrial societies, invisibility is just a matter of perception—or lack thereof. And sometimes, if you don't observe and acknowledge who you are, you risk becoming invisible to yourself, which is the worst invisibility of all.

Completing the Circle of the Aging Process

"It all begins in innocent childhood when you gradually enter the realm of consciousness of a temporal reality destined to end. Soon, usually in the pubescent years, you become empirically and intellectually aware of the reality of *duhkha*, as the First Noble Truth is revealed to you either you are mindful of it or not. By the time you head toward the final stage of this complex evolutionary journey, the completion of the circle seems to lead back to a similar stage of the one it began, except that the second time around *duhkha* has transformed consciousness, though not always for the better," I said looking at Roger's face trying to read his reaction. He was a gerontology graduate student I'd known since he was in high school. I liked the young man and enjoyed conversing about philosophical issues regarding old age; perhaps almost as much as he enjoyed challenging most of my arguments.

"C'mon man, you're always bringing up Zen Buddhism concepts into an issue that should be delegated to scientific analysis and interpretation," he retorted in customary fashion. "It's amazing how you can turn a black and white topic around and make it sound as if it were a colorful arching rainbow in a summer afternoon. And you should know better than I that there is no pot of gold at the end of the rainbow of aging."

"I'm afraid that you're the one with a monochromic vision, my friend," I said beginning to delight myself in the conversation. "And since you mentioned the rainbow, let's suppose that the spectrum of time is akin to the spectrum of light. In one end you have the bright shining yellow of childhood followed by the passionate red in adolescence that transitions to a grounded green of adulthood, until it keeps turning grey through mid-life as it turns into the white elderhood."

"Where are you going with this?" Roger questioned my analogy askance.

"Well, as black is the absence of color, it is in the color white that all others converge into. So, if in this hypothetical spectrum of time the color white represents that stage in which everything converges to the completion of the circle of time, then the possibilities for amassing all the experiences of a lifetime into one self-empowered being are as endless as time itself."

Roger lowered his head while scratching the back of his neck. Raising his chin slightly upward and in sync with his raised left eyebrow, he looked at me as if he were infused with *Dai-gidan* (Great Doubt). "I think you've been spending too much time in meditation, man. It might be altering your consciousness more than you think."

"And from my light grey color perspective, I think that when you're smack-dab in transition from passion red to grounded green you cannot yet experience the rainbow; not until you become white," I said looking straight into his eye. "In the meantime, I suggest your starting to spend time in zazen, for it might open up your consciousness, too, and allow you to recognize the color white when it comes to greet you."

After the day of that encounter with my young friend, I started thinking about the aging process from a multi-colored perspective; a kind of psychedelic angle if you will. I realized from my own analogy of bright yellow at the beginning of the spectrum of time and white at the opposite end, all the different stages of time (colors of life) had the opportunity to converge into one solid luminous white of wisdom in which I could become whole.

However, I wasn't content with my newly discovered intellectual perception alone. I could feel in the depth of my entrails that there is much more to the Living Process than the mere mindfulness of it. The Living Process abounds with life seamlessly, therefore demanding action. Inertia and indifference are characteristics of a different kind of process; a lifeless stationary experience in which only the appearance changes, while at the core everything remains the same. But even if I had an incalculable amount of time to spare, if I kept my mind always focused on a distant future, I'd waste all that abundance of time by squandering each moment that I failed to live in the now. What a waste of eternity that would be!

Then, one day when I was reflecting on the nature of the traditional culture of the samurai, I became aware of the importance of service in the productive use of whatever time I have left. I realized the impeccable manner in which this warrior class of fearsome and fearless men dedicated themselves, their lives, to the Shogun they committed to serve. In fact, the word samurai is based on the Japanese verb, *samurau*, which means to serve.[9] They observed a strict code of honor, *Bushido*, in which the tripod sustaining it was said to be *Chi*, *Jin*, *Yu*; respectively, Wisdom, Benevolence, and Courage.[10] Eventually, I realized that if I were to replace my silent anxiety with the aging process and focus my attention on the Living Process instead, both my experience and quality of life would become significantly enhanced. Indeed, if I were to apply an unswerving commitment to service, I would become a sort of Samurai of Life, no matter how old I am. Service, wisdom, benevolence, and courage could well become the Four Noble Principles.

What a surprise to recognize that my own egocentric concerns was one of the main obstacles to a fulfilling old age. As I looked for some esoteric truth about aging outside myself, I was astonished to realize that the obvious had been staring at me in the eye from the inside while I searched for an exotic answer to my quandaries. It was as though my selfish worries and personal obsessions obstructed my vision from seen truth fluttering around without my ever noticing it.

ZENior CitiZEN

All that was left for me to do was to delve into serving with the abandon of a samurai—before it was too late.

Chapter 11

The Tao of Power Aging

Giving in Without Giving up

Every time we commit to a purpose or cause, we will most certainly be challenged along the way. It is a prerequisite for advancing through the course set by the seeker; like an academic exam that evaluates the aptitude of the student to continue on the educational program. It seems that as soon as the aspirant to self-empowerment develops Great Faith (*Dai-shinkon*) in her ability to go forth, Great Doubt (*Dai-gidan*) appears to put to the test the strength of her Great Determination (*Dai-funshi*). In the face of the trial of self-confidence, there seems to be no better strategy than complete surrender to the natural progression of the events taking place, especially when they have unfavorable effects. It's giving in without giving up. This is particularly important as the latter stages of life as the aging process unfolds.

In my own efforts to develop self-empowerment as I age, I realized the importance of dedicating my time to service, cultivating wisdom through self-development, exercising benevolence in my daily actions, and embodying courage in the face of life's continuous challenges. By switching the focus of attention from my selfish aspirations to the needs of others, I amplified both the objectives and results of my ultimate personal purpose to become empowered. Thus, in addition to launching an educational and coaching venture to help individuals in their pursuit of a meaningful experience of aging, I became engaged in local causes that resonated with my Four Noble Principles of service, wisdom, benevolence, and courage, which I was inspired by the example of the noble Prince Siddhartha Gautama.

As it was the case in the development of Zen Buddhism, which evolved in Japan through centuries, it all began when Siddhartha Gautama was awakened by the revelation of The Four Noble Truths. Sitting under the Bodhi tree deeply immersed in meditation searching for the truth within, Siddhartha, the prince, became Siddhartha, the Enlightened One. The Four Noble Truths turned out to be the foundation upon which a profoundly simple religion and pragmatic philosophy of life rose as tall as the Himalayas. Since my own individual search has been based on a Zen approach, it made sense to me that I'd learn from those who have walked the path before. First, I examined every single step of the process that led Prince Siddhartha Gautama to become The Buddha. Then, I analyzed the stages of the aging process to see if I could find any parallels between his dilemma and mine, which narrowed down to one simple question: that's got to be more to life—in my case aging—than it meets the eye. And here is when the process of enlightenment of The Buddha and the aging process bifurcate. If The Four Noble Truths were the gateway to Siddhartha's path to enlightenment, then The Four Noble

Principles that manifested to me during my long search could exert a similar enlightening effect to my quest. Indeed, if there was a way to mastering the art of aging the Four Noble Principles was the roadmap to it.

Convinced that the Four Noble Principles were a legitimate pathway to self-empowerment, I decided to promulgate my thoughts whenever an opportunity arose. Thus, I began submitting proposals to deliver my message to several events, until a regional conference on aging invited me to participate. I was excited and curious to how my concept would be received.

"I'll be glad to take your questions now," I said after delivering my first presentation on the topic to approximately fifty people assembled in a large hotel conference room. A distinguished looking man dressed in an elegant dark suit and red tie matching the handkerchief sticking out of his jacket's upper pocket raised his hand.

"Fascinating," he said with sarcasm disguised under his thick British accent. "But what I'd like to know is how these principles could have any positive impact on the daily experience of an aging citizen?"

I looked at the beautiful friendly face of a middle-aged woman sitting in the front row to siphon inspiration before proceeding. It was apparent that the bloke was having issues with his own aging process and was desperate for some answers. Maybe I was overly defensive making my first presentation on the topic, but I felt as if I were under an intellectual attack. At the same time, I was in no mood to be intimidated.

"Let me turn the explanation into a process by and of itself before I get to the stage in which your question can be answered; perhaps even to your satisfaction," I said with a tinge of sarcasm of my own. "Sometimes the best way to understand the whole is by analyzing its parts."

The First Noble Principle: Service

"Service is the ultimate action of kindness. It is compassion manifested in physical form through the practical results it generates. In The Four Noble Truths of The Buddha, the first is the spring board from which all the others vault into being. The initial awareness that life means suffering, led to the realization of the second, third, and fourth noble truths, as well as all the eight elements of the latter. Service, which functions as an antidote to suffering, is what I perceive as The First Noble Principle that can subdue the anxiety of aging through selfless action."

The gentlemen had his arms crossed with the indicator finger vertically across his lips touching the tip of his nose. In spite of his defying stance, his eyes revealed the looks of a scared little boy who was terrified of growing older.

"Just as the awareness of *duhkha* instigated the entire enlightenment process of The Buddha, so service is the vehicle delivering the other three principles into action. In fact, it relates to each of the three divisions of The Eightfold Path: Wisdom (right view, right intention); Benevolence (right speech, right action, right livelihood); and Courage (right effort, right mindfulness, right concentration). Service, like The Eightfold Path, is the umbrella under which the initiatives of wisdom, benevolence, and courage originate. Service is the tangible manifestation of compassion that cannot be restrained."

"What does compassion have anything to do with the aging process? If anything, older people are the ones in the receiving end of it," the curmudgeon with a charming accent said disclosing even more the aging wounds of his resentment.

I walked slowly to the edge of dais and looked at him with compassion. "An essential element of the truth that The Buddha realized under the Bodhi tree was that to live morally was to live for others.[1] And if that is applicable to his Four Noble Truths, it most certainly applies to my Four Noble Principles of Living. Service is the vehicle that can deliver wisdom, benevolence, and courage for those who need the most. And what is remarkable about it is the fact that in the action of delivering service often times the giver is the one who benefits the most. In that sense, the point that you made about the older population being in the receiving end is correct, because by turning service into compassion in action, they automatically reap the rewards of the giving."

"Rubbish!" He discarded uncrossing his arms and dropping them to the side as if he'd lost both interest and hope.

"Perhaps not. When you focus your mind's attention beyond your self-centered interest, the anguish that it causes naturally vanishes away. That's one of the main reasons people become the stereotypical 'workholics,' because they want to forget themselves in the work they do. But the self-empowered person lives not for himself; he lives for others. So, if the work happens to be genuine humanitarian service, then not only the labor distracts him from his worries, but also rewards him with an enormous satisfaction of contributing to the common good." I paused furtively glancing at the beautiful and pleasant female face that nurtured me with a welcoming smile. "Albert Schweitzer, for instance, gave up a prestigious career as a doctor in his native Germany and went to Africa to build hospitals for the poor indigenous people of the region. He remained there until he died at the age of 90. He worked until the very end of his life while maintaining an exuberant zest for living. He said that 'the only essential thing in life is to seek truth, and to practice it as far as we understand it.'[2] And for him, as it is for many others, the truth they seek they find in service, and this is why I consider service to be the First Noble Principle."

He didn't contest my arguments any more. He seemed so deeply consumed by his own morose attitude toward aging that it was unlikely that anything I could say or do would ameliorate his case. Maybe he'd reached a point of no return; like a fire of despair burning through the meadows of hope for miles rendering it difficult to extinguish.

Suddenly, the gracious woman who'd been nurturing me with silent support raised her hand. Looking into her eye while acknowledging her request for attention, I realized that she was exerting a much more poignant effect on me than the authoritative-looking Englishman.

"The Four Noble Principles approach that you espouse makes sense to me," she said. "What I don't understand is why you delegate service as the first principle when it seems to me that wisdom is what defines personal power?"

"Perhaps wisdom sits on the top of the mountain of power, but it is service that moves it downhill to face its purpose. If wisdom remains latent and isolated, its power is diminished by lack of productive activity. Service does not allow it to happen and makes sure the wealth of meaningful knowledge is delivered wisely."

I was about to continue when I noticed the cantankerous gentleman was looking in my direction displaying interest in what I had to say. I smiled internally basking in the joy of service.

"The ancient Chinese teacher, Lao Tzu, said that the sage does not accumulate for himself. The more he uses for others, the more he has himself. The more he gives to others, the more he possesses of his own.[3] This wise man already knew some 2,500 years ago that service is the power vehicle with which to deliver and receive the benefits of wisdom. And because I'm a pupil of his teachings, I understand how in the Tao, the Way of self-empowerment, service is the fundamental principle according to the Living Process. Now, as for wisdom, it demands its own individual analysis."

The Second Noble Principle: Wisdom

"What's the main difference between knowledge and wisdom?" I asked a group of enthusiastic high school seniors to whom I was teaching a workshop on developing self-empowerment as you grow up.

"No-brainier," a witty and smart-looking young man wearing a round tortoise frame glasses blurted out. "Knowledge is power and wisdom is what older folks like you think you have and try to pass it on to young dudes like me."

The students burst into laughter. I waited until the merry uproar subsided before replying. "Wrong in both counts. Does anyone else want to offer another amusing input?"

"I'm sorry, sir, but Jonathan is not wrong in both counts. Of course he was joking about the wisdom bit, but knowledge is power; and that is undeniable," a petite brunette voiced assuredly.

"Atomic energy is power. It took a great deal of accumulation of knowledge to develop it. No doubt both atomic energy and knowledge are power; the power to build as well as destroy. The same nuclear power plant that can generate electricity to a large urban area can also produce an atomic bomb that would incinerate that very same city in a matter of minutes," I said noticing how the loud mirth suddenly turned into dead silence. Their attentive and somewhat scared-looking faces stared at me. "Knowledge in and by itself is not power, and certainly not wisdom either; and as my example indicates, it can even be dangerous. In fact, knowledge, not wisdom, is what I think I have and that's what I'm trying to pass on to dudes like you."

They laughed, but this time timidly and short-lived. They looked at me as though I were a prey to their starving minds in the hunt for knowledge.

"On the other hand, I couldn't possibly pass wisdom on to you, which I don't claim to possess any way. Wisdom can be acquired only through a self-discovery process, and it's impossible to be taught. In a way, wisdom is a journey through the road of knowledge that leads to self-empowerment for those who have earned it. What they seem to have in common is the need for time; time to accumulate, as it's the case of knowledge, and time to mature as it's the case of wisdom."

"I get it," said Jonathan who was now revealing his intelligent mature side. "Wisdom comes with time."

"You're wrong again, dude," I said to the amusement of the young people who seemed to have enjoyed the reversal behavioral role that Jonathan and I swapped; he as the serious young man and I as the prankster geezer. "Wisdom blossoms with time, but it does not come from it. It's not a given that a person who has been journeying through time for a long time is guaranteed to acquire wisdom. Conversely, often times in the early stages of the journey, in the youth phase that you are now, wisdom can reveal itself in all its splendorous power."

"Well, that I don't get it at all," Jonathan said.

Amazed at how much change had occurred since his first interaction with me, I thought I'd give him some nourishment for his mind to digest. "Let me give you two examples that will illustrate what I said and make it immediately comprehensible to you. Not too long ago, it was reported in the news that a 74-year-old man had been sentenced to death for promoting hatred, committing murders, and bringing his community to a total state of chaos and terror.[4] I don't think that any person in this room would consider this man a paragon of wisdom. In fact, his ignorance transcends the basic intellectual level of what it means to be human; and there are numerous others like him who don't make the news. My point is that age is not a guarantee of success in the pursuit of wisdom."

"What about the possibility of a young person possessing wisdom?" Jonathan questioned. "That doesn't seem realistic either."

"A young woman named Malala Yousafzai was awarded the Nobel Peace Prize, one of the highest honors reserved to the best among the best in the world, at the tender age of 17. She was recognized for her commitment to the activism of a cause she believed in: education liberation for the women of her native country, Pakistan. Gaining fame, she launched many other initiatives on behalf of her cause and the benefit of others. Wouldn't you say that this young woman has had a brush with wisdom somehow? Hasn't she raised to a level of wisdom that the old man I just mentioned knows nothing about? Well, I think I've proven my point once again that age, though it can be an asset for those who know how to make the most of it, it's not synonymous with wisdom."

Later in the day I was thinking about it further. Wisdom requires Right View and Right Intention. Time doesn't seem to be a determining factor. What is of utmost importance to accomplishing wisdom, which is tangled in a perennial pursuit process, is viewing life with compassionate eyes and with the intention of being a force of good in a wicked world. Although it sounds so simple, evidently, this is not an easy task; and maybe why there is not much wisdom going around in the world these days. It can feel like hitting a brick wall every time you try to take a step forward. You want to foster your brotherly feelings, but the cultural demands of the socioeconomic system insists that selfish individualism is the only way to go. Then you set your right intention to counteracting the nefarious condition of modern society, just to see it fade away in the dense nebula of alienation that the masses are lost in. But for those who are committed to going through the Living Process in earnest, achieving at least a modicum of wisdom is a feasible task.

Only through the acquisition of wisdom can you achieve self-empowerment. Knowledge is not enough. Time is but a factor. And you, once you find wisdom, you realize that you've just lost yourself.

The Third Noble Principle: Benevolence

Be good. Be kind. Be generous. This is the triad supporting the principle of Benevolence, and it is evinced by dictionary definition: benevolence is disposition to do good; an act of kindness; a generous gift.[5] When the giving becomes habitual, it turns into a code of ethics that you carry out without even being aware that you're doing it. Benevolence not only encompasses the elements of a compassionate nature, but also represents the ethical conduct of Right Speech, Right Action, and Right Livelihood of The Buddha's Eightfold Path.

"Sure, I can see benevolence as a noble principle," said Carl, a man in his mid-thirties who worked in the same building where I had my private office. Every now and then, we walked together to a local eatery at lunch time. He'd first learned about my interest in Zen Buddhism when he came into my office and saw the small Zen rock garden I kept on the corner of my desk. Since that day, he started asking me a lot of questions about it as his curiosity and enthusiasm seemed to grow.

"Yes, and it must start with you," I said. "You must say the right words of encouragement to yourself, make sure that you take the right action toward your self-development, and that your livelihood is right according to your own principles and values."

"I think I got the first two pretty good, but I'm afraid I'm going to need to find another job to abide by the right livelihood factor," he said in good jest while dodging to the side to give way to a fast moving woman who talked on the phone even faster than she walked.

When we got to the deli, there was a long line of impatient hungry customers. It didn't take long for Carl to begin griping about the wait and the rapidly passing time of his lunch break that would soon be over. Then, probably aggravated by low blood sugar levels, he started complaining about the slow pace in which the clerks besieged behind the counter kept the assembly line of sandwiches moving forth.

"Sometimes silence is the only right speech," I whispered to Carl.

"Yeh, right. You should tell my wife that," he replied right away revealing an intimate aspect of his domestic life.

"You're beginning to sound like many older folks I know who do nothing but grumble all day about how bad things are and soon their time will be over. Their words do plenty of harm and yields no good whatsoever; to the contrary, it aggravates a situation that will not be changed by complaining. They are neither good, kind, nor generous to themselves, or to others for that matter," I said trying to gauge his physiognomic reaction.

"Now you're comparing me with the old farts you know," he said in the same tone of voice he was bitching about the slow-moving line.

"No, not you, just your attitude. I have to say that you definitely sound like a young fart; someone who will turn out to be and old fart when your time comes," I replied. "The Noble Principle of Benevolence can only be activated when it's initiated by a wholesome mind that disparages neither oneself nor others. It is actually a very simple progressive motion: the way you think determines the way you feel, and the way you feel influences the way you act; and your speech both conveys and reinforces a negative experience you want to avoid in the first place. You see, Right Speech leads to Right Action; no wonder you feel like you don't have the Right Livelihood. You may be talking yourself away from it."

Soon, we were watching the young clerk assemble our mouth-watering sandwiches. She looked distraught as if she were mentally and physically spent. Suddenly, she noticed me noticing her distress and we made eye contact. I gave her a broad smile followed by a lighthearted small talk that seemed to have affected her disposition in a positive way. For the first time since we got to the line she looked relieved and smiled back at me while commenting on the busy day it'd been. Observing my friendly interaction with the deli clerk, Carl glanced at me looking surprised and puzzled. As she is cashing us out, I put a generous amount in the tips jar, which she repaid with a glowing grateful smile that subtly muffled the sounds of the words "thank you."

"Benevolence is a big word that can be expressed in very small acts," I said as Carl and I headed to one of the outside round tables on the sidewalk. "It doesn't require grandiose acts or meaningful causes to be exercised. Every day opportunities arise for small acts of kindness to make a difference to the Living Process of everyone involved."

"I feel like I just witnessed Right Speech and Right Action in motion," he remarked unwrapping his sandwich. He looked embarrassed. "You were right; maybe my poor attitude is what blocks off opportunities for me to find my Right Livelihood."

"And imagine what can happen at an older age when you're already feeling your strength waning piecemeal. By then, because you're not as resilient as you used to be, any negative self-talk will trigger a negative action of behavior that will likely make you feel like sh..., well, we're eating now. I guess what I'm trying to say to you is that benevolence is a way of being not doing, and it happens as a natural outcome of being benevolent," I said.

"What if you're not?"

"Then, you need to work on becoming; that is, if you want to experience the Living Process in earnest. Otherwise, you're just going through life dragged by the current of our selfish individualistic culture until you drown in your own isolated accomplished misery. In this case, my friend, you're just an old fart in training; someone experiencing the anxiety of the aging process that offers no rewards in the end." I paused to dig in my avocado-turkey sandwich.

"I think you're giving way too much weight to the role of benevolence to an individual's well being," he said.

"Oh, no, you're missing the point altogether," I immediately replied with my mouth full. After a brief moment of chewing I proceeded. "It's not about an individual; it's about the common good. Benevolence, if it were to become a cultural trademark, could drastically alter, and perhaps even reverse, the current dangerous course of history. It's not about me, you, or them; it's about all of us, and in all stages of our lives."

"I guess I was thinking more like 'brownie karma points,'" he joked. "But man, it takes a lot of effort and concentration to become benevolent in a highly competitive environment."

"It takes more than concentration and effort to defy the odds of what holds us back from becoming self-empowered," I said. "It takes courage."

The Fourth Noble Principle: Courage

If it takes courage to be, it takes indomitable courage to work on becoming courageous, especially if the process of becoming begins in old age. At this latter stage in life when you are face-to-face with your aging image in the mirror reminding you that the expiration of time is ticking closer every day, overcoming the anxiety of death and the fear of the consequences of aging can be a daunting task. Acceptance and resignation in the face of what cannot be altered is, indeed, a manifestation of courage in non-action, or as in Taoism is called *wu wei*, a state of affairs in which all human actions become as spontaneous and mindless as those of the natural world.[6] You no longer resist the mighty currents of the river of life; to the contrary, you flow with it effortlessly, or at least in accordance with Taoist philosophy. But achieving the supreme state of tranquility that Chuang Tzu referred to as *Ying ning* (tranquility in the action of non-action)[7] when even your non-actions are paralyzed with fear, now, that takes an inordinate amount of courage; even for a "Man of Tao." The question, then, is how can you develop that state of being? How can you become courageous when your fears rule sovereign over your mind and emotions?

"So, where do you begin?" Ms. Thompson asked me as I coached her in my office. The late sexagenarian woman had attended my workshop on developing self-empowerment and became my first coaching client. The professional link eventually led to a friendship bond.

"Everything begins at the moment when awareness is born. Once you realize that your unfounded fears about aging and death are not in your best interest, then you have just started spinning the wheel," I said thinking of the Wheel of Dharma, which I did not mention concerned of switching the focus of our conversation to a philosophical rather than practical results I intended to deliver to her.

"Unfounded fears? They are as real as aging and death themselves!" She contested.

"The mind is everything. What you think you become," I said quoting a popular saying attributed to The Buddha. "Your fears, as well as the natural occurrence of aging and dying, only have a foundation if you build one for them. And if you have already done it, then it would behoove you to tear it down."

"It seems like we're back to square one," she said. "Where do you begin?"

I stood up and started pacing back and forth while collecting my thoughts. "Granted that the spinning of the wheel of awareness is already in motion, then the process of cultivating the qualities of courage and fearlessness begins. Facing your fears and overcoming difficulties without hesitation, sprout from the core of the awareness of the conditions of human life as is, not as you wish it were. At that juncture in consciousness, you realize that your fears are not only useless, but worse yet, detrimental to the development of your self-empowerment and well being. Therefore, you must not allow them to take hold of you and focus only on what is to be done."

Noticing the expression in her eyes that begged me to provide a practical answer to her question, I sat down again at my desk to maintain direct eye contact with her as I resumed talking.

"Because of the natural human tendency to search for pleasure and avoid pain, you resist the arrival of discontent and hurt whenever it knocks on your heart's door. And among all the anxieties and suffering in the course of a lifetime, perhaps none is more frightening than the prospect of disappearing into the unknown while deteriorating alive. What's a woman to do in the face of such a seemingly tragic perspective? Well, let's begin with common sense; that is, realizing and accepting the fact that this is the way life happens. Everywhere and in all different forms it manifests its power, life displays the common characteristics of birth, aging, and death. These are the rules of the game you enlisted to play, and agonizing over the rules or expecting them to be different is to forfeit the opportunity to win; to win self-empowerment through living instead of losing to aging and dying.

"Tough rules," she said.

"Yes, but with great rewards," I remarked. "It is the man and woman who courageously conquer their fears and anxieties who have a shot at becoming empowered.

"Then, why there are not more people living in this self-empowered state of being?" She asked.

"Because wisdom belongs but to a selected few; an elite of courageous life-warriors committed to embarking on the difficult path to acquire this special virtue. The masses are snarled in the bondage of desires and illusions of a temporal reality that is as ephemeral as their swinging moods. However, sometimes their anguish becomes so poignant that they're compelled to jump over the fence, for as the Roman philosopher Seneca said, 'no courage is so great as that which is born of utter desperation.'"[8] I paused observing how intently she seemed to absorb my words. That's when I realized it was time to increase the volume of the message. "But you, Ms. Thompson, you belong to the category of life's courageous warriors. You are in the pursuit of victory over the cowardly self hiding under the camouflaged blanket of insecurities created by circumstances you cannot control. The wheel of awareness is already spinning within you and you now know that self-affirmation is the affirmation of life. Like the Taoist approach of *wu wei*, your very self is starting to become your action in no-action. You're giving way to the unfolding of courage of your spirit; and the good life is the courageous life. It is the life of the powerful soul."[9]

"It sounds like courage does to the spirit what Botox does to the sagging skin in my face," she said laughing out loud. I could tell that she was trying to allay the intense level of our conversation while absorbing its content.

"Sure, except that, unlike the effects of Botox, the injection of courage leaves permanent and indelible results in your being. And a self-empowered woman becomes a force of nature to be reckoned with," I said observing her welcoming reaction to my words.

I walked to the corner of my office where I kept an electric water boiler and offered her some green tea. She turned it down as quickly as she resumed our dialogue.

"Heavens know how much I want to become a force of nature to be reckoned with. I just don't know where to begin. If only there were a formula that I could apply; a system I could follow; or better yet, some sort of prescription for the ailments of my aging self...," she said as a gentle wisp of wistfulness filled the air.

Cup of tea in hand, I sat down at my desk again eager to deliver her some good news. "Actually, there is," I said watching her literally jolt on the chair. "There is a mystical belief that there are six virtues that can lead to the development of courage in the heart of the soul. These virtues are supposed to be connected with the blossoming of the twelve-petalled lotus flower near the heart. These six virtues are: control of thoughts and actions, perseverance, patience, faith, and equanimity.[10] However, it's not a formula, system, or prescription that automatically allows the magic of transformation to take place. It is you, the person exercising the elements of the formula, the six virtues, day in and day out in the face of continuous challenges. It's not easy to control your thoughts and actions when you feel harassed by the circumstances of your life. Persevering when defeat repeats itself over and over again requires strong determination. To have the patience to continue persevering demands an unwavering faith. And in the midst of this unrelenting struggle and immense doubt, harnessing even a modicum of equanimity is an undertaking for Titans. As you can see, Ms. Thompson, it takes a truly self-empowered woman to become a force of nature to be reckoned with. She must cultivate courage and fearlessness in the inmost depths of her being, and at the same time must learn not to be discouraged by failure."[11]

"Oh, boy, what's harder: to succumb to despair or climb above it?" She questioned her own self doubts.

"It all depends on what you want to achieve. Succumbing is certainly easier, albeit much more painful. Climbing above it can be exhausting, but infinitely more rewarding, for at the top of the mountain power awaits to greet you," I said.

"Any chance of a third option?" She asked sardonically.

"Developing courage is a mandatory prerequisite in the pursuit of self-empowerment," I said noticing that our time would be up soon. "It's what gives you the strength of mind and spirit to conquer whatever comes to challenge your well being. It can be something as banal as a passing negative thought, or as complex as a major life crisis, your courage is the invisible sword with which you can ward off whatever assails you. Courage is an essential life skill that you can strive to acquire through practice. Courage is the backbone of power."

The Power of Purpose

In my next coaching session with Ms. Thompson, which was a couple of weeks after I had seen her last, she looked exuberant and radiant, as though she had injected her wrinkled approach to aging with the attitudinal Botox of courage. Wearing a flowery spring dress, smelling like a rose, and a blooming smile, she sauntered into my office with gaiety.

"It's nice seeing you so invigorated," I said flashing a bright smile of my own.

"I'm very excited about my latest findings," she said eager to tell me her latest discovery. "I found out what makes some people seem to stop living in old age while others thrive."

"That's very exciting, Ms. Thompson. I can't wait to hear about it," I said with anticipation and a great feeling of satisfaction to witness her becoming self-empowered.

"I read about the results of a recent brain research that concluded that people who have more purpose in life, their brains function better and indicated to researchers one of the main reasons people aged differently," she said with the enthusiasm of a child sharing the stories of a sleep-over birthday party. "I figured, that's it! Purpose! Purpose! this is what I need to propel my life forward no matter how old I get. Sadly, however, in the same reading, I learned that the main debilitating factors of old age are physical or mental disability and extreme poverty.[12] Now, here is the punch line: I realized there is nothing I can do to stop physical or mental disability, neither in myself nor anybody else. However, I can, should, and will do anything in my power to put the kibosh on the spread of poverty among older citizens. And since purpose is the ticket to well being in old age, what a better way to do it than throwing my hat in the ring of social affairs."

"That's awesome, Ms. Thompson. I can easily picture you involved in some social cause and I'm confident that you can do plenty of good to a lot of people," I said rejoicing vicariously.

Suddenly, her high-spirited energy dimmed. I looked at her puzzled with the unexpected and inexplicable transformation. "What's the matter, Ms. Thompson?"

She looked down to the floor as if it were sapping her energy underground. She seemed embarrassed and disappointed. "The problem is that I have no idea how I can go about doing it."

I smiled feeling relieved that it was nothing serious about the matter. "Well, that's the easiest part of the equation. There are many possibilities for you to get involved in whatever your heart's calling happens to be."

"Like what? How can a 68-year-old woman like me get started in social activism? I'm no longer the young woman prowling the streets of the San Francisco Bay Area in the 1960s promoting the counter-culture cause. I'm an older woman now."

"Yep, but not quite old enough to join the ranks of some illustrious activists who have and are still putting their will power into action," I said.

"And who are these eminent ladies?" She asked slightly raising an eyebrow of curiosity.

"Well, there are so many, though I'm thinking of one particular group of ladies. But perhaps I should start with one of the original ones; the mother of them all, if you will. Her name is Mary Harris Jones, or as she became popularly known, Mother Jones," I said noticing her leaning forward toward me as if moved by anticipation and interest.

Mother Jones

"Mary Harris Jones was an Irish-American schoolteacher and dressmaker who was destined to become one of the most prominent labor and community organizers in the history of the United States," I continued. "A sequence of tragedies in her life led her to pursue a purpose that was beyond her own selfish interest; something bigger than herself. After the yellow-fever epidemic of the mid-nineteenth century claimed the lives of her husband and four children, her workshop burned down in the great Chicago fire of 1871 leaving her without any possessions. Having had her heart shredded into pieces by the pain of losing it all, she turned the focus of her attention and will power to a cause of social justice that had long been dear to her heart. In other words, she devoted her life to her purpose."

"Purpose!" Ms. Thompson exclaimed instinctively. "Tell me about her purpose."

I resumed talking as I walked toward the bookshelves in my office. "It all began with her indignation with child labor exploitation. She was outraged that children as young as seven years of age were coerced, by both their miserable economic situation and the immoral cruelty of captains of industry, to work arduously in hard conditions for fourteen hours and longer. Among the many inhumane consequences of the Industrial Revolution in the eighteenth century, the abusive and degrading exploitation of child labor sits at the top. Since coal was the fodder that nourished the new economic beast, children became important tools with which to extract the supply from underground; and in the end, they became a sub-product of the fodder themselves as cheap manual labor. Once she learned about the exploitation of those children, her concern widened to all members of the lowly working class. Soon, she made sure that her voice would echo through the squalid working conditions in the mines as well as the deaf ears of society."

Ms. Thompson looked pensive but didn't utter a single word. I walked back to my desk holding a book in my hand. "It was a matter of time and she'd be labeled 'the most dangerous woman in America,' a phrase coined by the district attorney of West Virginia."

"The most dangerous woman in America?" Ms. Thompson repeated interrupting my train of thought. "It sounds hyperbolic to me."

"Not at a time when women didn't have a voice and couldn't even cast a ballot. So, you hear the speech that the 65-year-old woman delivered to an agitated crowd of exploited workers on September 6, 1912, you can't help but agree with the district attorney's assessment," I said with the open book in my hands. "Listen to this passage of her speech on that day: 'This great gathering that is here tonight signals there is a disease in the State that must be wiped out. The people have suffered from that disease patiently; they have borne insults, oppression, outrages...When we were on the Capitol grounds the last time you came here, you had a petition to the Governor for a peaceful remedy and solution of this condition. The mine owners, the bankers, the plunderers of the State went in on the side door and got a hearing, and you didn't. And the crowd erupted in a raucous applause'."[13]

Ms. Thompson's undivided attentive expression demanded me to proceed without saying a word.

"The point I'm trying to make, Ms. Thompson, is that if a 65-year-old lady from the early twentieth century, which was at the time a much older age than it is today, could have such a tremendous impact in the society of her time, wouldn't you agree that an older woman of the early twenty-first century can achieve even more?" I asked and paused noticing her eyes drifting toward the ceiling as if she was thinking about it. "As an elder woman, Mother Jones demonstrated to both her contemporaries and the generations of elder citizens to come that the exercising of self-empowerment has no age barriers, no gender specification, social status, or any other self-imposed limitation. Indeed, Mary Harris Jones proved that an older citizen, or any citizen for that matter, committed to a cause not only can ignite a social movement, but also become a movement in and by herself. And many others have followed on her footsteps."

"Really? Who else?" She inquired right away, seemingly eager to learn about her own possibilities.

The Tao of Power Aging

Maggie Kuhn and the Gray Panthers

"In 1970 the United Presbyterian Church decided to let 65-year-old Maggie Kuhn know that she would no longer hold her executive job in the organization. She was being forced into retirement because of her age. Big mistake. Instead of bemoaning her unfortunate fate, she got together with five friends with similar predicaments and established the Gray Panthers, an organization committed to changing the rules of the game. Aware that old citizens had long become a neglected and forgotten class, the Gray Panthers championed a new empowered role for the elders in society as no other organization had ever done before. She believed that the older citizens have the benefit of life experience, the time to get things done, and the least to lose by sticking their necks out for the larger public good.[14] Maggie Kuhn was a model of independent womanhood and of the importance of having goals larger than ourselves and of growing old with dignity and respect. Her story is an important chapter in the history of twentieth-century social reform in the United Sates. At a time when the role of women was a second-class function and only a handful of female executives existed in a male dominated society, she pulled the rug from under the feet of the status quo."

"She sounds like a remarkable woman," Ms. Thompson remarked.

"Indeed, especially considering the dominant culture of her time," I said. "Outspoken and fiercely determined in her activism, Kuhn refused to bow to convention in her personal life as well. She never married, choosing to pursue an exciting career instead of the drudgery of domesticity, and free love affairs instead of the false sense of safety of marriage. The story of her life is a testimony to a pioneer woman who affirmed all the rights of women, including their sexual rights.[15] But more importantly, Maggie Kuhn was a fighter against ageism who believed that old people and women were America's biggest untapped and undervalued human energy source. She also dedicated her life fighting for social and economic justices, human rights, among many other important social issues. She was a woman with a purpose on a mission."

"That's right. Now that you're talking about a woman with a purpose on a mission, I remember a long time ago when I was watching the news and they reported about a 90-year-old woman who was walking across the United States protesting something or other; I don't quite remember what it was. Do you happen to know whom I'm talking about?" She asked.

"It must be the story of Doris Haddock, or Granny D, as she became known," I guessed with a great deal of confidence. After all, there are not many 90-year-old ladies out there walking cross-country to protest political corruption.

"That's it. The granny moniker rings a bell," she said with renewed enthusiasm.

Doris "Granny D" Haddock

"You know, Ms. Thompson, sometimes thousands of people set out on marches and rallies to change society. Sometimes it takes only one with strong convictions, idealism, vision, and, of course, the courage to do it. Granny D is one of the most notable examples of a single person's determination to achieve, solo, what usually takes thousands to do. Granny D, however, did it at the age of 90!

꙳ The Tao of Power Aging ꙳

Doris Haddock was one of the oldest political activists in the world. A former housewife and office assistant, Doris was content enjoying her retirement for more than 20 years when her husband passed away. After her best friend died a few years later, she started questioning her lifelong beliefs and convictions. Like you, she searched for a purpose that would make a difference; something she could do to honor the memory of the people she loved. And like Mother Jones, she wanted to turn her personal pain into a meaningful gift to the world," I said thinking that the impulse to serve a common cause is often triggered by *duhkha*.

"And what was Granny D's motivation?" She asked.

"She believed what has been proven to be the obvious: democracy in the United States has been hijacked by private interests buying out the democratic process from the people through 'investments in politicians' in electoral campaigns. Thus, she laced her sneakers and set out to walk across America to rally against the influence of big money in the people's government. She'd no longer tolerate the betrayal of democracy by money in politics, and she was going to do something about it. Hence, in February 2000, the 90-year-old Doris "Granny D" Haddock embarked on an epic walking journey across the country galvanizing popular attention to a political system gone awry. Starting in Los Angeles, she walked 3,200 miles in fourteen months to Washington D.C. to bring attention to the issue of political campaign finance reform."

"That's remarkable! No wonder she made the news," Ms. Thompson observed in awe.

"Well, even though the very fact that a nonagenarian crisscrossing the country at a snail's pace is newsworthy by itself, the media was lukewarm at best in covering Granny

D's movement; no pun intended, to garner attention to the objectionable influence of big money in the United States political system. After all, it was not in the best interest of the corporate-owned media in the country. I remember reading about television networks pooh-poohing her story calling it a 'soft-news story in a hard-news world.'[16] It was not until The New York Times ran a story about Granny D that she received the national attention she deserved; or as it would be called today, she went viral."

"I can only imagine that the media at-large really picked up on it, then," she said. "I mean, how could they not?"

"Yes, soon afterwards the media went on a frenzy to cover the story of this 'innocent elderly lady' whose vitriolic message against the prostitution of democracy exposed many politicians as if they were pimps hiding under their fedora hats of public servants. Media outlets suddenly realized that Granny D's story was not quite as soft-news as it was originally dubbed. In fact, her message was as hard as a brick smashing through the window of political corruption. In a memorable speech she delivered in 1999 that awakened many citizens to critical issues threatening the nation's democratic process, she said that democracy is not something we have, but something we do," I said leaning forward over my desk with my fingers interlaced under my chin. "Ms. Thompson, the only reason I'm telling you all of this is to bring to your awareness that many an older woman is imbued with purpose and exerting a positive impact for the common good. And you or anyone else with purpose, passion, and determination can do it, too."

"This is all very interesting," she uttered without looking at me with an air of wonder. Apparently, she'd not heard a word I said in my last sentence. "I never thought there were old, and I mean very old citizens like this lady getting involved in important social issues. Do you happen to know where I could find this speech?"

I stood up and walked back to my bookshelf to retrieve the source of information she wanted. I handed the open book to her on the page of the speech. She gently took it from my hands in began reading out loud.

"It is said that democracy is not something we have, but something we do. But right now, we cannot do it because we cannot speak. We are shouted down by the bullhorns of big money. It is money with no manners for democracy, and it must be escorted from the room...While wealth has always influenced our politics, what is new is the increasing concentration of wealth and the widening divide between the political interests of the common people and political interests of the very wealthy who are now able to buy our willing leaders wholesale...What villainy allows this political condition? The twin viral ideas that money is speech and that corporations are people. If money is speech, then those with more money have more speech, and this idea is antithetical to democracy. It makes us no longer equal citizens."[17] She stopped reading, placed the book on the desk, and released an spontaneous sound of astonishment. "Wow! What an amazing woman!"

"Wow is the sound of purpose and service in intimate union; and there is no age limits or requirements to express it," I emphasized strategizing my way to her mind. "What Mother Jones, Maggie Kuhn, Granny D, and many, many other unsung heroines hidden behind the faces you encounter on the streets do with and for their lives, anyone committed to a purpose can achieve. These ladies are not thinking about the aging process because they are too busy engaged in the Living Process."

She looked at me in silence with her eyes full of yearning before picking the book back that she'd just put down. She examined the front and back cover with attention. "Very impressive, indeed. Even a distinguished member of the political party that steadfastly opposes her views of anti-capital in political campaigns endorses her work and calls her a 'representative of all that is good in America.' A former President of the United States calls her 'a true patriot and our nation has been blessed by her remarkable life.'[18] A remarkable new life that began at 90! Absolutely fascinating!"

"It sounds like at 68 you're ahead of the due date of giving birth to a self-empowered woman," I said. "The truth is that self-empowerment is always in labor and it can come to life at any moment, no matter how old you are."

"Well, thank you so much," she said abruptly standing up ready to head out the door. "This has been one of the best sessions we've had to date. I feel like now I know exactly what I need to do to go forth."

We shook hands and exchanged farewell greetings. It would be two weeks before I saw her again for our next meeting.

From Wild Youth to Raging Maturity

I always regarded the 1960s as the most remarkable decade in the history of cultural and political movements in the twentieth century. At a time when the economy was growing strong and the living standards at one of the highest point ever in the United States, the youth of this era ignited a counterculture movement that spread like an intellectual wildfire throughout the world. Ironically, it was the privileged and educated youngsters with extraordinary opportunities to profit from the robust economic environment who struck the match that set society ablaze. The generation born in the post-atomic bomb era that witnessed the devastating effects of this technology of destruction was leery of the dominant culture that allowed it to happen. Thus, they noticed right away that behind the beautifully painted images of prosperity, hid a grotesque carbon pencil drawing of socioeconomic injustices they were in no mood to behold, much less embrace it. Like an atomic bomb that assembles the atoms before releasing their energy in explosive fashion, the youth of the 1960s came together and unleashed a disruptive power never seen before. The Atomic Generation had come of age.

But as it is with everything under the domain of *duhkha*, the flower-power generation withered into old age. Half century after their extraordinary accomplishments in social transformations that established women and minority groups' rights, environmental protection awareness, and the demand for socioeconomic justice, among many other contributions of great humanitarian value, many of them were willingly corrupted by the cultural yuppie trend of the 1980s, while others were arm-twisted into the status quo against their will. However, the genuine hardcore members of this turning point generation remained true to their cause; and not even old age was going to stop them from carrying out their unfinished business.

"I can't wait to share the news with you," a very excited Ms. Thompson barged into my office minutes before our appointed time. "I discovered my purpose and I found an outlet through which to express it to the fullest."

"Have a seat, please," I said while clearing my paper-cluttered desk afraid that the unexpected wind of enthusiasm might blow them away. After she settled down on the chair across my desk, I offered her some water thinking that it would quench the heat of her excessive gusto. "Let's start with purpose first."

She took a big gulp of water followed by a deep breath and I could feel the satisfaction in her being when she breathed out. "O.K., let me start from the beginning. When I was a young woman attending UC Berkeley in the early 1960s, I participated with abandon in the Free Speech Movement that would soon spread around the country and the world. It started out in my freshman year when I was at Sather Gate on the UC Berkeley campus helping distribute pamphlets to spread the word of our cause. Oh, those good old days," she said wistfully. "We were a bunch of idealistic kids who desperately wanted to create change, to have a purpose that was not confined to the regimented functionalistic and humanly irrelevant nature of the educational system. It was at that time that I learned the lifelong lesson that in purpose lies the happiness that cannot be attained with a hefty bank account alone. But I also learned, though not until many years later, that purpose may change as we grow older."

I ruminated in my mind, without saying anything to her, that purpose was not different than anything else in life that changes in the natural process of impermanence imposed by *duhkha*. I just kept my eyes fixated on hers showing both my interest and support to the unfolding of her self-empowerment process. Like everything and everyone, she was changing, too.

"Well, since our last conversation when you introduced me to the story of Mother Jones and Granny D, I've been thinking a lot about it in relation to my own desire for purpose. I realized that while the subject of purpose may change, the inner drive that sets it in motion is always closely associated to who we are as individuals. So, when I learned that there were older citizens out there like Doris Haddock, it became clear to me that the fire that burned in the heart of my youth had been dwindled to an ember, but it's never been extinguished. As it is, my purpose just needed a new focus through which it could express itself. And at the core of my purpose lies a passion for activism for social change; just as it was in my young rebellious days at UC Berkeley. What all of this means is that I've rediscovered my purpose and I've been fanning the ember and now the fire is back."

"Excellent!" I said leaning backwards in my swiveling black leather armchair. "I'm glad to know that you've found the entrance of the path to self-empowerment. Now I'm curious to hear about the outlet through which you'll set your purpose into action."

"It's one of the most bizarre things that ever happened to me," she said and for the first time her eyes dodged away from my gaze. "The other day I was driving and I noticed this commotion on the street. There were quite a few people gathering around a group singing what sounded like odd songs that made the bystanders laugh. Unable to restrain my curiosity, I pulled my car over and walked toward them to check it out. And there they were, a number of rowdy old ladies wearing frumpy hats and colorful clothing singing their hearts out. The lyrics were in protest to a federal environmental approval for building a pipeline and port facilities for shipping Rocky Mountain natural gas to Asia via the Oregon coast. This is a 230-mile pipeline route going through farmlands that is grievously opposed by landowners and conservation groups.[19] When I found out who they were, I was ecstatic and eager to join them. I'd found the channel through which to express my purpose."

"The Raging Grannies!" I blurted out. "I remember thinking of telling you about them but I got sidetracked talking about Granny D that escaped me altogether." I wonder why I didn't suggest your joining them in the first place."

"Perhaps because I'm not that old," she said with a smug smile. "Let's face it, those ladies are mostly in their eighties and beyond."

"Go ahead, tell me what you learned about them that excited you so much," I requested feeling excited for someone I'd been trying to help.

"Well, as soon as I got home that evening, I researched them and this is what I found out. The Raging Grannies began in 1987 in Victoria, British Columbia. What started out as a protest against atomic-powered and nuclear-armed US Navy vessels harboring in the British Columbia, soon expanded to other important political and economic issues that the Raging Grannies deemed critical to social welfare: housing for the poor, feeding hungry elders and children, improved treatment of Victoria's streets vagrants; and yes, even opposition to the city's dumping of raw sewage in the ocean. Although they claim that they never intended to start a widespread movement, it was a matter of time for their presence to be felt throughout North America, and they eventually became Raging Grannies International."[20] She paused to take a sip of water before continuing. "Both their agenda and their street theatre style of performance approach resonated with my own inclinations. Following the principle of Canadian author, Margaret Laurence's prescription that 'as we grow older we should become not less radical but more so,' they realized that time is limit and of the essence. Getting older reminded them that they didn't have a lot of time left, so they'd be better get busy. Also, they realized that anger is an appropriate emotion in response to the mess that's being made of our world, and that rage is not a stage, but a transformative, focusing force.[21] I'll tell you, after learning all of this, I felt this could be like going back to Berkeley in a time machine."

And this is how Ms. Thompson found her purpose—and the vehicle through which to deliver it. Her decision to taking positive action with her time, would strengthen her courage to face the limitations that aging imposes on the individual. By dedicating her time and energy to a cause in which she focused her mind on the interest of the common good, instead of feeling preoccupied with the aging process, she developed a new reason for being alive.

"Here Ms. Thompson. I want you to take this with you," I said handing her an oversized card with a beautiful picture of a lighthouse on a cliff at sunset looking over the magnificent Oregon coast. Inside the card, there was a quotation by George Bernard Shaw. "I think this shall inspire a new perspective for your life and give you the courage to continue living with purpose while making a difference in the world."

Standing up and ready to head out the door, she took the card in her hands, opened it up, and smiled before reading it out loud. "This is the true joy in life, the being used for a purpose recognized by yourself as a mighty one, the being a force of nature instead of a feverish selfish little clod of ailments and grievances complaining that the world will not devote itself to making me happy. I am of the opinion that my life belongs to the whole community and, as long as I live, it is my privilege to do for it whatever I can. I want to be thoroughly used up when I die, for the harder I work the more I live. I rejoice in life for its own sake. Life is no brief candle to me. It is a sort of splendid torch with I've got to hold up for the moment and I want to make it burn as brightly as possible before handling it on to future generations."[22]

"Thank you, thank you very much," she said while still looking at the card. "Both this quote and your gesture mean a lot to me. I'll do my utmost to make sure that for as long as I hold on to the splendid torch of life, I'll shed some light along the way. I'm determined to leave my legacy to the world."

When she walked out of my office her last words were left behind in my mind: "leave my legacy to the world." What did it really mean? How can an average person living an average life leave a legacy to the world? Perhaps influenced by cultural standards, I always thought of leaving a personal legacy as something grandiose that prominent people do; like establishing philanthropic foundations bearing their names that outlast their lifetime. Or even average citizens of means who bequest significant amounts of moneys to organizations whose mission resonate with their principles. But what about the millions of people who have neither the means nor the eminence of social status? How can they leave a personal legacy? I wondered about it for a long time, until I met a humble elder man who had been doing it for his entire life, as he showed me what it means to leave a personal legacy to the world.

The True Meaning of Personal Legacy

On one of those typical early December rainy days in Oregon, I was sitting by the window in my favorite coffee shop enjoying two activities that give me great simple pleasures: reading and people watching. Alternating between the book I read and looking outside where people strolled by indifferent to the steady falling rain (they're Oregonians, after all), I placed the book on the table next to my green tea mug to think about the concept of *Anatta* (meaning "non-self" or "substanceless"), which I was reading about. It is a difficult concept for a Westerner brainwashed by the touted pseudo-values of selfishness and greed to understand, much less to embrace it. After all, we identify ourselves with our names, physical characteristics, likes and dislikes, and the accumulated experiences of our lives, all of which develop into whom we become as the years go by. In traditional Indian thought, the *Atman* (self) was permanent, distinct from the physical body and capable of passing from life to life. It was the true essence of a person, separable from experiences and actions performed in the present and ultimately identified with Brahma, the supreme reality (the heavenly father that Christianity alludes to as the destination of the saved departed souls). By contrast, The Buddha taught that there is no such eternal self, for everything arises in dependence upon causes and conditions; and as far as human beings are concerned, each person is made up of five separate bundles or *skandhas*:

the physical body, feelings, experience, habitual responses, and consciousness, all of which are constantly changing.[23]

I was about to pick up the book and resume my reading when a transient outside caught my eye. The disheveled-looking old man didn't seem to blend in with the more conventional crowd that paraded on the sidewalk, even though the increased numbers of his kin were becoming a growing common sight in the landscape of mainstream society. Wearing a worn out navy blue jacket with a small hole near the lapel and a brown beanie on his head, he ambled along not showing any signs of insecurities or distress. Suddenly, he stopped right in front of the window from where I stared at him and we established eye contact. His bright green eyes gleamed with wisdom of years well lived, which made me wonder how could, what seemed to be a homeless old man, exude so much liveliness in such a desolate condition. I greeted him with a gentle nod and a smile in order to break the uncomfortable silent ice that our eyes communicated, and he reciprocated in kind before walking away.

I tried to resume reading but I was having a difficult time focusing on the content. My mind had drifted away in the memory of that man's radiant eyes smiling at me with a hypnotic effect. I kept forcing the issue to no avail. I just couldn't read or even ponder the subject matter of the book. Some half-hour later, after musing, daydreaming, and watching people go by as fast as I wasted time (though I'm aware that time I enjoy wasting is not wasted time), I decided to step out into the rain and head home for a nice hot lavender bath.

As I turned around the corner of the fourth block on my way home, I stopped abruptly when I saw the man in the navy blue jacket and brown beanie sitting on the steps of a building under a ledge across the street talking to a young fellow street dweller. With the rain dripping down my face, I observed him from afar noticing his right arm around the other's man shoulder as they seemed to talk with each other. Tired of getting drenched and curious about the interaction I was witnessing, I crossed the street and walked toward where they were to avoid the rain and, with a self-conscious sense of guilt, to eavesdrop their conversation.

"Don't worry about it. You're still young and tomorrow is another day full of surprises; and you never know what it'll bring," the old man said to his much younger companion. "I'll tell you what: why don't you just go to the men's shelter tonight, get a good night sleep, and see what tomorrow is gonna be like, and the tomorrow after that."

"Tomorrow, and tomorrow, and tomorrow, creeps in this petty pace from day to day, to the last syllable of recorded time...," I recited the passage of Act V Scene V of Shakespeare's play Macbeth in my head after hearing the old man's comment. But before I could finish it, their interaction distracted my thoughts.

"Here, take this and get yourself something to eat before you head to the shelter," the old man said handing the young man some crumpled wet bills he got out of his trousers' pocket. "And remember, tomorrow is another day."

The young man grabbed his small backpack and stood up. Then, without thanking the old man, he snatched the money and walked off into the ill-fated downpour of his life.

Shortly afterward, the old man looked up and saw me there staring at him, again, though this time I probably disclosed a puzzling astonishment in my face. He looked surprised to see me standing next to him.

"I was walking home and needed a break from the rain," I said feeling embarrassed and in need to give him an explanation for my being there. "I couldn't help witnessing your interaction with that young man. Forgive me for asking, but don't you need that money you gave him as much as he does?"

His bright green eyes twinkled as he looked into mine while standing up to face me. "Maybe. But not more than I need what I'm getting for giving it away."

I frowned confused. With my eyes fixated on his, I tried to understand the meaning of his words without having to ask. Not a chance. "And what exactly is it that you're getting, sir?"

"The satisfaction of leaving my personal legacy to the world," he answered with the conviction of someone who knows exactly what he's doing.

Now I was more baffled than before. How could an old impoverished man think that he's leaving a legacy to the world by giving away his much needed pecuniary reserves. Certainly, it was a noble act of kindness, but a far cry from leaving a personal legacy; at least from my perception at the time that seemed to be as limited as his material resources.

"You see, I don't know how many tomorrows I have left in my allotted time. So, every day, whenever I have a chance, I give of myself as I try to forget my own situation and focus instead on the needs of those who are worse off than I am. That way, they get what they need at the moment, and I get what I need in the long run," he explained without my asking. Then, his eyes smiled and he started walking away.

"Wait!" I said compelling him to stop and turn around to face me. "Please, take this with you. Let the rewards of your tomorrows begin today. And thank you for leaving your personal legacy to me. I've just learned a most valuable lesson."

Later that evening while soaking in a lavender infused hot bathtub listening to Miles Davis' *Kind of Blue*, I mulled over the true meaning of leaving a personal legacy that I'd just learned from an old destitute man. We don't establish a legacy of our being with money or fame, but with kindness of heart in our everyday actions, even—or especially—when no one knows about it. A thoughtful word of support to someone who's struggling and feeling helpless; a sympathetic smile to a stressed out clerk in a supermarket checkout line; or the gesture of handing out a small monetary contribution to someone in desperate financial need. In these and many other similar instances, we are leaving a personal legacy to the world. I realized that this was at the core of The Buddha's Dharma, as the First Noble Truth of *duhkha* meant empathizing with the sorrow of others; the doctrine of *anatta* that implied that an enlightened person must live not for her or himself but for others.[24] In the end, personal legacy seems to be of two kinds: that of the ego in the pursuit of recognition and self-importance, and the other of *anatta*, the absence of ego, whose only goal is to be a vehicle through which good is delivered.

The Ultimate Personal Legacy

"You only live once," so the popular adage says. But some people seem to be capable of multiplying once by a thousand, which by mathematical principles, they turn the value of one lifetime into a thousand fold experience. It is as though they can live several lives in one by expanding what otherwise would be the existence of a solitary egoistic self clinging to people, things, events, and even life itself; all of which must pass. Those rare and unique individuals seem to be aware of the delusional fallacy of an independent ego "that struts and frets his hour upon the stage until it's heard no more." Apparently, they have a clear understanding that their isolated self is but a cell among billions in a large body of human life to which they hold an enormous responsibility for its well being. As scientific evidence demonstrates, it only takes one cancerous cell to wreak havoc in a healthy body. But those few dignified people are more like powerful Thymocytes cells (T-cells) that combat invasive destructive organisms threatening the body of the human life they belong. They accomplish the ultimate personal legacy of their lives, even if no one will ever know who they are.

Unfortunately, most people do not even think about leaving a personal legacy until much later in life when they grasp the reality that time will soon expire. But personal legacy is not supposed to be a postmortem remembrance of achievements and good deeds of a life long gone. It is meant to be a mindful activity that happens in the now; the time when the one who's bequeathing the legacy is engaged in the transformations she's contributing to create. And the first and most important transformation of all is the one that takes place within; the one that turns the infinitesimal self into a self-empowered unit of the whole; a T-cell ready to ward off the adversaries of life, be it old age or death. It is only by transcending the selfish attachments of a conniving ego that tricks us into believing that our exceptional existence is the nucleus around which the electrons of life rotates that we surpass mortality itself. Once we overcome this delusional misperception, then our lives become a gift, "for it is in giving that we receive; it is in pardoning that we are pardoned; and it is in dying that we are born to eternal life."[25]

But it's not only individuals who strive to leave a legacy. Generations and societies do it as well. In fact, leaving a collective legacy as a member of a group can carry significantly more weight than any citizen could accomplish alone. Ms. Thompson's quest to make a difference later in her life is a good example of the blending of the personal and collective legacies. Since her young college days, she'd been passionate about social issues that were important to her. And even though the circumstances of her adult life led her temporarily astray from her ideals, throughout the years she remained committed to her values. Therefore, when the time was right, she jumped right into it by joining a group of likeminded women who shared her passion for social justice. Both Ms. Thompson and all the feisty ladies of the Raging Grannies, all of whom will likely pass away unknown to their fellow-citizens, their individual and collective legacy will be indelibly etched on their self-empowered awareness of their unassuming actions while they were alive—and the recognition of people like me who admire and respect their commitment to aging with meaningful purpose.

However, the most valuable lesson about leaving a personal legacy I learned from a homeless old man. It'd never occurred to me that someone who is down and out at rock bottom of the social strata can leave a personal legacy, too. It was an experience that reiterated my belief that self-empowerment is something anyone under any circumstances can develop. In spite of living in such an inhumane condition, that old homeless man discovered a power within himself to overcome his personal misery through the development of his compassionate heart. It is an intelligence of the spirit that supersedes by far our highly regarded intellectual capabilities.

In the end, everyone can leave the ultimate personal legacy by giving of himself to the world in all its manifestations. It doesn't matter whether it's a group of elder ladies singing protest songs to call attention to a cause, or a homeless old man sharing the contents of his deep heart and shallow pockets with those needier than he, every person has an opportunity to make her mark in the world, even if no one will ever learn about the good deeds done. And as time speeds up toward the end of our temporal existence, the aging process becomes the catalyst to the realization that being a force of good is the gateway to self-empowerment, which often begins with the unconditional acceptance and surrender of ourselves to what is now.

Thus, by flowing with the Tao of time without resistance or regrets, we find the serenity of surrender that becomes the Tao of Power Aging itself; like a river flowing back to the ocean it belongs. And that's where the Nirvana of Aging can be found.

Chapter 12

The Nirvana of Aging

Synchronicity Calling

I was so excited to have been selected for an interview that I left home well in advance. Aware that dozens of people had applied for a once-in-a-lifetime employment opportunity with a reputable international company in Geneva, Switzerland, I felt elated to be one of the three finalists invited for the first round of interviews. As good fortune was smiling at me, I grinned right back at it with anticipatory optimism. Determined to leave nothing to chance, I made a point of heading out the door early with plenty of time to spare in case I ran into some unexpected traffic jam, got a flat tire, or any other setback that could add even a small amount of stress to my well-prepared state of mind. I'd spent a lot of time and energy getting ready for the occasion and my resolve to be at my best during the interview was not going to be compromised by unforeseeable events.

ZENior CitiZEN

"All along the watchtower...," I sang along with the music on the radio as my voice echoed the excitement coming from within. Opportunity had knocked on my door and my hand was on the doorknob ready to turn it wide open to let it come in. But as I turned left on the next street, I realized that I was about to drive by the house of my good old friend, Hermann, whom I'd not seen in a long time. I glanced at my watch and it dawned on me that I'd exaggerated my precautionary timing by a long shot. Since I'd probably have to wait some 30 minutes in my parked car before walking into the building where the interview was going to take place, I felt a strong impulse to stop by just for a few minutes to greet my friend. However, I was a man on a mission, and extra time or not, I had a lofty task ahead of me. Then, I thought how his positive attitude could actually be quite beneficial to me, for he'd likely pump up my spirit with his customary optimistic outlook. But then again, I needed to stay focused on the assignment ahead. As I'm getting closer to his house, there was an internal battle taking place within me between my rational mind telling me to keep going and my intuition demanding that I stopped by Hermann's house. A few yards away from his residence and the winner of the struggle between mind and intuition was yet to be determined. Then, without my even noticing it, I abruptly turned the steering wheel onto my friend's driveway.

Hermann was a late septuagenarian German-American I befriended when I responded to an advertisement of an oak bookshelf for sale. We hit it off right away, became friends on the spot, and he ended up giving me the item, which made me most appreciative of his generosity and I decided to pay for it with the valuable currency of my loyal friendship. Since we first met many years ago, we'd gotten together numerous times to talk about a wide range of subjects ranging from the esoteric to the mundane—and often with a bottle of red wine to enthuse the conversation. I enjoyed listening to the wisdom of the intelligent, well educated, and worldly traveled man with a wealth of life experience. Unfortunately, because I'd been so busy with some personal affairs, work, and preparing for the coveted employment opportunity, I'd dropped the ball on touching base with him. But there I was, unexpectedly standing outside his door ready to knock on it at a time when opportunity was knocking on mine.

After several attempts without getting a response, I opened the unlocked door and walked in repeating his name out loud while slowly making my way inside. Since I saw his car in the garage, I knew that he was home. Perhaps he was in the backyard tending to his small flock of chickens. But as I walked by his bedroom door, there he was lying in bed under the black and red checkered wool blanket.

"What's the matter my friend? Aren't you feeling well?" I asked moving toward him with an eerie hunch that there was something wrong. His eyes were wide open but he didn't say anything. By the time I reached the outskirts of the bed, he turned his head slowly toward me and his eyes twinkled in sync with a faintly smile.

"I am dying," he said softly, his voice filled with resigned serenity.

"You're what?" I said noticing that my heart started beating faster. "What kind of nonsense is it? You probably just got the flu. It's going around this time of the year."

"I am dying," he repeated. "I knew it was going to happen when I went to bed last night. By the time I closed my eyes, I was convinced that I was going to die in my sleep. I was actually quite surprised when I woke up this morning. Who knows, maybe I just needed to see you one more time."

I could see in his eyes that he was telling me the truth. Suddenly, I could feel the goose bumps rippling through the skin of my forearms, as I thought of the synchronicity of my urge to stop by his house at the time of his dying. Having never witnessed the moment of anyone's death in my life, I felt somewhat timorous not knowing how to proceed.

"Why don't you pull that chair over and sit here by my side," he said nodding with his chin in the direction of a green cushioned chair on the corner of the room. "For an old widower who's been living alone for a long time, it will be nice to depart from this world with a friend by my side. Thank you for being here."

When I moved toward the chair, I noticed that I was shivering from head to toes. What did I get myself into? I was on my way to one of the most important occasions of my life when I was compelled by intuitive forces to stop by Hermann's house. And now I was being asked to stay by my old friend's deathbed. What a momentous crossroads! I couldn't possibly walk away within the five to ten minutes I'd originally intended to spend at his house. But if I stayed longer, I'd miss one of the greatest professional opportunities of my life. I dragged the chair to the side of the bed feeling devastated with the dilemma that I unwittingly put myself into. But when I looked into his shimmering eyes, I knew there was no choice for me. There was some mysterious reason for the untoward turn of events that I could not fathom at the time. What I did know with certainty, however, was that at that moment his death was more important than the death of a potentially extraordinary professional opportunity in my life.

"I've been preparing for this occasion all my life," Hermann said looking into my eye as though I reflected the time of his younger years. "We do not have to wait for the painful death of someone close to us or the shock of terminal illness to force us into looking at our lives. Death is a mirror in which the entire meaning of life is reflected.[1] Death is not supposed to be the most fundamental and terrifying problem of human life; instead, a moment of liberation and rebirth into a new unknown."

"It's what it is, isn't it? One unknown after the other," I said thinking of the unexpected situation that completely sabotaged the diligent search, meticulous application, and dedicated preparation for a rewarding employment situation that would never happen. "If there is an unknown we can really prepare for, I guess death is the only one we know for sure will arrive sooner or later. All the others can change on a dime."

I kept staring at his countenance and he seemed to be so peaceful and self-asserted. It made me wonder about the effectiveness of preparing for what is likely the most important transitional moment in human life.

"Tell me, Hermann, how do you go about preparing for death all your life?" I asked hoping to harvest a few more crops of wisdom from the rich soil of Hermann's mind.

He smiled faintly before releasing a deep sigh. "You can only prepare for death by living life to the fullest, but at the same time having no attachments to it. If I were to put it into a simplistic formula, I'd say that it boils down to awareness, acceptance, and achievement. Awareness that death is as natural as it is inevitable; acceptance that there's no way to avoid it; and achievement in the act of surrendering to it."

"And at this pivotal moment, do you feel that you've lived your life to the fullest?" I asked filled with curiosity about the effectiveness of his strategy.

"Absolutely!" He replied right away without a modicum of hesitation.

"And how did you manage to accomplish such a lofty goal?" I asked with great anticipation.

He turned his head slightly toward me with his eyes deeply anchored into mine. He didn't utter a single word and the long silence made me feel uncomfortable. But the way he looked at me was part of the answer itself. He was living to the fullest to the very last moment.

"How can you live to the fullest?" He repeated to himself filling the quiet with words. "Well, in my case, I surrendered to all the circumstances of my life with abandon. I loved intensely, though I knew that I'd have to pay a hefty price for the experience when the death of the love arrived, either through physical death or the simple end of it. I took risks in my personal and professional life going after what was meaningful to me, though the failures and disappointments piled up along the way. I was a loyal friend to many, though a few betrayed my friendship and trust. I pursued happiness relentlessly, though I knew that the amount of sorrow often outnumbers the experiences of joy. But above all, I lived to the fullest by dedicating my life to what lies beyond this little self that is dying now. All the people I loved, the friends I made, the positive influence I exerted in so many people, many of whom I'll never know I did; all of it combined makes me confident that, yes, I have lived my life to the fullest, indeed."

Instinctively, I reached out and gently touched his cheek with my right hand. Without the use of words, I wanted to convey to him that at that moment, even though he stood on the thin edge that separates life and death, he was still living to the fullest; to the very last breath of life. Many of the fundamentals of what he referred to as a definition of living to the fullest were taking place right then, especially the exerting a positive influence on a friend who'd happened to stumble into his moment of dying. In my turn, I was living to the fullest, too. Besides the synchronicity of being called to be with a dying friend, I'd learned to trust and surrender the end results of even what I aspired to achieve or acquire the most. In a sense, the death of my potential employment abroad gave birth to a lifelong lesson that I'd treasured for years to come. Living to the fullest established the foundation upon which I would build my self-empowerment. Now I understood what he meant by preparing for death.

It was not long afterwards that he smiled at me for the last time before taking flight in the wings of death toward the Great Mystery. It was my first time witnessing someone exhaling the last breath of life—and what a powerful experience it was. Observing the peaceful expression in his face, his last smile still delineating the contour of his mouth, I wondered what happened to the powerful life-force that had expressed itself for 78 years as a man named Hermann, who would no longer animate that used up bio-chemical machine. As I sat there, quietly beholding his lifeless body for a long time, I imagined his spirit being hurled out through the Earth's stratosphere into an unimaginably endless Universe, at the same time that many other souls came in the opposite direction to begin their earthly tour. Swept away by a whirlwind of emotions and thoughts, I leaned my head downward to touch his forehead with mine and a teardrop rolled down my left cheek when I felt the cold temperature of his blood paralyzed in his veins. Suddenly, I felt my own temperature dropping at the moment of witnessing death for the first time—and realizing the twist of fate that led me to it. It's all a Great Mystery!

It'd been almost two hours since I arrived at Hermann's moment of death. For some reason, I felt quite content just to be sitting there by his deathbed in a silent and quasi-referential vigilance of my friend's dead body. Eventually, I would have to get up and make the necessary phone calls and arrangements. Meanwhile, all I wanted to do was to recollect my many encounters with the man who contributed to my understanding of what it means to master the art of aging, living, and dying.

Learning to Age, to Live, and to Die

"I have learned many things, old man," the young Shaolin monk said.

"You have learned discipline and acquired many new abilities," Master Po remarked. "However, never forget that a priest's life is a simple one and must remain free of ambition."

"Have you no ambition, Master Po?" The young monk asked.

"Only one. Five years hence, it is my wish to make a pilgrimage to the forbidden city. It is a place where even priests receive no special status. There, in the temple of heaven, will be a festival, a full moon of May. It'll be the thirteenth day of the fifth month of the year of the dog."[2]

That was the day Master Po was killed by the regal guard of the Chinese Emperor.

Since I first watched that episode of the television series, *Kung Fu*, I never ceased marveling about the message of the scene. The fact that Master Po was able to foresee the day he would die was not farfetched to me. After all, with a lifetime of meditation, seclusion, and rigorous training of the mind, body, and spirit, it's not in the least discreditable that the Shaolin Master would achieve high levels of divination. What absolutely astonished me was the purpose of his life's ambition: his own death. Why, I wondered, would anyone, even a highly evolved individual, have death as the ambition of living? I broached the topic in a summer afternoon when I stopped by Hermann's house to help him with his chicken-coop remodeling project.

"Pass me the hammer, will you," Hermann said stretching out his arm in my direction. "As for your Master Po question, I think your confusion is in your misinterpretation of what he meant to say. It's not like the old man was looking forward to die; to the contrary, he was probably eager to reach that moment in life when the conclusion of his life's purpose reached the apex."

I frowned watching Hermann place three protruding nails in his mouth not understanding how the moment when existence supposedly comes to an end can be perceived as a life's ambition; purpose fulfilled or not. He looked at me from a slanted angle over his right shoulder and smiled shaking his head. Obviously, he noticed how flummoxed I looked, therefore he didn't waste any time to clarify his words.

"I can definitely relate to Master Po's life ambition, or at least as I interpret it to be," he said after hammering the third nail in the roof of the coop. "The way I see it, the moment of death is the culmination of life's accomplishments. Everything that the individual was supposed to do has been fulfilled within the timeframe designated for the purpose of his life. All the joy and pain experienced; all the challenges and rewards conquered; all the gains and losses endured, they all become conjoined at the moment of death of the individual empowered by the education of living. In that sense, when Master Po shares with his pupil that the only ambition in life he has is the day that he foretells he's going to die, is like a student looking forward to graduation day. And once you complete the studies you have set yourself up to do, there's no reason to remain in school."

"It's hard to picture the old blind sage man as a student yearning for his school days to be over," I said with an off-the-cuff observation.

"Sure, but don't forget that even a master must be a neophyte at some point. And when it comes to navigating the realm of time, it seems that we are all beginners, always relearning how to grow older and face the inevitable death."

I noticed a subtle somber tone in his voice, as though some relearning was taking place right at that moment. That triggered a recollection of my transitions from one stage to the next in my own aging process: Childhood to adolescence, to adulthood, to middle age, and now on the threshold of elderhood; a time when I became viscerally aware of my mortality.

❧ The Nirvana of Aging ☙

"Tell me, Hermann, how do you adapt to the constant beginner status? How can you learn, much less relearn, how to surrender to a gradual deteriorating process that leads to your ultimate demise? I asked in earnest.

He put the hammer down on the workbench and paused for awhile before responding. "I have long realized that the aging process, especially after the sixth decade, is the most challenging phase of a lifetime. There's no way that anyone can surrender to it by simply applying intellectual theories or sheer optimistic views of old age and death. Usually, this inherent human desperation is handled by either giving in to scientific explanation or succumbing to religious fervor. The former is motivated by arrogance and the latter by fear, and both fail miserably at what they attempt to achieve: resilience. They blow but a faint breath of solace into the grieving nature of the human spirit."

"What do you do, then?" I insisted on specifics.

"You just live, day by day, to the fullest," he said almost dispassionately. "Sometimes when I say it, people question that the concept itself is an intellectual theory or just an optimistic cliché for good living, and therefore I'm contradicting myself. But how can I respond to an intellectual question with an experiential answer? Living to the fullest is something whose meaning varies from person to person; it's not a universal experience. For instance, the fictitious Shaolin Master Po, for him living to the fullest was to empower himself through rigorous spiritual training so that his death would become the most coveted moment of his life. It was the only ambition of his life that he lived it to the fullest. On the other hand, for the empathetic type, living to the fullest is to pursue what Master Po did, but beyond the limitations of the interest of the self. For this kind, it's all about turning the gift of his individual life into a gift to the world he belongs, no matter how modest the contribution may be. And of course for some others, may be something as mundane as gardening or devoting to a hobby; or better yet, making art of one's passion."

"Yeah, but sometimes living to the fullest is often disturbed by the unwelcome changes in life that siphons the fullest out of the living," I said. "The unexpected untoward events, the mean-spirited people, the unalloyed evil that exists in the world; all of it and then some, at times makes me feel like I'm living on an empty tank of *joie the vivre*. How do you refill the tank when it gets to emergency-level low?"

"Remember, you're the only one living your life to the fullest, or the emptiest, if that's what you get down to. But in spite of ill-fated changes or even all the malevolence in the world, if the meaning of living to the fullest is rooted in an unswerving commitment to self-empowerment, like Master Po, then even what you perceive as a disadvantage becomes a stepping stone toward your ultimate objective." Hermann took a few steps in my direction to look me in the eye when he resumed speaking. "Out of evil much good has come to me. By keeping quiet, repressing nothing, remaining attentive, and by accepting reality—taking things as they are, and not as I wanted them to be—by doing all this, unusual knowledge has come to me, and unusual powers as well, such as I could never have imagined before."[3]

"What kind of unusual knowledge and powers are you talking about, Hermann?" I asked.

"Self-knowledge and self-empowerment. The knowledge that I'm equipped with the mental and emotional wherewithal to accept the circumstances of my condition, and the power to know that I can prevail over whatever comes my way, for I've done it many times before. In the end, it is all about developing self-empowerment, which in turn begets the confidence that refuels the engine of life so you can live it to the fullest, again."

We walked to the covered patio to take a break from the work and the heat. He opened up a cooler nearby and grabbed a couple of beer cans out of it before inviting me to sit down.

"Now that I'm well into my seventh decade of living, I can look back and see how much pain and suffering I've been enduring through my life," he said while handing me one of the beer cans. "But I would be remiss if I failed to acknowledge the extraordinary power that I've acquired through sorrowful experiences and agonizing doubts. And of course, I wouldn't discount the many memorable moments of joy and happiness; after all, they've also contributed to the development of my self-empowerment, though not as significantly."

"It sounds like self-empowerment is what's all about," I said popping my beer can open.

"Yes, but unfortunately only a few venture to earn it, for it takes a mammoth amount of mettle to face a multitude of unpredictable changes with a leveled mind," he said as his eyes drifted away from my gaze for a moment. "However, the most important element of the equation is the common denominator that is anything but common these days: the ability to love; not the love that you fall in or out of, but the love that you grow from."

Über Knowledge

"I just don't want to make the same mistake that so many people do, not to mention to pay the costly price for failing to live in the moment," Hermann said one evening after dinner when he invited me over for supper in appreciation for my helping him with his chicken-coop remodeling project. "I once met a terminally ill woman who shared with me that her parents raised her to live preparing for the future where life would eventually happen. Thus, she grew up always in a hurry to get to the next phase of her life. By the time she was in high school, she was dying to finish secondary education and start college. By her sophomore year, she was dying to finish college and start working, which prompted her desire to marry and have children. Soon, she was dying for her children to grow old enough so she could return to work. And then she was dying to retire and begin enjoying her life. At the time she realized she was actually dying, she learned that she'd forgotten to live."[4]

"What a terrible time to realize that you've wasted your life," I said. "At that point, there is just no chance for redemption."

"That's exactly the mistake I don't want to make. Dying never has been the greatest fear in my life. Not living is. For this reason, I've been empowering myself while living to the fullest."

"You sound like the symbolic representation of Nietzsche's Übermensch; the man of power that has transcended the mundane human experience. That's a lofty goal," I said.

~ The Nirvana of Aging ~

"Indeed, but a doable lofty goal," he replied before sipping on the Irish cream he served along with dark chocolate for dessert. "Nietzsche, my fellow-German citizen and one of the most brilliant philosophers ever to be misunderstood, also gave a roadmap leading to the ideal concept of the superman, the man who has transcended the limitations of his human nature. It is the 'will to power.' Life itself is 'will to power;' self-preservation is only one of the indirect and most frequent results.[5] Well, that's what I apply to my own self-empowerment in order to reach the level of the Übermensch; and as such, live my life to the fullest."

"But how can you live to the fullest when life is gradually emptying the tank of what makes for quality living? You've mentioned to me in the past that after the sixth decade of life things can get pretty rough along the way to the end," I said beginning to notice the effects of the wine we drank with our meals.

"That's when the Übermensch steps in to assert his valor, willpower, and liberation from fear. Nietzsche stressed that satisfaction can only be found within, and that resentment occurs when a person is unable to accept himself. And he claimed, boldly, that the secret to harvesting the greatest abundance and the greatest enjoyment from existence is by living dangerously.[6] And what's more dangerous than accepting yourself as you are at a time when your physical capabilities are dwindling piecemeal?"

"Yes, but at this point in life the Übermensch has turned into an altmensch," I joked combining the German words for old (alt) with man (mensch). "The living conditions become quite a bit more dangerous then. Health tends to decline and physical abilities diminish concomitantly. Losses keep coming in droves and become but memories piled up in an obscure corner of the mind. And if all that were not bad enough, some even risk losing the very mind where those precious memories of a lifetime are stored. It must be tough to be a Übermensch under these conditions."

Hermann frowned and his raised eyebrow revealed that he'd plunged into a pensive state of mind. He placed his right elbow on the table, and with his indicator finger across his tight lips, he remained silent for a long time. Suddenly, he dropped his hand and looked at me straight in the eye and spoke with a strong tone of conviction. "This is the time when the Übermensch rises like a shining Sun. These are the moments that remind him how he developed Über in the first place, for he knows that the Holy Grail of self-empowerment lies atop the pinnacle of every challenge he overcomes. And the more challenges he has the more opportunities to drink from the Holy Grail of Über, therefore becoming even more powerful. And since it is in old age that the Übermensch encounters the last challenges at the last phase of his life, it is a momentous opportunity disguised in daunting adversity."

I looked at him in awe and with utmost respect for this Übermensch disguised as an ordinary man. He was like a gardener of his own spirit who always seemed to sow a positive harvest. He was a man committed to his own self-development and somewhat unattached from the troubles of the world. He once told me that he can always do something to improve himself, but not much he could do to improve the world, which I disagreed. Nevertheless, he was not a selfish person by any means; to the contrary, he was a loving and giving man. He just had a strong sense of *amour de soi* (love of the self) and at the same time an unspoken disdain for *amour-propre* (self love).[7] He was a man who lived entirely in the present without remorse for the past or anxiety for the future. Sometimes I wondered whether Hermann already had transmuted into the Übergeist, the self-empowered spirit that transcends time and space. After all, in the end, even the Übermensch must die.

Memento Mori (remember that you're going to die)

It'd been a year since Hermann passed away and much had changed in my life. The coveted employment interview that I "accidentally" missed ended up being a blessing in disguise. It was one of those occasions that seemed unfavorably serendipitous in the unknown of the moment, but in hindsight ended up being important events in my life. In any case, I've always felt that what happened that day had much more to do with me than Hermann. As the strong and brave Übermensch that he was, he needed neither me nor anyone else to walk him through the threshold of death. In some eerie happenstance, he had called me over so I could eyewitness his passing. And that was his last gift to me.

For the past twelve months, I'd been thinking a lot about the aging process and death that awaits at the end of it—or unexpectedly at any time. I knew that during the time of my friendship with Hermann, I'd been influenced by the intellectual prowess of incisive German philosophers, particularly Friedrich Nietzsche, and that I'd been blending it, unwittingly, with the pragmatic wisdom of Eastern thinkers. Soon, I was merging the concepts of the Übermensch with the Taoist principle of *wu wei*; like a superman living in the now while letting things unfold effortlessly. Having adopted this attitude, I was finally ready to play the game of life and death receptive to whatever came my way; without resistance, resentment, or remorse.

But I was getting older and now soundly aware of my mortality. I kept noticing how many people my age and younger died regularly of various causes. My concern wasn't so much with the inevitable arrival of death, but the unpredictable manner in which it arrived as I marched on toward the latter years of my life. Now I was aware that my death was stalking me and wouldn't give me time to cling on to anything, and most certainly not the years of my youth long gone. Instead, the awareness of my death, which was magnified by my witnessing a friend die, it'd become an abstract guide that advised and reminded me that time would not go on forever and I'd better do the most with what I had left. Although I shared Hermann's goal of becoming self-empowered, a Übermensch, I wanted to empower others as well; and in the process, contribute with the common good before my time expired. As I continued my journey, I realized that the road to the Nirvana of aging was paved with surrender, service, and self-empowerment.

Surrender, Service, and Self-Empowerment

Although it sounds like an action characterized by immediacy, surrender is actually a process. Depending on the purpose that demands surrendering, it takes time for surrender to come into being; sometimes it takes a long time others not so much. Regardless of the time it takes to come to fruition, surrender entails change, and often of dual nature: the internal decision to yield to the circumstances that triggered the surrendering and the external manifestation of the action, which is often evinced in behavioral and attitudinal modifications. Evidently, for the latter to take place, the former must happen first, for without the intellectual and emotional decision to surrender, whatever it is that calls for change won't be manifested into being. Within this context, the aging process is one of the most persuasive motivations to surrender to inevitable change of the most difficult kind.

Among all the expressions of surrender, the surrendering of the self is the ultimate and most difficult task to accomplish. However, those who achieve such a towering undertaking are handsomely compensated with self-empowerment. As oxymoronic as it may sound, it's through the giving up of the self that we gain it. Furthermore, the relief that comes from letting go of the unattainable endeavor to control the circumstances of our lives, leads to a Nirvana-like state of being that has been described as the fearless state that one is able to face everything without the fear that comes from the narrow and ultimately fruitless quest for self-protection,[8] And the best—if not the only—path leading to the complete liberation of the self is by losing it through service beyond selfish interest. By nurturing a selfless compassion for the suffering (*duhkha*) in and of the world—and there is an abundance of it all around us—we can free ourselves from our own *duhkha*, which is the objective of the Third Noble Truth of The Buddha.

"The thing that lies at the foundation of positive change, the way I see it, is service to a fellow human being."[9] When I first read this quote without knowing the source, I thought it was likely attributed to some humanitarian individual of the caliber of Albert Schweitzer. After learning that it'd been written by a top-notch corporate executive, I began wondering whether it was part of some cunning publicity campaign to shed positive light on the business of Chrysler Corporation. But it didn't matter. The only relevant point of the quote was its meaning: the foundation of positive change is service. And my inference was that since aging is the quintessential change, making it positive would involve service.

As I started putting all the pieces of the puzzle together, a new image of the aging process began appearing before my eyes. It was an image of power—Power Aging—demonstrated in quiet bravery rather than fiery bravado. First the gentle surrender, the yielding to a formidable force of nature that cannot be opposed; and by doing so, perhaps become capable of tempering the potent impact of its gradual grueling changes. And if service is the foundation of positive change, the combination of the two certainly would lead to self-empowerment, which is the ultimate beneficial transformation. Alas, it takes the Übermensch to effectuate such a difficult undertaking. However, in the case of the aging process, the characteristic of the Übermensch that is the most important is not "the will to (self) power," but another principle of Nietzsche's philosophy: *amor fati* ("love of fate"); the sentiment of resignation where peace can be cultivated. As the creator of the Übermensch concept said, "My formula for greatness in a human being is *amor fati*: that one wants nothing to be other than it is, not in the future, not in the past, not in eternity. Not merely endure that which happens out of necessity, still less to pretend it isn't real—but to love it."[10] This is the ultimate triumph of the Übermensch in old age.

It was a matter of time for my realizing that there was an enormous resemblance between Nietzsche's

ꕥ The Nirvana of Aging ꕥ

Übermensch and Chuang Tzu's "Man of Tao," both of whom require courageous surrender to what is and how we must flow with it regardless of circumstances. In Nietzsche it was expressed in the resignation of love of fate (*amor fati*), and for Chuang Tzu was about the true character of the Taoist philosophy of *wu wei*, which is not mere inactivity but perfect action in non-action. It is not sheer passivity, but it is action that seems both effortless and spontaneous because it is performed "rightly" in perfect accordance with our nature and with our place in the scheme of things.[11] It is the ultimate act of surrender in trust.

Since Nirvana is liberation from the obstinate fetters of fears and anxieties that hold an individual hostage to himself, the mating of the wisdom of the East and West gave birth to my own experience of a Nirvana of aging: unconditional surrender with love for what is while flowing with the Tao of life—and death—without resisting the perpetual forward motion of time. But considering that both the strength and circumstances of the fetters of trepidations vary from person to person, would the path that I discovered to my own Nirvana of aging lead others there, too? Maybe. But as a Zen teacher once told me, "As for a Zen secret regarding the aging process, if there is one, you must find it within yourself, for you are the very essence of what Zen is supposed to be; the mindfulness of your living experience." Hence, you'll find out only if you begin the process on your own terms.

As for me, now I understand that becoming a ZENior CitiZEN requires combining the wisdom of the East and West in the perspective of the aging process. In the end, the Übermensch who surrenders to the flow of the Tao is the one who becomes capable of mastering the art of aging.

Notes

Introduction

[1] D.T. Suzuki, *What is Zen?* (New York: Harper & Row Publishers, 1972), 1.
[2] *Power Aging* is one of the fundamental concepts of this book. It supersedes what is commonly known as "healthy aging" or "successful aging," both of which relate to dealing with the natural changes that occur during the aging process. Power Aging distinguishes itself as the development of fortitude of the being to overcome the limitations of aging in mind, body, and spirit.
[3] *Eldergeddon* is a term I coined to describe the silent apocalyptic fear of old age. Unlike thanatophobia, which is the psychological term to describe the fear of death, my concept of eldergeddon reflects the unspoken anxiety of older adults with future age-related calamities such as dementia or institutionalization.
[4] Seng-t'san, *Hsin-Hsin Ming*, verses of the perfect mind, an interpretation by Eric Putkonen (Mound, MN: Awaken to Life, First Edition, e-book format (PDF)).

Chapter 1: The First Step of a Thousand-Mile Journey

[1] Taisen Deshimaru, *The Zen Way To The Martial Arts* (New York: Penguin Books USA, Inc., 1991), 1.
[2] Mel Thompson, *101 Key Ideas, Buddhism* (New York: Contemporary Books, a Division of McGraw-Hill Companies, 2000), 22.

Chapter 2: The Reawakening of Zen

[1] Alan Watts, *The Way of Zen* (New York: Vintage Books, 1985), 111.
[2] Eugen Herrigel, *Zen in the Art of Archery* (New York: Vintage Books Edition, 1989), vii-ix.
[3] Sun Tzu, *The Art of War* (Boston, Massachusetts: Shambhala Publications, Inc., 2001), 9.
[4] Sun Tzu, *The Art of War*, 12.
[5] Koichi Tohei, *What is Aikido?* (Tokyo, Japan: Rikugei Publishing House, 1973).

Notes

[6] John Stevens, *Aikidō* (Boston, Massachusetts: Shambhala Publications, Inc., 1996), 102.
[7] Collected Quotes from Albert Einstein, http://rescomp.stanford.edu/-cheshire/EinsteinQuotes.html
[8] Waysun Liao, *T'ai Chi Classics* (Boston, Massachusetts: Shambhala Publications, Inc., 1990), 3-19.

Chapter 3: The Holy Trinity of Zen

[1] Philip Kapleau, *The Three Pillars of Zen* (Boston, Massachusetts: Beacon Press, 1965), 58-59.
[2] Theodore Roszak, *The Making of an Elder Culture* (British Columbia, Canda: New Society Publishers, 2009), 176.
[3] Paul Mutimer, *Zen Tennis* (New York: HarperCollins Publishers, Inc., 1997), 48-51.

Chapter 4: Dreaming of Being Awake

[1] Inazo Nitobe, *Bushido, The Soul of Japan* (Boston, Massachusetts: Tuttle Publishing Company, Inc., 1969), 32.33.
[2] Lord Byron, *The Works of Lord Byron* (Hertfordshire, England: Wordsworth Edition, Ltd., 1994), 380.
[3] Carlos Castaneda, *Tales of Power* (New York: Washington Square Press, 1974), 106.
[4] Carlos Castaneda, *Tales of Power*, 196.
[5] Albert Schweitzer, *The Light Within Us* (New York: Philosophical Library, Inc., 1959), 3.

Chapter 5: The Awakened One

[1] Karen Armstrong, *Buddha* (New York: The Penguin Group, 2001), xii.
[2] Walter Henry Nelson, *Buddha, His Life and His Teaching* (New York: The Penguin Group, 1996), 17.
[3] Walter Henry, *Buddha, His Life and His Teaching*, 27.
[4] Jacky Sach, *Buddhism, Everything You Need to Understand This Ancient Tradition* (Avon, Massachusetts: Adams Media, 2006), 16.
[5] Walter Henry, *Buddha, His Life and His Teaching*, 52.
[6] Luke 14:25-27.
[7] Karen Armstrong, *Buddha*, 2-3.

Notes

[8] Jacky Sach, *Buddhism, Everything You Need to Understand This Ancient Tradition*, 20.
[9] Karen Armstrong, *Buddha*, 6.
[10] Jacky Sach, *Buddhism, Everything You Need to Understand This Ancient Tradition*, 22.
[11] Karen Armstrong, *Buddha*, 92.
[12] Walter Henry, *Buddha, His Life and His Teaching*, 103.

Chapter 6: The Dharma of Power Aging

[1] Karen Armstrong, *Buddha* (New York: The Penguin Group, 2001), xiii.
[2] Nicole S. Dahmen, Ph.D. and Raluca Cozma, Editors, *Media Takes on Aging* (Sacramento, CA: International Longevity Center - USA, 2009), 13.
[3] Theodore Roszak, *The Making of an Elder Culture* (British Columbia, Canda: New Society Publishers, 2009), 272.
[4] Chögyam Trungpa, *The Truth of Suffering and the Path of Liberation* (Boston, Massachusetts: Shambhala Publications, Inc., 2009), 64.
[5] Erich Fromm, *Psychoanalysis & Zen Buddhism* (London: Unwin Hyman Limited, 1960), 80.
[6] Karen Armstrong, *Buddha*, 71.
[7] Ian P. McGreal, Editor, *Great Thinkers of the Eastern World* (New York: HarperCollins Publishers, Inc., 1995), 164.
[8] Jacky Sach, *Buddhism, Everything You Need to Understand This Ancient Tradition* (Avon, Massachusetts: Adams Media, 2006), 43-44.
[9] Bhikkhu Bhodi, *The Noble Eightfold Path: The Way to the End of Suffering* (London: Buddhist Publication Society, 1999), 13-14.
[10] Jacky Sach, *Buddhism, Everything You Need to Understand This Ancient Tradition*, 44.
[11] Susan Jeffers, *Feel the Fear and Do it Anyway* (New York: Ballantine Books, 1987), 194-195.
[12] Karen Armstrong, *Buddha*, 178.
[13] Walter Henry Nelson, *Buddha, His Life and His Teaching* (New York: The Penguin Group, 1996), 109.
[14] Theodore Roszak, *The Making of an Elder Culture*, 175.
[15] Walter Henry Nelson, *Buddha, His Life and His Teaching*, 113.
[16] Jacky Sach, *Buddhism, Everything You Need to Understand This Ancient Tradition*, 49.
[17] Jon Kabat-Zinn, *Wherever You Go There You Are* (New York: Hyperion, 1994), 3.

Notes

[18] P.D. Ouspensky, *The Psychology of Man's Possible Evolution* (New York: Vintage Books, 1973), 11, 33.
[19] Paul Tillich, *The Courage to Be* (New Haven, CT: Yale University Press, 2000), 16.

Chapter 7: The Myths of Aging

[1] Ken Dychtwald, *The Power Years* (New Jersey: John Wiley & Sons, Inc., 2005), 13.
[2] U.S. Census Bureau, Decennial Census, Population Estimates and Projections: Data for 2010-2050 projected populations.
[3] Nancy R. Hooyman, H. Asuman Kiyak, *Social Gerontology: A Multi-disciplinary Perspective*, 9th Edition (Boston, MA: Pearson Education, 2011).
[4] Cary S. Kart, Jennifer M. Kinney, *The Realities of Aging: An Introduction to Gerontology*, 6th Edition (Needham Heights, MA: Allyn and Bacon, a Pearson Education Company, 2001), 9.
[5] Etta Clark, *Growing Old is not for Sissies, Portraits of Senior Athletes* (Ronhert Park, CA: Pomegranate Calendar & Books, 1993).
[6] Bruce Grierson, "Going the Distance," *Parade Magazine*, December 29, 2013, 9.
[7] "Completing the Kona Ironman at Age 70," *Spirituality & Health*, March/April 2015, 32.
[8] Kart, Kinney, *The Realities of Aging*, 10.
[9] Mary S. Furlong, *Turning Silver into Gold: How to Profit in the New Boomer Marketplace* (New Jersey: FT Press, 2007), 4-6.
[10] Associate Press, "For jobless over 50, the search is rough," *Corvallis Gazette-Times*, 22 October, 2013, A8.
[11] Matt Sedensky, "Employers recognizing older workers for experience," Associated Press, *Corvallis Gazette-Times*, 14 September, 2013, A1-A8.
[12] Kart, Kinney, *The Realities of Aging*, 13.
[13] William H. Masters, Virginia E. Johnson, Robert C. Kolodny, *Masters and Johnson on Sex and Human Loving* (Boston: Little Brown and Company, 1988), 179-180.
[14] Shere Hite, *The Hite Report* (New York: Dell Publishing Company, Inc., 1976), 508, 510.
[15] As quoted from a 61-year-old woman interviewed for this project who requested to remain anonymous. She started a relationship with a male divorcee in her age group with whom she claims to have the best sex of her life.

Notes

[16] *A Profile of Older Americans: 2011.* Administration on Aging, U.S. Department of Health and Human Services.

Chapter 8: The Facts of Aging

[1] Walter Hamilton, "Many Americans foresee working until age 80," Los Angeles Times, *Corvallis Gazette-Times*, 25 November, 2011, A6.
[2] "The Big Challenges Ahead," *AARP Bulletin*, November 2012, 21.
[3] Matthew Gonzales, "The hidden hungry: shining a light on the growing problem of senior hunger," *Kiwanis*, February, 2012, 17-19.
[4] Yoshiaki Nohara and Andy Sharp, "Elderly Japanese turning to crime," Bloomberg News, *Mid-Valley Sunday*, 21 July, 2013, A4.
[5] United Nations, Department of Economic and Social Affairs, Population Division. *World Population Ageing 1950-2050.*
[6] Kristen Gelineau, "Global Study: World not ready for aging population," Associated Press, *Corvallis Gazette-Times*, 1 October, 2013, B5.
[7] For comprehensive statistics about global aging, visit http://www.globalagewatch.org. The Global Age Watch Index was created by elder advocacy group Help Age International and the United Nations Population Fund.
[8] Yamamoto Tsunetomo, *Hagakure, The Book of the Samurai* (Tokyo, Japan: Kodansha International, 1983), 57.
[9] Rob Romasco, Caregiving's Journey, *AARP The Magazine*, December 2012/January 2013, 66.
[10] Susan Jacoby, *Never Say Die, The Myth And Marketing of The New Old Age* (New York: Vintage Books, a Division of Random House, Inc., 2011), 122-123.
[11] Jimmy Carter, *The Virtues of Aging* (New York: Random House, Inc., 1998), 27.
[12] Rana Foroohar, "Inequality isn't just a social issue—it's putting the future of the U.S. economy in peril," *Time*, 10 February, 2014, 23.

Chapter 9: It's About TIME

[1] Roger Waters, "Time," Lyrics, *The Dark Side of the Moon* (London: Pink Floyd Music Publishers, Ltd.), 1973.
[2] Patricia Barnes-Svarney, Editorial Director, *The New York Public Library Science Desk Reference* (New York: A Stonesong Press Book, MacMillan, 1995), 77.
[3] Patricia Barnes-Svarney, Editorial Director, *The New York Public Library Science Desk Reference*, 68.

Notes

[4] William Shakespeare, *The Complete Works of William Shakespeare* (New Jersey: Outlet Book Company, Inc., 1975), 107.
[5] Merriam-Webster's Collegiate Dictionary, Eleventh Edition (Springfield, MA: Merriam-Webster, Inc., 2007), 990.
[6] Lizzie Parry, "The real life Peter Pan: Teenager diagnosed with 'an intense fear of growing up' stopped eating, stopped to appear shorter, and spoke in a higher voice," www.dailymail.com/uk, 5 February, 2015.
[7] Chuang Tzu, *Basic Writings*, Translated by Burton Watson (New York: Columbia University Press, 1964), 6.
[8] Roger Waters, "Eclipse," Lyrics, *The Dark Side of the Moon* (London: Pink Floyd Music Publishers, Ltd.), 1973.
[9] In their excellent book, *Generations, The History of America's Future, 1584 to 2069*, William Strauss and Neil Howe detail the succession of generational biographies that make up the national identity of the American people.
[10] Tom Brokaw, *The Greatest Generation* (New York: Random House, Inc., 2001).
[11] Mel Thompson, *101 Key Ideas Buddhism* (Chicago: Contemporary Books, 2000), 67.
[12] Heard from a gypsy man in the sleepy Portuguese seaside small town of Quarteira as we conversed about self-empowerment.

Chapter 10: The Obstacles to Power Aging

[1] "At 90, musicians still going strong," *Corvallis Gazette-Times*, Monday, August 11, 2014, A6.
[2] William Shakespeare, *The Complete Works* (New York: Gramercy Books, 1975), 1088.
[3] Marie de Hennezel, *The Art of Growing Old* (New York: Viking Penguin, 2012), 58.
[4] Grace Bonds Staples, "As Boomers age, need for memory-care facilities grows," The Atlanta Journal Constitution, *Corvallis Gazette-Times*, 28 September, 2013, B8.
[5] Matthew Craft, "Elder care costs keep climbing," Associated Press, *Corvallis Gazette-Times*, 10 April, 2015, A8.
[6] Caregiving in America 2015, *AARP Bulletin*, November 2015, 6.
[7] William Shakespeare, *The Complete Works*, 239.
[8] Yamamoto Tsunetomo, *Hagakure, The Book of the Samurai* (Tokyo: Kodansha International, Ltd., 1983), 29, 30.
[9] Scott Shaw, *Samurai Zen* (ME: Weiser Books, 1999), 19.

Notes

[10] Inazo Nitobe, *Bushido, The Soul of Japan* (Boston, MA: Tuttle Publishing, 1969), 94.

Chapter 11: The Tao of Power Aging

[1] Karen Armstrong, *Buddha* (New York: The Penguin Group, 2001), 96.
[2] Nido Qubein, *How to Get Anything You Want* (High Point, NC: High Point University Press, 2006), 88.
[3] Selected by Peter McWilliams, arranged by Jean Sedillos, *The Life 101 Quote Book* (Los Angeles, CA: Prelude Press Inc, 1996), 258.
[4] Tony Rizzo, The Kansas City Star, "Death sentence given to avowed anti-Semite," *Corvallis Gazette-Times*, 11 November, 2015, B7.
[5] *Merriam-Webster's Collegiate Dictionary*, Eleventh Edition (Springfield, MA: Merriam Webster, Inc., 2007), 114.
[6] Translated by Burton Watson, *Chuang Tzu Basic Writings* (New York: Columbia University Press, 1964), 6.
[7] Thomas Merton, *The Way of Chuang Tzu* (New York: Penguin Books, Inc., 1969), 26.
[8] Paul Tillich, *The Courage to Be* (New Haven, CT: Yale University Press, 2000), 16-17.
[9] Paul Tillich, *The Courage to Be*, 28-29.
[10] Rudolf Steiner, *How to Know Higher Worlds* (Great Barrington, MA: Anthroposophic Press, 1994), 139.
[11] Rudolf Steiner, *How to Know Higher Worlds*, 67.
[12] John Leland, "Growing Old, Yes, but Refusing to Fade, *The New York Times*, 18 October, 2015, 28, 29.
[13] Edward M. Steel, Editor, *The Speeches and Writing of Mother Jones* (PA: University of Pittsburg Press, 1988), 106.
[14] Theodore Roszak, *The Making of an Elder Culture*, (Gabriola Island, BC: New Society Publishers, 2009), 72.
[15] Maggie Kuhn, with Christina Long and Laura Quinn, *No Stone Unturned, The Life and Times of Maggie Kuhn* (New York: Ballantine Books, 1991), back cover jacket flap.
[16] Doris Haddock with Dennis Burke, Granny D: You're Never Too Old to Raise a Little Hell (New York: Random House, Inc., 2003), xi-xii.
[17] Haddock with Burke, *Granny D: You're Never Too Old to Raise a Little Hell*, 267.
[18] Haddock with Burke, *Granny D: You're Never Too Old to Raise a Little Hell*, front and back cover.

Notes

[19] Jeff Barnard, "LNG plan gets environmental OK," Associated Press, *Corvallis Gazette-Times*, 1 October, 2015, A1, A6.

[20] For information about the Raging Grannies International, visit http://www.raginggrannies.org. Also, watch the "Raging Grannies" documentary film trailer at https://www.youtube.com/watch?v=KnnNPxk3vgI

[21] Alison Acker, Betty Brightwell, *Off our Rockers and into Trouble: The Raging Grannies* (Victoria, BC: Touch Wood Editions, Ltd., 2004), 2-3.

[22] Susan Jeffers, *Feel the Fear and Do it Anyway* (New York: Ballantine Books, 1987), 186.

[23] Mel Thompson, *101 Key Ideas, Buddhism* (Chicago: Contemporary Books, A Division of The McGraw-Hill Companies, 2000), 4.

[24] Karen Armstrong, *Buddha*, 116.

[25] The last verse of the Peace Prayer of St. Francis of Assisi

Chapter 12: The Nirvana of Aging

[1] Sogyal Rinpoche, *The Tibetan Book of Living and Dying* (New York: Harper Collins Publishers, Inc., 1993), 11.

[2] Created by Ed Spielman, developed by Herman Miller, and produced by Jerry Thorpe, *Kung Fu*, The Complete First Season (Burbank, California: Warner Bros, Inc., 2004), disc 1, scene 9.

[3] Translated and explained by Richard Wilhelm with a commentary by C. G. Jung, *The Secret of the Golden Flower, A Chinese Book of Life* (New York: Harcourt Brace & Company, 1962), 126.

[4] Allen Klein, *The Change-Your-Life Quote Book* (New York: Random House, Inc., 2000), 90.

[5] Robert C. Solomon and Kathleen M. Higgins, *What Nietzsche Really Said* (New York: Schoken Books, 2000), 78.

[6] Shelley O'Hara, *Nietzsche Within Your Grasp* (Hoboken, NJ: Wiley Publishing, Inc., 2004), 44.

[7] Leo Damrosch, *Jean Jacques Rousseau, Restless Genius* (New York: Houghton Mifflin Company, 2005), 238.

[8] Mel Thompson, *101 Key Ideas, Buddhism* (New York: Contemporary Books, a Division of McGraw-Hill Companies, 2000), 53.

[9] Lee Iacocca, "The thing that lies at the foundation of positive change, the way I see it, is service to a fellow human being (httpp://www.brainyquote.com/quotes/l/leeiacocca387555.html?src=t_service)

[10] Shelley O'Hara, *Nietzsche Within Your Grasp*, 18.

Notes

[11] Thomas Merton, *The Way of Chuang Tzu* (New York: New Direction Publishing Corporation, 1969), 28.

ABOUT THE AUTHOR

Sebastian de Assis, is a writer, teacher, philosopher, and independent scholar. A former traditional educator and the author of the acclaimed *Teachers of the World, Unite!*, he's transitioned to becoming an independent teacher and writer focusing on human development and self-empowerment.

He has traveled extensively through Europe, South and North America, Africa, and the United States. An alumnus of the University of Hawaii and California State University, he is a bona fide expert in cross-cultural communications, multiculturalism, and promoting diversity. He is fluent in Spanish, Portuguese, and French.

When he is not writing or reading in his personal library while listening to Johann Sebastian Bach or Miles Davis, he is probably on the tennis court competing with the same passion he devotes to everything he engages in.

For more information about Sebastian and his work visit www.sebastiandeassis.com.

www.ingramcontent.com/pod-product-compliance
Lightning Source LLC
Chambersburg PA
CBHW020642300426
44112CB00007B/205